CONTEMPORARY
STUDIO PORCELAIN

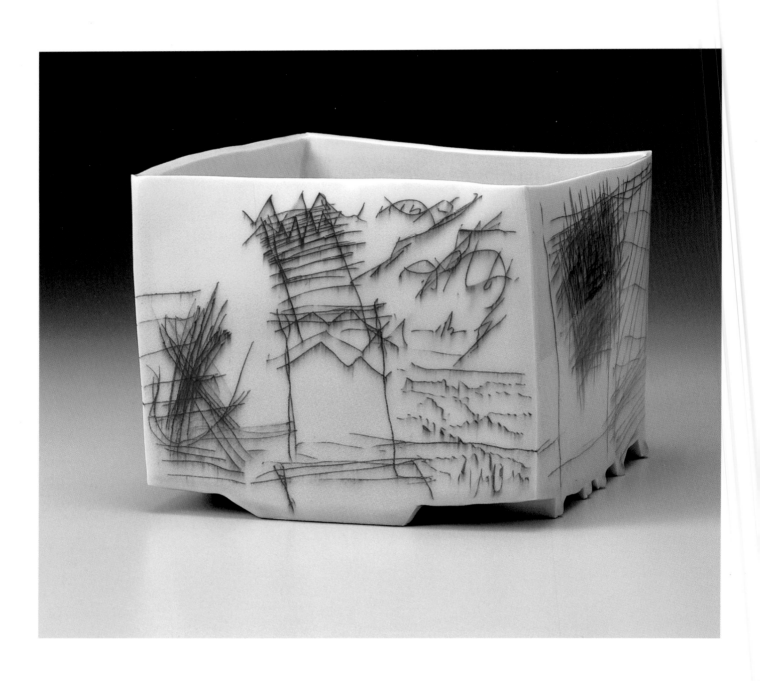

CONTEMPORARY
STUDIO PORCELAIN

Peter Lane

Second Edition

A&C Black • London

University of Pennsylvania Press • Pennsylvania

First published in Great Britain 1995
Second edition published in 2003
A & C Black Publishers Limited
Alderman House
37 Soho Square
London W1D 3QZ

www.acblack.com

ISBN 0-7136-6637-4

Published simultaneously in the USA by
University of Pennsylvania Press
4200 Pine Street
Philadelphia, Pennsylvania 19104-4011

ISBN 0-8122-37722

Copyright © Peter Lane 1995, 2003

CIP Catalogue records for this book are available from the British Library
and the U.S. Library of Congress.

Peter Lane has asserted his right under the Copyright, Design and Patents Act, 1988,
to be identified as the author of this work.

Book design by Penny and Tony Mills
Cover design by Dorothy Moir

Printed and bound in Singapore by Tien Wah Press Pte. Ltd

A & C Black uses paper produced with elemental chlorine-free pulp,
harvested from managed sustainable forests.

Cover illustration: *Blue and White Dyad*, by Marc Leuthold (USA), 2002. Unglazed coloured porcelain, deeply carved, 53 x 71 x 10 cm (21 x 28 x 4 in.). *Photograph by Eva Heyd.*
Half title page illustration: Porcelain bowl, by Peter Lane (UK), 1999. Wheel-thrown, double glazed, height: 15 cm (6 in.). Firstly, a pale blue transparent glaze was sprayed on and incised when dry. A second, satin-matt glaze containing copper and rutile was then sprayed on top before firing in a reduction atmosphere to 1280°C (2336°F). *Photograph by the artist.*
Frontispiece: Blue and White, by Masamichi Yoshikawa (Japan), 2000. Sculpted porcelain form, 29 x 27 x 23 cm (11 ½ x 10 ⅝ x 9 in.). *Photograph by Sokrates Mavromatis.*

CONTENTS

Acknowledgements

Any author of a book of this kind must rely heavily upon the goodwill and cooperation of many people. I am deeply indebted to all the porcelain makers who have so generously given of their time and expertise in helping me to gather new material for this book. Like myself, any artists who work in clay find themselves members of a unique global community that willingly shares information about ideas, techniques, successes and failures. I have been greatly encouraged and enthusiastically supported during my research for this book by numerous friends and colleagues in the International Academy of Ceramics who responded to my quest for appropriate images and detailed information about their work. This has enabled me to demonstrate some of the new directions that have taken place in porcelain making since the publication of earlier books. I am especially grateful for superb photographs showing the works of so many potters from around the world and to the photographers for allowing their reproduction as illustrations for the text. In particular, I would like to thank Hein Severijns (Holland), Jan Schachter (California), Curtis Benzle (Ohio), Thea Burger (Illinois), Gabi Dewald (Germany), Karl Scheid (Germany), Moyra Elliott (New Zealand), Lenka Velínská (Czech Republic), Louana Lackey (USA), Ann Mortimer (Canada), Dorothy Feibleman (UK), Peteris Martinsons (Latvia) and others who were all extremely helpful in various ways, and Georgette Strobino at the Secretariat of IAC in Geneva for addresses of artist members. My sincere thanks are due also to Chris Hogg and Harry Fraser for their helpful technical notes on the search for porcelain and bone china bodies with good working properties. To Chris Hogg, also, more thanks are due for notes on his experiments with copper red glazes. Many potters, gallery owners and collectors at home and abroad have all given me the encouragement needed to produce this new book on contemporary studio porcelain. I am indebted to my editor, Alison Stace, and especially grateful to Linda Lambert, at A & C Black Publishers who persuaded me that it was time to address the subject again. To my dear wife, Jean, for her patience, tolerance and constant support while I spent long hours communicating only with my word processor, and who regularly interrupted her own creative work to keep me supplied with good food and endless cups of cocoa or tea, a very special thank you.

Peter Lane, 2002
New Alresford, Hampshire

FOREWORD

by David Leach, OBE

David Leach (*portrait taken in his studio by Peter Lane, 2002*).

In 1980, I was privileged to write a foreword to Peter Lane's first book, *Studio Porcelain*. In it I dared to prophesy that the book would have a broad appeal. It has. Since then, we have had his *Contemporary Porcelain* in 1995 and, now, this new, expanded volume in full colour illustrates some of the most imaginative applications of porcelain by individual ceramicists from many countries who are making vessels, sculptural objects, conceptual installations, and architectural works.

It is my impression that these books by Peter Lane have done more than any other single agency to popularise the making and appreciation of porcelain in its many varied forms all over the world. They reveal the increasingly wide range of porcelain makers, their thoughts and inspirations, their diligence, their technologies and their problems. Peter's patient persistence to discover, research and so lucidly expose all this creativity is truly remarkable.

David Leach,
28th October 2002

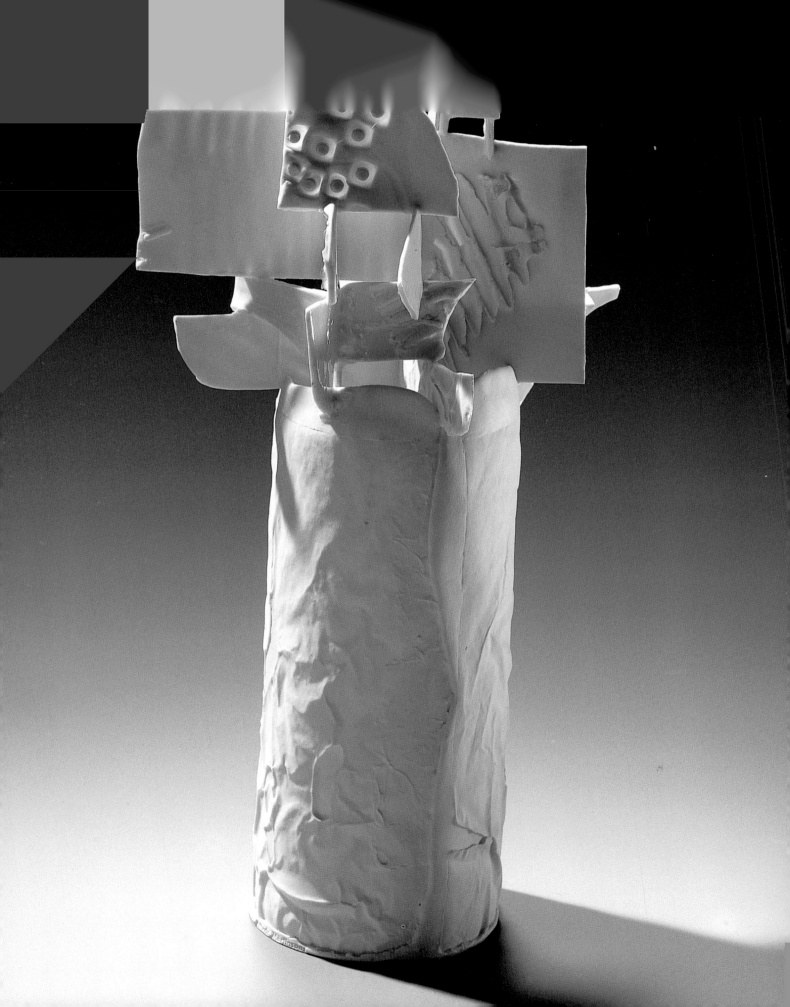

INTRODUCTION

There have been many exciting developments in the field of contemporary ceramics since my first books on the subject were published in 1980 under the titles of *Studio Porcelain* and *Contemporary Porcelain: Materials, Methods and Expressions* in 1995. These were attempts to examine an area of the discipline which, despite its long history, had been largely neglected by studio potters. This new book endeavours to address the subject afresh and to investigate what changes in attitude or in approaches to design and making, if any, may have occurred during the intervening years and how they fit within the context of the new millennium. In the course of my research, I have consulted a large number of ceramicists in many countries who regularly work with porcelain and tried to discover something of their personal philosophy towards their art and its place in modern society. Particular emphasis is given in the book to the enormous diversity and rapid development that took place in international studio porcelain over

the latter part of the 20 th century and continues at the start of the 21st. This is an opportunity to examine some of the aesthetic concerns, technical achievements and working methods of these ceramicists currently working with porcelain and its close relative, bone china in various parts of the world.

Porcelain offers a far wider range of options and applications than those most popularly perceived for it. The basic qualities usually associated with or required of high-fired porcelain such as delicacy, translucency, fineness, whiteness, density and purity remain available, of course, but many potters have chosen to break with traditional expectations of the medium. Often, those singular physical properties will be still evident in a porcelain object but the emphasis on any or all of these will depend upon the manipulative processes employed at various stages from wet to dry; the thickness of sections; the application of colour in oxides, stains, slips or glazes; and on the final firing. The primary concern of most artists is more likely to be in the exploration and realisation of three-dimensional form in porcelain. To achieve this they have incorporated or developed various techniques for their purposes.

(Left) *Sails in the Mountains*, by Peteris Martinsons (Latvia), 1997. Porcelain sculpture, slip-cast and handbuilt, partly glazed, 38 x 20 x 19 cm (15 x 7 x 7½ in.), Martinsons' work exploits complexity, translucency and fragility.
Photograph by Maris Kundzins.

It has been generally accepted that porcelain, as a plastic material, can be somewhat daunting both to use and control until one becomes familiar with certain unique aspects of its character. In previous books I tried to clear away much of the fog and mystique surrounding the successful production of porcelain and to offer advice and suggestions for its imaginative use. Today, there appear to be virtually no boundaries that cannot be stretched and few rules that can remain inviolate in this area of human invention. There exists an immense variety of forms, surface treatments and imagery produced by porcelain potters from around the world, examples of which have been assembled together in this new book. Originality, flair and skill combine in the best work to present us with numerous stimulating images: vessels, tiles, wall panels, figurative sculptures, and abstract objects all created in an unusually 'unforgiving' medium. There are a number of potters who, after several successful years using porcelain, have returned to working with earthenware clays because they offer options that are easier to control at lower firing temperatures. Others have persevered in using this fine, white body and gained fresh inspiration by pushing it to the very limits of their ability. They have been joined by an increasing number of younger artists, excited by the whiteness and purity of the material, who are producing ever more extravagant expressions in form or in new conceptual installations.

Not all the pieces illustrated will be immediately recognisable as porcelain because they seem not to fit into any of the familiarly held perceptions. One might question, therefore, whether porcelain was the proper medium to use for them, but for one reason or another, it was decided that a different clay body would fail to satisfy all the practical and aesthetic requirements which the artist deemed essential

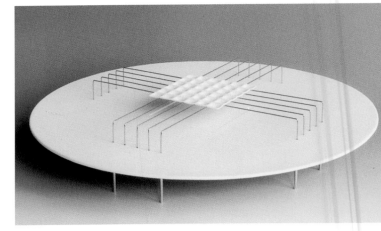

Untitled, by Wil Broekema (Holland), 1998. Limoges porcelain with steel wire, 30 cm (11¾ in.), fired to 1240°C (2264°F) in an electric kiln. *Photograph by the artist.*

for his/her personal ideas. Nevertheless, in each case, porcelain acts as the common denominator linking all the works chosen to illustrate this book. Techniques and processes described are, in many instances, similar to those identified with other branches of ceramics adapted, where necessary, to suit individual needs.

The work of the contemporary ceramicist has grown out of a long and glorious history. One might expect that countless generations of potters have explored every practical, technical, social, cultural and aesthetic aspect from the preparation and composition of clay bodies and glazes to the construction and firing of many different types of kilns in producing the vast wealth of ceramics which we all inherit. In truth, it is often stated that since so much has gone before, there is little scope for truly fresh invention. Still, ceramics will continue to offer us an appropriate, universally understood, medium to express individual thoughts, ideas and feelings. In this respect one can make an analogy with words or with musical notes in that they, also, can be infinitely reworked to communicate anew.

I have selected a wide range of images to demonstrate that imagination and inventiveness is still very much alive today. I tried to discover

(Top) *White/White Millefiori Bowl*, by Dorothy Feibleman (UK), 1999. Porcelain, d. 21 cm (8¼ in.) *Photograph by Mark Johnston.*

(Bottom left) *Reminiscence of a Pot*, two mobiles, by Hubert Kittel (Germany). Slip-cast elements partly coloured with cobalt solution unglazed, polished hard-paste porcelain, fired at 1400°C (2552°F), h. 29 cm (11½ in.). (The spout is connected; cylinder and cone aren't connected; the pedestal is a rolling vehicle). 'I like to play with the functional elements of a coffee – or teapot to find new design solutions. These elements (corpus, spout, handle,

lid, bottom) are old, traditional images and standards of our tableware culture. Sometimes I need this interplay between nonsense and sense in designing new products.' *Photograph by Klaus E. Göltz, Halle.*

(Bottom right) *Closed Second Inversion* by Sarah-Jane Selwood (UK), 2001. H. 13 cm (5 in.), d. 10 cm (4 in.), thrown porcelain (Limoges). The form is precisely cut multiple times, sections inverted and rejoined, bisque fired, 1000°C (1832°F), Ice Crackle glaze fired 1280°C (2336°F) in reduction. *Photograph by Shannon Tofts.*

Porcelain vessel, mounted on stoneware pedestal by Tim Gee (UK). Southern Ice Porcelain body painted with a shellac resist solution and washed back to create several levels of translucency, 19 x 9 cm (7½ x 3½ in.). Fired to 1290°C (2354°F) in an electric kiln and polished with silicon carbide (Wet 'n Dry) paper after both bisque and final firings. *Photograph by the artist.*

Dots & Lines, by Bai Ming (China), 2000. Wheel-thrown porcelain, 46 x 19 cm (18 x 7½ in.). *Photograph by the artist.*

how individual artists develop their ideas and come to terms with their materials and processes. This book attempts to examine the current situation and to explain the motivations, methods and techniques of some leading studio potters working almost exclusively in porcelain. Their work can be considered in relation to those traditional qualities which have made fine porcelain ceramics so highly prized by emperors, princes and commoners alike for hundreds of years. In addition, we can look

(Left) Incised porcelain bird and leaf bottle, by Elaine Coleman (USA), 2002. Iron blue celadon glaze, h. 19 cm (7½ in.), w. 9.5 cm (3¾ in.), fired to cone 10 in reduction. *Photograph by the artist.*

Covered jar, by Mahmoud Baghaeian (Canada), 2002. Porcelain freely painted with wax resist brushwork, d. 23.5 cm (9¼ in.), fired to cone 9. *Photograph by the artist.*

Still Life No. 58, by Elsa Rady (USA), 2002. Porcelain on painted aluminium shelf, 26.5 x 9.5 x 28 cm (10½ x 3¾ x 11 in.). *Photograph by Paul Sanders.*

Thrown lidded jar with bone china fin on lid, by Peter Beard (UK). H. 22 cm (8¾ in.). *Photograph by the artist.*

Porcelain Object No. 5, by Geoffrey Swindell (UK), 2002. H. 10 cm (4 in.), wheel-thrown and altered. *Photograph by the artist.*

beyond recognisable boundaries to see how porcelain is being used to contribute important elements in different kinds of three-dimensional expression. An enormous range of sculptural and architectural porcelain has been produced and examples appear throughout the book. Included, also, are a variety of vessel forms, some of which may be familiar while others are unusual in shape or concept.

There are many potters for whom those delicate and varying degrees of translucency, remain the supreme attraction and ultimate goal. Certainly, the interplay of light onto and through a finely-made piece provides one of the most satisfying experiences in both seeing and touching. However, this aspect may not appeal to everyone to the same extent. Some ceramicists, for example, are attracted to porcelain more for its smooth, dense texture that

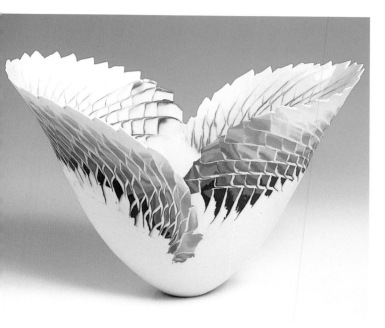

White Winged Bowl, by Judith De Vries (Holland).
Porcelain in white and coloured Limoges body, 18 x 24
cm (7 x 9½ in.), fired to 1220°C (2228°F) in oxidation.
The bottom is wheel-thrown and nerikomi elements built
up and adjusted. *Photograph by Ron Zijlstra.*

Porcelain sculpture, by Sueharu Fukami (Japan), 1998.
Slip-cast under pressure, glazed, pale blue celadon glaze,
reduction fired in a liquid petroleum gas kiln, 89 x 26 x 31
cm (35 x 10¼ x 12 in.). *Photograph by Takashi Hatakeyama.*

allows them to create extremely fine, incised, pierced and carved surfaces at various stages from wet to dry. Others will prefer to exploit whiteness for its own sake or as a 'canvas' for colour. For there is no doubt that much of the appeal of porcelain (and even more so with bone china) owes much to its unique brightness, so that uncontaminated by iron or other impurities, an unblemished colour spectrum is at their disposal.

At the time of writing and as will be confirmed later in this book, more and more ceramicists are content to work solely in pure white porcelain, often in a minimalist way. Some may clothe their pieces in a simple transparent glaze but the majority of these are satisfied to produce objects without disguising the plain, white surface. Often, such pieces are polished until absolutely smooth. Several artists have close links with industrial production, especially in slip-casting, and they are able to make use of factory facilities and expertise in their personal work. In a number of other individual studios, where a particular kind of colour response is required, the work is not even fired to its normal maturation point. In these cases, porcelain has been chosen to form the whole or a significant proportion of the body composition for making quite low-fired ceramic objects. This is because the artist is no longer concerned to meet the normal requirements of domestic use (e.g. to hold liquids) and the extra strength and durability afforded by firing the body to maturity is not essential. All porcelain bodies must be fired to temperatures in excess of 1200°C (2192°F) if they are to become impervious to water. But, even when fired as low as 1000°C (1832°F), porcelain still offers an extra-fine, smooth, white body, superior to most others. It provides such excellent opportunities for surface treatments that they compensate for any physical weakness. In some cases, potters have chosen to use porcelain merely as a slip to coat and conceal any coarser clay they chose to create the piece. Porcelain-based slip offers a good,

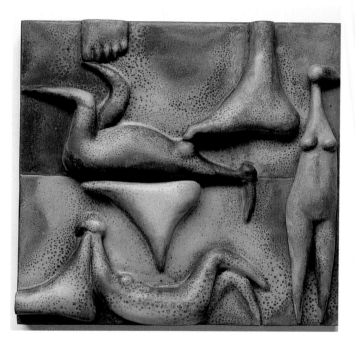

(Above) *Struggling Form*, by Harumi Nakashima (Japan), 2002. Hand-built porcelain, 50 x 40 x 50 cm (19 x 16 x 19 in.), fired to 1230°C (2246°F). *Photograph by Taku Saiki.*
(Top right) *The Lake of the Landscape*, by Wolfgang Vegas (Venezuela), 2001. Porcelain mixed, construction with stalks of wheat, electric firing 1200°C (2192°F), metal 14 x 34 x 31 cm (5½ x 13½ x 12½ in.). *Photograph by Gilles Boss.*
(Bottom right) Wall panel by Ruth Duckworth (USA).
Photograph by James Prinz.

white ground for colour while a thicker application can be compacted and burnished to a silky-smooth sheen.

Ceramicists, perhaps, are more intimately occupied with (and to a certain extent conditioned by) the materials, techniques and processes of their discipline than any other artist-craftsmen. They must understand sufficient of the practical physics and chemistry involved if they are to avoid frequent frustrations. Even the most experienced suffer disappointments from time to time when results are not quite what had been intended. Their search for personal ideals is continuous and, in many cases, their appetite for technical understanding is voracious. This interest has spawned an enormous number of books which have been published on every aspect of ceramics during the years following the Second World War but the demand for yet more information about technicalities remains undiminished.

Despite the inveterate curiosity of most potters, I have discovered a surprising number who admitted that they have little or no interest in ceramic chemistry for its own sake.

They obtain all their commercially-prepared materials from reliable sources knowing how they will perform in use so that they can concentrate all their creative energies to procure fairly predictable results. Above all it is the expression that matters. During more than 40 years of making and teaching ceramics, my own interest in and respect for the diverse ways in which individual artists around the world resolve technical as well as aesthetic problems of design remains strong. I firmly believe that as experience grows so does the realisation that there is so much more than anyone can possibly comprehend in a single lifetime. Therefore, we have to be selective, concentrating upon particular aspects that appeal to us and, in that continuous enquiry, we are limited only by the time we can devote to it and by our own capacity to understand. This fact, for me, contributes to the continuing excitement of ceramics and of porcelain in particular. The main aim of this book, therefore, is to examine and give details of the personal thoughts, feelings, approaches and techniques currently employed by individual ceramicists in this specialised field. However, it is important to stress that techniques can never be a satisfying end in themselves. They are only the *means* employed to achieve that end. Any discussion about methods and processes, therefore, must be directly related to the more significant aesthetic achievements of the work illustrated.

It is highly unlikely that the reader will find that *all* the objects depicted in this book appeal to his or her personal taste. Nor has it been possible to include reference to every notable

Eraser House, by Richard Shaw (USA), 1996. Porcelain with over-glaze transfers, 32 x 24 x 32 cm (12½ x 9½ x 12½ in.). *Photograph by Schopplein Studios.*

potter working in porcelain at the time of writing. Nevertheless, I believe that, as an author, it is essential to exercise a broadly catholic choice which gives a reasonably wide representation of studio porcelain at the beginning of the third millennium. I consulted a great number of ceramicists working in porcelain and bone china around the world all of whom have been most generous in providing me with information about their thoughts, feelings, aims and processes.

As a teacher of ceramics, it was incumbent on me to encourage and motivate my students to observe, learn, think, feel and experiment. Equally, as an artist, my own curiosities extend to discovering the how, why and wherefore behind the inspirational sources and working methods of professional ceramicists whom I meet. To this end, I have included comments made by individual artists using their own words, wherever possible, to assist further understanding and appreciation of the works illustrated in this book. There are detailed descriptions, also, of the working methods employed by many potters from different social

Hybrid Creature, by Dalit Tayar (Israel), 1995. Wheel-thrown and modelled porcelain with underglaze painting, h. 17.5 cm (6 ⅞ in.). *Photograph by Leonid Padrut.*

Ship of Fools, by Michael Flynn (UK/Germany), 2000. Hand-made in Meissen porcelain, glaze and enamels, h. 39 cm (15 ⅜ in.). *Photograph by the artist.*

and cultural backgrounds. Of course, the materials they use in the execution of their art are common to all ceramicists, but the stimuli, influences, approaches, techniques and objectives cover a very wide spectrum.

My own personal preference, for example, is for the making and enjoyment of 'vessel' forms, especially bowls, since they are open to infinite variation both subtle and extreme, whether or not concerned with function. The purity of a simple bowl shape, with its natural flowing profile springing from a narrow base and swelling out and upwards to open like a bud, has always appealed to me. Although countless millions of container forms have been produced in ceramics to serve a multitude of purposes from the humble to the sublime, there will never be an end to their

aesthetic possibilities. The best of such objects transcend utilitarian needs to become the purest form of three-dimensional art.

Throughout history, ceramics presents us with a magnificent kaleidoscope of human expression, functional, figurative and abstract. But, frequently, art critics have tended to dismiss sculptural work executed in clay as being of little relevance to the field of 'fine' art and arguments concerning its status remain unresolved. Today, it would appear acceptable to produce fine art from any and all kinds of different materials and in numerous guises from the familiar to the shockingly bizarre or as purely transient imagery. Art as photography, video and film have gained respect in this setting. Fired clay, on the other hand, irrespective of purpose or scale

(Above) *Three Helmet Bowls*, by Neville French (Australia), 1998. Porcelain, h. 7 cm (2 ¾ in.), d.16 cm (5 ¼ in.). *Photograph by Terence Bogue.*

(Below) *Tripod Bowl*, by Greg Daly (Australia), 2001. Wheel-thrown porcelain with enamel and gold leaf over glaze, fired to 1300°C (2372°F) followed by a lustre firing between 720°–800°C (1328–1472°F) in an electric kiln, d. 21 cm (8 ¼ in.). *Photograph by the artist.*

(Top) Vessel form, by Karin Bablok (Germany), 2002. Wheel-thrown porcelain painted with basalt glaze, h. 19 cm (7 ½ in.), d. 26 cm (10 ¼ in.), fired in reduction atmosphere 1280°–1300°C (2336°–2372°F), by *Photograph by Joachim Riches.* (Above) *Windlights*, by Piet Stockmans (Belgium), 1997. Slip-cast porcelain, 14 x 14 cm (5 ½ in.), *Photograph by E. van Sloun.*

may receive only reluctant recognition in some quarters however expressive the work or its relevance to, or comment upon, modern life. Unreserved confirmation that the best contemporary ceramics are worthy of the definition 'fine art' is, I believe, long overdue.

Uncompromising attitudes raise questions as to whether criticism of any ceramic work can be truly objective other than in matters of fact, to be judged in those measurable, quantifiable aspects such as pure craftsmanship. Indeed, to what extent can critical criteria remain constant in the face of continuing development? The unrelenting speed of change affects us all. What one generation adores the next often abhors as in other areas of the visual arts. It would seem virtually impossible to identify a definitive kind of 'public' taste that might indicate what should be expected of ceramic art today. After all, we do not *need* individually produced, handmade ceramics as in past periods. They are not essential for everyday, practical purposes. Of course, there will always be those who prefer not

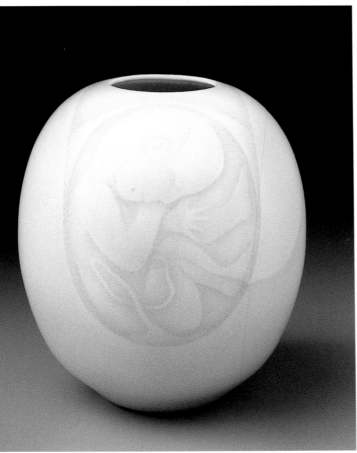

(Top) Porcelain, by Victor Greenaway, (Australia), 2002. Spiral-lipped bowl, eggshell white, w. 33 cm (13 in.) x h. 19 cm (7 ½ in.). *Photograph by Terence Bogue.*
(Bottom) *Linda's Treasure*, by Scott Malcolm 2002. Porcelain, wheel-thrown and incised under celadon glaze, h. 8 cm (3 ¼ in.), reduction fired to cone 12. *Photograph by Peter Lee.*

to use industrially-made ceramics, or glass, or plastics, etc. in a domestic situation and, doubtless, their needs will continue to be supplied, but the modern potter is not *bound* to cater for them. Therefore, the only certain restrictions, apart from economics or individual sensibilities, are those imposed by the potter's own ability to control the material processes of his or her art. One can choose to build upon tradition or fly in the face of it. Above all else, contemporary ceramics should be accepted as a prime vehicle for tactile, visual expression.

Many questions came to mind during my enquiry into contemporary studio porcelain, some of which relate to ceramics in general. Although some answers may be found in the following pages, most will remain open for discussion and reassessment. It is extremely difficult to attempt a definitive analysis of a discipline in a state of constant flux, but by questioning, examining and observing developments around the world one can arrive at some small understanding and appreciation of the wonderful diversity to be found in modern ceramics. We can look at a piece and ask ourselves in what way it relates to traditional ceramics or how it fits within the context of the late 20th and early 21st century? Whether it has the power to evoke a sympathetic or antipathetic response in us? Are there references to, or influences from, any other branches of the visual arts? Does it seem to reflect a moment in time like the present or does it echo past moods, expressions or cultures? How 'original' is it and does it matter if it is not? Is it so esoteric that it only belongs in an exclusive gallery setting? Is the use of certain porcelain elements, set within an 'installation', that itself may be only of a temporary nature, a valid application of the medium? Are there are any guiding principles to help us appreciate the work beyond those of supreme craftsmanship? Should there be any need to universally justify acceptance of the totally unexpected? How or why does it appeal or repel us? The main problems often experienced when we are faced with unfamiliar imagery, or even with materials being used outside traditional contexts, seem to be with applying tolerance and respect for that which does not fit into a comfortable niche. No one kind of expression should be deemed superior to another, they are merely *different*. We can like or dislike some more than others and, in so doing, make our personal choices. Life would be infinitely dull if we all prescribed to a particular taste!

Writing these few sentences reminds me of a time, long ago, when I taught painting in an adult education evening class. One man clearly knew what he liked and liked what he knew. His mind was closed to anything else. Consequently, he made little progress. Other students were prepared to experiment. Their work improved rapidly and, consequently, their enjoyment grew week by week.

Judgment on the merit of any of the images presented is bound to be subjective to some degree. Whether the work succeeds in communicating to us on any level is, inevitably, an individual matter. Bernard Leach once wrote that we must beware of superficiality for, 'only the artist or craftsman of unusual perception and strength of character stands a chance of selecting what is best from the welter of ideas which rolls in on him today'. Open and receptive minds will enjoy that challenge!

We are constantly bombarded with images from so many different sources that few can fail to be affected by them. The natural world has long provided inspirational material for creative expression in ceramics but experiences of travel, transport, architecture, urban environments, civil or international strife etc. in addition to aspects of the human condition such as war, famine, social injustice and even family relationships can also act as trigger points for intensely personal work.

I have been extremely fortunate in being able to select examples of porcelain ceramics to illustrate the text from ceramicists whose earlier work has been included in my previous books and to have discovered and made contact with many others whom I did not previously know. I found the research involved to be both invigorating and, at times, frustrating. The frustrations

Nerikomi bowl, by Thomas Hoadley (USA), 1998. Handbuilt with coloured porcelain, d. 25–28 cm (10–11 in.). *Photograph by the artist.*

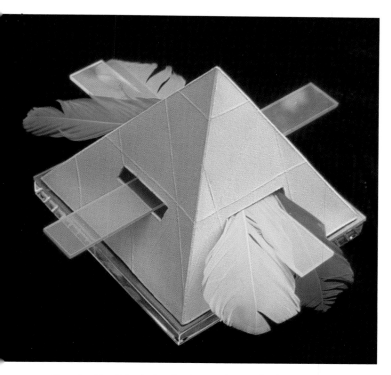

Carnival in Gizeh, by Jo-Anne Caron (Belgium), 2002. Porcelain pyramid with feathers, 20 x 20 x 23 cm (8 x 8 x 9 in.), fired to 1230°C (2246°F). *Photograph by the artist.*

were constant because the gathering and collating of material together with the concentrated effort of writing allowed no time for me to respond in my own ceramic work to the surge of creative energy aroused by such an amazing diversity of images, and the richness of invention and ingenuity, demonstrated in the work of so many ceramicists included in this book. It is my hope that the selection presented to the reader will prove both stimulating and thought provoking. In my previous books only about one third or at most half of all illustrations were published in colour and one had to rely on the captions for colours or detailed information in order to visualise the objects as they really were. Fortunately, full colour pictures have become the norm in books and magazines about works of art so that we can more easily appreciate them. The work of some ceramicists whom I know particularly well is described in more detail but I am aware that space does not allow me to do proper justice to every artist whose work is

Spiral I by Walther Sturmer (Germany). *Photograph by Fotostudio Schuster, Munich.*

illustrated. Indeed, it is impossible to show the full range of creativity through an inevitably limited selection of pieces from each ceramicist. However, it is my earnest wish that readers will become sufficiently interested and encouraged to seek more information about any individual whose work appeals to them.

CHAPTER ONE

QUALITIES AND PROPERTIES OF PORCELAIN

COMPOSITION OF PORCELAIN BODIES

It is not difficult to imagine the enormous impact made on Europe when the first shipments of elegant and refined porcelain objects arrived from China. This was at a time when few people possessed any more than coarse earthenwares. When Oriental porcelains appeared at European ports during the 16th century, their beauty sparked a major artistic revolution. An urgent search to discover the secret porcelain recipe and to manufacture porcelain from local materials soon began, but it was to be over 200 years before success was achieved.

Pottery manufacture in England had not been accorded the same degree of royal patronage enjoyed by many European factories, even though soft-paste porcelains were being produced from as early as 1745. While Chinese kaolin had proved to be satisfactory for manufacture in the natural state, the English equivalent, with its larger particle size, was highly refractory and it lacked the

plasticity of those traditionally used in the East. In order to make a good workable body, certain other materials had to be added to the composition. Extra silica in the form of flint or quartz is required to ensure compatibility between body and glaze. French kaolins are in the main rather more plastic than those from Cornwall, but they still fall short of the super plasticity of those found in China.

The major innovation in the English pottery industry was the development of a kind of hybrid porcelain by Josiah Spode towards the end of the 18th century. He added bone ash (calcium phosphate), made by calcining cattle bones, to the essential hard-paste ingredients, thus providing a much more manageable composition well-suited to factory production. This material became known as 'bone china' and it possessed those desirable and sought after qualities of whiteness and translucency. Bone ash acts as a powerful flux with clay and up to 50% may be present in a typical bone china body. There can be problems in the kiln, however, due to the high shrinkage rate and also to the fairly limited firing range. Its manufacture was confined almost exclusively to England and, for many years, the Staffordshire potteries supplied a worldwide market. Although

(Left) *Triple Porcelain in Dilapidation*, by Jeroen Bechtold (Holland), 2002. Green porcelain inlay in white, 7.5 x 7.5 x 47 cm (3 x 3 x 18½ in.) *Photograph by the artist.*

bone china remains a rather difficult medium, it has become a popular material for a number of studio potters today who are using industrial processes such as slip-casting, grinding and screen-printing with imagination and originality.

Few clays can be used 'as dug' in the making of refined ceramics. Therefore we refer to the clay mixtures as bodies. Varying amounts of clays and certain other materials such as quartz, flint, feldspar, nepheline syenite, Cornish stone, whiting, silica sand and talc are combined together to make workable plastic bodies for a whole range of purposes and firing temperatures. Porcelain bodies are usually composed of just three main ingredients: kaolin (china clay), feldspar and quartz with smaller amounts of ball clay or bentonite added to ensure plasticity. Unfortunately, ball clays impair the whiteness and affect translucency whereas bentonite is less likely to do so. However, bentonite (a highly plastic, colloidal substance with a very fine grain size), which is widely used for preparing porcelain with good throwing properties, can increase problems of shrinking and cracking if more than 6% exists in the composition. Other plasticisers of vegetable origin are used in some modern porcelain bodies.

Porcelain, therefore, is simply a composition of fine, relatively similar-sized particles of kaolin, silica and feldspar that provides for complete fusion at high temperatures. It is the extra silica content in porcelain which contributes its glassy translucent quality but, at the same time, makes it more susceptible to stress due to its high rate of expansion and contraction. All potters are aware of the importance of slow cooling following a kiln firing, but porcelain is especially vulnerable to dunting, if cooled too quickly, at those points where the silica inversion takes place at 570°C (1058°F) and 226°C (439°F) respectively.

Despite differences in composition, most porcelain bodies possess the potential to be translucent but the degree to which that state is

Glas Maol: Spring Pillow, by Tony Franks (UK), 2000. Bone china, 58 x 44 x 18 cm (22 ¾ x 17 ¼ x 7 in.), fired twice to 1200°C (2192°F), then 1220°–1230°C (2228°–2246°F), sand-blasted, polished and coloured after bisque firing. *Photograph by Shannon Tofts.*

achieved depends on the thickness, or rather thinness, of the clay and on the temperatures reached in the kiln. Nevertheless, if translucency alone is held to be the key to defining 'true' porcelain, it may be argued that many of the bodies currently available are no more than white porcellanous stonewares. Therefore, the definition of porcelain becomes open to question. However, this is not an issue that concerns us here. My research has discovered an extremely wide range of applications for white, porcellanous bodies having a very high content of the essential kaolin, feldspar and silica supplying the main qualities expected of porcelain. Some body compositions are considerably more translucent than others but that particular property may be of little interest to the ceramicist for whom form, surface, colour or texture is sufficient for their personal expression. Porcelain bodies generally become vitrified when fired to temperatures well above 1200°C (2192°F) and the higher this is, the greater the proportion of glass that will be formed in the body. This is the main factor assisting the passage of light through it, although complete vitrification is not necessary for this to occur.

Regardless of an abundance of fairly reliable prepared materials available from commercial sources, the search for the ultimate porcelain body free from any disadvantages seems set to continue. The ideal would be a supremely white body which would be very plastic, easy to throw or handbuild, be able to support itself when wet, have minimal shrinkage, resist cracking or splitting at every stage from wet to dry, be translucent when relatively thick, be strong when fired, and to mature around 1200°C (2192°F) while performing to perfection in any kind of kiln or atmosphere. Even with the advanced technology available to the ceramics industry today, it is unlikely that all these requirements can ever be met but ceramicists continue to explore possibilities.

A translucent porcelain body recipe, specially developed for use by the late Audrey Blackman (well-known for her rolled modelled porcelain figures), was published in *Ceramic Review* (No. 100) in 1986. It remains popular with a number of British potters and is as follows:

Super Standard Porcelain China Clay	50
(Imerys Minerals, *previously English* *China Clays*)	
Westone – H (sodium activated white Texas bentonite)	5
FFF Feldspar	27
Quartz (300s mesh)	17
Whiting	1

Another recipe for a throwable bone china body was prepared by D. Christopher Hogg and this, also, appeared in *Ceramic Review* (No. 113) in 1988. I am indebted to him for allowing me to quote the following information:

Bone ash	50
Super Standard Porcelain China Clay	25
MF4 flux	2.5

2.5% Westone – H white bentonite is added to this recipe.

From a scientific point of view, whiteness and translucency of porcelain are well understood to the extent of being calculable, given the right information. The properties are dependent on two fundamental properties: light absorption and light scatter. (I am here ignoring the influence of thickness, which, although very important, I take as being obvious.)

Light is absorbed by colouring metal ions, usually iron and titanium in clay bodies. Light is scattered at interfaces between the glassy matrix and the crystalline phases present such as mullite from the clay, and undissolved quartz. Colouring metal ions reduce both translucency and whiteness. Crystalline phases reduce translucence but increase whiteness. The whiteness and translucency actually achieved are the result of the balance between these two parameters.

To make a porcelain that is both white and translucent requires the minimum of colouring metal ions and a fairly low level of crystalline phases. This means using pure clays, no ball clay for example, and a high feldspar content to give plenty of glass on firing and only a small quantity of crystalline phases. Needless to say, these requirements conflict with the plasticity required for throwing, and stability during firing. Compromises are inevitable.

Firing porcelain in reduction helps, converting yellow ferric iron to pale blue ferrous iron that is less strongly colouring, provided that no titania is present to interact with it. Cornish china clays contain little titania, but many china clays from other parts of the world can contain as much as in many English ball clays.

Another technique is to add something that reacts with the iron and bleaches it. This is what happens in bone china, where the phosphate from the bone ash in effect bleaches the iron. The result is an almost pure white body that is very translucent. Unfortunately, a lot of bone ash is needed to ensure that all the iron is combined with the phosphate, and a bone china body can be described as a porcelain body mixed with an equal weight of bone ash. This halves the clay content and so greatly impairs the plasticity.

In the extreme, the two properties of whiteness and translucency are conflicting: a material is either extremely white and opaque or extremely translucent and not white. If nearly all the light is reflected back to you, there is none left to pass through, and conversely if much of the light passes through, less is reflected back. White opaque glazes are opaque because they are white; window glass is very translucent but not at all white. In practice, things are not that extreme, and most people have an appreciation of what is white and translucent in porcelain, compared to what is not.

In addition to all that, there is the property of plasticity that I have mentioned only in passing. Here, I'm afraid science has still a long way to go in understanding the fundamentals. There is plenty of practical experience and many empirical tests for plasticity, but not much science. The simplest solution to poor plasticity is to add a little bentonite, and use the purest you can get. A sodium-activated bentonite is best, acidified after mixing it in to ensure good flocculation. Preferably use an organic acid that burns away, such as acetic acid (vinegar). Mineral acids give off unpleasant fumes during firing. An alternative method of flocculating is to add a very little slaked lime (and I mean a very little, if you value the skin on your hands). Some china clays produced in Czechoslovakia and much used in German porcelain are flocculated this way.

A good, reliable porcelain body introduced to many potters in Britain during the 1960s and 1970s and which became extremely popular was the David Leach Porcelain Body. I used it myself almost exclusively for several years. This body is still available from commercial sources today and can be obtained in many parts of the world as, indeed, can most other prepared bodies. The porcelain from Limoges in France is the preferred vehicle for the work of several potters whose work is illustrated in this book. Others use a porcelain based on the Zettlitz kaolin from Czechoslovakia. One of my current preferences is for the Harry Fraser Porcelain Body produced by Potclays Limited in Etruria, Stoke-on-Trent, England. I have found this body to be generally most reliable to use. It throws well, fires white and, although it has a reasonably wide firing range, it is translucent when used thinly enough at temperatures as low as 1220°C (2228°F). Harry Fraser explained the process of developing this particular porcelain for me as in the following notes.

There are many recipes for porcelain bodies. Most of them are blends of kaolin with a flux (usually feldspar) and free silica in the form of flint or quartz. Some recipes include additions of ball clays, bentonite or other plasticisers. The incorporation of ball clay is very desirable from a plasticity viewpoint but, if present in any significant amounts, tends to prevent translucency. Consequently, its use in porcelain bodies is usually confined to recipes where translucency is not a requirement – for example, in porcelain insulators.

Development of a plastic, throwable but white firing and translucent porcelain is very dependent upon the type of kaolin used. Grolleg features in many recipes and, indeed, it was the basis of the well-known David Leach Porcelain Body formulation in the 1960s and 1970s. However, an even more plastic kaolin was then produced by English China Clays; this was known as Standard Porcelain China Clay. This china clay has a very slightly lower iron content than Grolleg and thus fires slightly whiter as well as being slightly more plastic. I, therefore, selected it as the basis for a new porcelain body, using FFF Feldspar as the flux and 200s mesh quartz to develop thermal expansion. Preliminary mixes were not sufficiently plastic and so Quest white bentonite was progressively introduced until the plasticity seemed to be reasonably good – and certainly as good as any other porcelains then available.

A problem is that we all know what plasticity is

but nobody has yet succeeded in devising an instrument that can properly measure it. Plasticity is closely linked to green strength and that we can measure by means of a Modulus of Rupture machine. MOR tests done on clay samples of the new body showed that green strength was well up to that of other porcelains. However, previous experience had indicated that the handling properties could, perhaps, be further improved by slight flocculation. This also would enable filter pressing times to be significantly reduced and thus lower production costs.

Trials were done using whiting and other flocculants as a part replacement for feldspar in the body recipe. Whiting does, however, become a very vigorous flux at high temperatures – especially where a glassy matrix is developed – and so refractoriness tests had to be carried out to quantify the extra fluxing effect. In this way, an optimum flocculant addition was incorporated which produced a slightly better throwing body, the clay seeming more flexible and standing up better. It was incidentally interesting that the improvement in throwing properties of the clay body could not be detected on the MOR machine. Flocculation also reduced the filter pressing time from around ten hours to about seven, enabling production in the normal working day.

The quartz grain size was also important. In porcelain bodies, the effect of the quartz content on thermal expansion depends on its particle size, and this is influenced by the firing temperature and amount of glass formation which takes place. Glass formation dissolves the free silica, converting it to silicate which lowers thermal expansion and thus has an opposite effect to free quartz. The finer the particle size the more effective free silica becomes in promoting thermal expansion but also the more easily it can be taken into glaze solution by the solvent action of the fluxes. A 200s mesh grade of quartz was selected which, in trials, gave the best combination of craze resistance and fineness.

The new porcelain body was then sampled to porcelain users whose production trials confirmed that it threw exceptionally well and fired to a good colour and translucency.

A most important consideration was the production plant upon which to produce the new porcelain. Hitherto, production of studio porcelain bodies had been by slotting the production in between batches of other white firing bodies, e.g. white earthenware and white stoneware types. In a sliphouse system one can clean out blungers, agitation arks and pugmills but not very easily, and it is impractical to clean out interconnecting pipework to the pumps etc. In a factory, therefore, it is likely that when switching from one body to another there will be some degree of contamination with what was previously processed. For this reason, the practice of rejecting the initial production and progressively feeding it back into the system is generally used to minimise any contamination with the previous body. Nevertheless, this procedure cannot be as good as the use of plant dedicated only to porcelain production.

Production of the new body was, therefore, withheld until dedicated plant could be made available. Eventually, suitable plant became available at Potclays Limited and the body was launched into production.

'Southern Ice Porcelain' is a fairly new body now produced commercially in Australia and marketed around the world. This porcelain resulted from a long period of research carried out in Hobart. In the mid-1980s, **Les Blakebrough** (Australia) began working with unglazed white porcelain using many of the plastic bodies that are available from France, England and Australia but none had all the properties he felt were necessary for his purposes. They were either difficult to work with in that some would not respond well to simple tasks like kneading, some tended to laminate in the preparation process, or they were not a good enough colour when fired. Blakebrough set himself a precise target.

Forest Floor, large bowl, by Les Blakebrough (Australia), 2002. Southern Ice Porcelain, thrown, deep etched, unglazed, polished, d. 25 cm (9 ⅞ in.), h. 20 cm (7 ⅞ in.). *Photograph by the artist.*

Wood-fired bottle by Janet Mansfield (Australia), 2002. Made from Three Ways Porcelain. *Photograph by the artist.*

I had in mind a clay that would look and feel good when left unglazed in the fired state. I wanted it to be a clean, white colour, with a sensible overall shrinkage rate – like 12%. I wanted it to work easily in all making processes – throwing, slab building or slip-casting, and to perform well on a semi-automatic roller-head machine.

This was an ideal research project and, having established the Ceramic Research Unit at the University of Tasmania – Centre for the Arts, in the late 1980s, Blakebrough obtained the first of several Australian Research Council grants in 1994 to investigate the development of a fresh porcelain clay. This clay project continued for five years until a body was produced that fulfilled all his requirements. It proved to be whiter than any other porcelain body offered, a reasonable clay to work with and very plastic. It can be thrown, cast or worked on roller machines. It matures to a good translucent body at 1280°C (2336°F) and fires equally well in oxidation or reduction. It requires care to join – as in applying handles which need to be fixed with both parts as close

as possible in consistency. Cast handles can be attached very easily with slip.

In 1999 the result of this research was commercialised through Clayworks of Dandenong, Victoria who began production of Southern Ice Porcelain. Local and export markets quickly opened up. This is one of the most exciting white and translucent porcelains that I have ever used.

Janet Mansfield (Australia) has developed a porcelain clay body, in conjunction with another Sydney potter, Judy Boydell. One of her purposes in this project was to explore the potential of local materials, especially the clays and feldspars in the area around Gulgong NSW, Australia. She explained her motivation for this enterprise:

Many Australian potters are importing porcelain from overseas companies and it seemed to me that we should be developing what was at hand.

Gulgong is an area rich in natural resources and, by using them, it should be possible to find an individual and personal aesthetic for my work. When thrown and turned thinly, and fired to 1300°C (2372°F), this clay body is vitreous and translucent. It blushes orange when partially protected from the wood flame, possibly because of a small percentage of titanium in its composition. The recipe is a simple one, just clay blended with a local siliceous feldspar. We are continuing to test these blends looking for optimum strength and whiteness. The porcelain is available commercially, sold under the name, 'Three Ways Porcelain', and we have had some good reports from ceramic artists using it.

Another excellent porcelain body has been produced by **Tom Coleman** (USA). He started working with porcelain in the late 1960s with very little information on the subject and only a few porcelain formulas published that used materials available in the United States. One common recipe that some potters tried during that time came to be known as 'equal parts porcelain'. This clay contained the same amounts of kaolin, ball clay, silica and feldspar. He soon understood why few potters persevered with this imperfect material. He described it as like 'window putty that fired to a similar colour'. Since then, the ceramic industry has made great advances in mining natural resources and in manufacturing new materials. For some 30 years or so, he formulated and tested hundreds of different porcelain bodies until the invention of a manmade plasticiser enabled him to compose a body that throws as well as any stoneware or white clay on the market today.

The real secret for me is being able to use more than 30% silica for glaze fit without sacrificing the throwing properties of the clay body. As a traditionalist, I think a true porcelain should be very white, translucent, ring like a bell, and create a non-crazing marriage between the surface of the

Porcelain bottle, by Tom Coleman (USA), 2002. Wheel-thrown and decorated on the surface with oxides and glazes, dipped in Coleman White Chun glaze, h. 23 cm (9 in.) w. 23 cm (9 in.), fired to cone 10 in reduction. *Photograph by the artist.*

clay and the glaze. To me, any formula that contains ball clay is a porceleanous stoneware. A true porcelain has an inner glow that reflects through the surface of the clay and continues through to the surface of the glaze. Any glaze applied to a good porcelain should take on a whole different texture and colour quality. This result cannot be achieved by applying porcelain slips over darker clays. It just won't have that glow.

PORCELAIN BODY RECIPES

Many potters choose to make their own porcelain bodies to recipes with which they have become familiar over a long period of time. In this way, they can avoid some of the problems encountered in the use of commercially-prepared bodies when ingredients are altered for one reason or another. **Tom Turner** (USA) gave me the following recipes for (A) a body which he made up and used for many years and (B) a recently revised composition:

Tom Turner Porcelain Bodies *(for cone 9 –10 Reduction)*

(A)		(B)		
Vee Gum –T	4	Vee Gum T	8	(Plasticiser from R.T. Vanderbuilt)
OM4 ball clay	12	OM4 ball clay	25	
Tile 6 kaolin	75	Tile 6 kaolin	150	
Kaopaque-20	38	Kaopaque-20	75	(delaminated, washed kaolin)
Custer feldspar	60	Custer feldspar	125	
Silica (200s mesh)	70	Silica (200s mesh)	125	
Epsom salts	0.25	Epsom salts	0.5	
		Alumina hydrate	10	(150s mesh C-31)

Porcelain vase, by Tom Turner (USA), 2002. Combed surface, honey ash glaze, h. 25.5 cm (10 in.), w. 12.5 cm (5 in.). *Photograph by the artist.*

Vee Gum-T is the whitest and most plastic material I've ever found. It is a plasticiser and lubricant that doesn't burn out. The Epsom salts are essential for throwing as a flocculated body will stand up and a deflocculated body will not.

Turner mixes the above bodies in a particular order. Firstly, the Vee Gum-T is blunged in warm or hot water and then he proceeds down the list of ingredients and, by adding the most plastic materials first, maximum plasticity is achieved. This body matures at cone 9 and will survive up to cone 10 but then begins to deform. For handbuilding, the Vee Gum-T content should be increased to between 2% and 3%. To lower the maturation point, 1% of talc is added for each lower cone number required. Recipe (B) was developed because Turner wanted to improve the throwing properties and strengthen its ability to support itself in the process.

The addition of mullite, Molochite or a grog made from the same body either leaves spots or a rough surface when fired. I happened to have a slightly coarse alumina hydrate that I have used for a kiln wash for 30 years. Adding 2% to my porcelain body has made positive changes to the way it performs.

Sandra Black (Australia) suggested a porcelain body recipe developed by Mike Kusnik in Western Australia:

No. 1	Cresta B.B. kaolin	60
	Potash feldspar	40
	Zinc oxide	3

She altered this recipe in 1983 in order to improve the whiteness as follows:

No. 2	Cresta B.B. kaolin	30
	Eckalite No. 1 kaolin	30
	Potash feldspar	40
	Zinc oxide	3
	Zircon	2.5

Cresta B.B. kaolin	40
Eckalite No. 1 kaolin	32
Zinc oxide	3
Silica	26
Bentonite	3

This clay is a very white and plastic porcelain. The feldspar, zinc oxide, silica and bentonite are milled for 12 hours. After 12 hours, add the kaolin and mill for a further four hours.

Black prepares her porcelain in batches of 10 kg (22 lb) dry weight, firstly making it into a slip which is stirred and sieved through a 100s mesh. The clay is then ball milled for between 16–24 hours. This removes any iron spots and grinds the clay to a fine consistency before it is poured into cloth bags to be hung up to dry in a shaded area. When the right consistency is obtained, the bags are dampened down with a water hose to remove dirt and to soften hardened slip around the opening. The clay is removed from the bags and wedged before storage. It is usable after its first wedging but storage is recommended to improve plasticity.

Michael Tannock (New Zealand) recently tested a series of porcelain body recipes for translucency, slumping at high temperature, whiteness, and shrinkage. While testing he was aware of trying to keep the levels of titanium dioxide and iron oxide to a minimum as their presence precludes translucency. He gave details of this research and his final recipe, quoted here, is based on those tests.

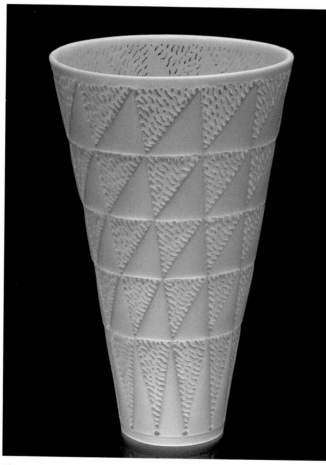

Slip-cast and carved vessel by Sandra Black (Australia), 2001. Made from Sealey's doll-casting porcelain, h. 19 cm (7½ in.), fired to cone 7 in an electric kiln and then polished with silicon carbide paper. *Photograph by the artist.*

China clay (Premium NZ)	41
Nepheline syenite	28
Silica 200s mesh	9.5
Silica 350s mesh	9.5
Clay Ceram (a sort of white ball clay)	10
Bentone CT	2
Epsom salts	0.5

Another variation provided by Black also comes from Mike Kusnik:

I fire this porcelain to Orton cone 6 in oxidation. It

develops very good translucency and is very white at this temperature. I use a commercially-available fritted clear glaze. My choice of materials depends on the amounts of iron and titanium that are present in them. Thus, 'normal' bentonite, ball clays and china clays are excluded and replaced with less iron- and titanium-bearing clays. Bentone CT is, I believe, hectorite, a whiter firing clay, from the smectite group of minerals (the smectite minerals are also called bentonites). It and the ball clay are used as plasticisers. I decided to use some ball clay to help to keep the cost down as the Bentone CT is expensive, and although the ball clay does contain higher titanium dioxide levels, the fired body does not seem affected by it. Premium China Clay is a white-firing china clay mined in New Zealand. It is composed mainly of halloysite, rather than kaolinite. It may not be available in other parts of the world, so a substitution may be necessary, with adjustment to account for any amount of feldspar and silica that another china clay may contribute. Rational analysis shows that Premium China Clay is about 91 halloysite (chemically the same as kaolinite) and 9% free quartz.

Bentone CT is a proprietary name for a bentonite substitute. I actually think that they use it as a paint additive. It is referred to as a hectorite clay. Geologically speaking there is a group of similarly structured clays which belong to the same group, the smectites. Bentonite belongs to this, and hectorite does also. Hectorite has a 'type locality' (where it was first described and named) of Hector in California USA I think. It is one of the constituent minerals that make up Gerstley Borate, along with Colemanite. It has the useful habit of swelling with the addition of water, because of the way that the layers of the minerals are structured which means that it can absorb a lot of water and makes it a good plasticiser.

Teapot and cup, by Michael Tannock (New Zealand), 2002. Wheel-thrown porcelain, oxidation fired to Orton cone 8 with a copper glaze in oxidation for the delicate blue colour. Teapot: 14 x 11 x 22 cm (5 ½ x 4 ¼ x 8 ¾ in.); cup: 9 cm x 7 cm (3 ½ x 2 ¾ in.). *Photograph by Studio La Gonda.*

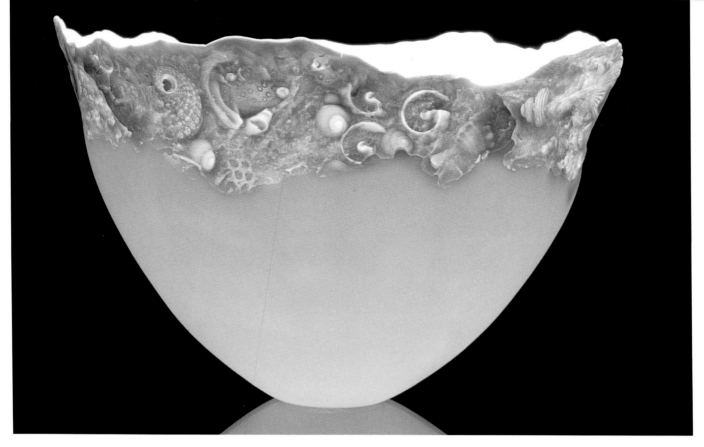

Cretaceous Bowl, by Angela Mellor (Australia), 2002. Bone china with paperclay inlay, h. 12 cm (4 ¾ in.), w. 18 cm (7 ¼ in.) x d. 18 cm (7 ¼ in.), fired at 1250°C (2282°F), oxidised. *Photograph by the artist.*

PAPER PORCELAIN

An increasing number of ceramicists have experimented with porcelain bodies mixed with other materials such as paper or textiles. Soaking textile fabric in slip enables them to wrap thin flexible sheets around a form and the organic matter is burnt away in the kiln to leave the 'skin' of fired clay behind. Cotton paper pulp mixed 50/50 with dry clay produces a heavy slip that can be poured on to plaster batts to make flat sheets or it can be cast to shape in plaster moulds. Stiffened sheets can be rolled out so that the surface resembles leather. These sheets can be torn or cut with scissors and assembled into various forms in the normal way. Firing should be carried out in a well-ventilated area to allow for the pungent gases that the mixture releases.

Paul Scott (UK) is one ceramicist who has explored the possibilities offered by mixing paper pulp with porcelain. He uses a mixture consisting of two parts porcelain to one part paper pulp. This proportion gives the material remarkable strength in both the leatherhard and dry states and it is possible to produce literally paper-thin sheets with it. Although Scott uses these ceramic sheets rather like a printmaker would use ordinary paper for making others have created sculptural expressions with similar material.

Angela Mellor (Australia/UK) uses pulp made from a soft, white tissue paper mixed into a bone china slip. This is converted into a plastic condition so that she can attach fragments to the rims of slip-cast vessel forms without any loss of translucency.

Maggie Barnes (UK) explained how she prepares paper porcelain by mixing dry porcelain powder (usually, Potclays HF1149) into a batch of paper pulp until the resulting slurry is similar to thick cream. She prefers to use 100% cotton fibres not only for purity and whiteness, but also for its extra strength. 'Some of the cheaper, commercially produced cellulose fibres sold for clay use are, in my opinion a poor substitute.' When combined, these ingredients form a pure white clay that she finds the perfect canvas with which to work. The mixture is left to stand for 48 hours to allow the clay and the fibres to amalgamate.

While pursuing a sponsored research project, Barnes produced a series of coloured tiles and panels with Southern Ice Porcelain. She believes that this body has a brilliant whiteness beyond any porcelain she has used previously, and its matt surface responds to colour in the same way as quality white paper. By combining it with cotton fibres, she created a hybrid material that performs perfectly for her purposes. The drying process must be slow and carefully monitored so that the slabs and tiles thus formed will behave well at all stages of production. Her work is fired to 1260°C

(2300°F) although this particular clay becomes translucent at 1250°C (2282°F).

During the papermaking stages of this research project, I had been incorporating surgical gauze into the paper 'tiles' to add strength. Various samples of this were still lying around in the studio, and I played with them on the workbench as I went about my habitual tidying of debris during kiln firing. By the end of the day I had a series of coloured panels created by using the gauze as a resist to coloured slip washes. Why colour in the middle of what was a pure white work period? This triggered something in the creative memory that resulted in a feverish search through sketchbooks and other source material in an attempt to find what had caused the mental detour. As is often the case, it came to the surface when I stopped looking. The answer lay in my shell collection. Seemingly endless variations of surface pattern – the mesh patterns on paperclay slabs were re-created 'memories' from my lifelong obsession with marine life; reinforced daily by the display in my sitting room.

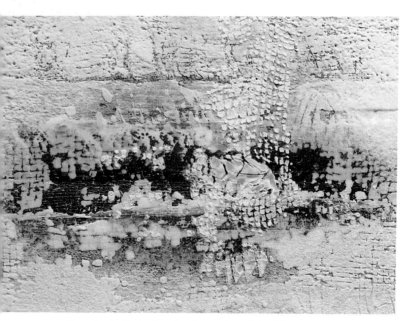

Panel, shell design (surface detail) by Maggie Barnes (UK), 2002. Porcelain paperclay with pure porcelain stained slip decoration, unglazed and polished, reduction fired 1260°C (2300°F). Created during a research project sponsored by Yorkshire Arts. *Photograph by Jerry Hardman-Jones.*

Barnes explained how she prepares porcelain paperclay from equal parts of Southern Ice Porcelain slip and 100% cotton fibres pulp. Ideally, the slip should be the consistency of thick cream and the prepared pulp should have as much surface water removed as is feasible. The mixture is well beaten in a glaze mixer, then poured onto plaster batts to remove surplus moisture. The resulting sheets are rolled to thin them for translucent work, or laminated together to create thicker slabs for tiles and panels. Embossed tiles and panels in both paper and paperclay are created to her own design. These are carved into lino, plaster or clay, or cast in silicone rubber. The carved plaster, bisque clay, rubber stamps and lino-cuts are all used to create impressed surface relief. The more flexible silicon rubber stamps and lino

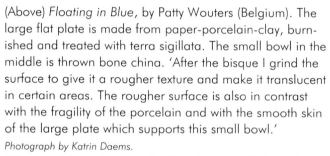

(Above) *Floating in Blue*, by Patty Wouters (Belgium). The large flat plate is made from paper-porcelain-clay, burnished and treated with terra sigillata. The small bowl in the middle is thrown bone china. 'After the bisque I grind the surface to give it a rougher texture and make it translucent in certain areas. The rougher surface is also in contrast with the fragility of the porcelain and with the smooth skin of the large plate which supports this small bowl.'
Photograph by Katrin Daems.

(Above right) *On the Edge*, by Patty Wouters (Belgium). Porcelain, 36 x 15 cm (14 ⅛ x 5 ⅞ in.). Little bowl: thrown with HF 1149 from Potclays, fired at 1260°C (2300°F). Before the bisque several thicknesses were obtained with a resist technique and washing away several layers. Large dish: thrown with HF 1149 from Potclays, burnished and treated with terra sigillata (outside). The inside was glazed with a crackle glaze in the green stage. Bisque firing at 1080°C (1976°F). After the bisque, coloured with iron sulphate and fired in a saggar at 850°C (1562°F). *Photograph by Katrin Daems.*
(Right) *We Are in Our Cups*, by Enid LeGrose Wise (Canada), 2002. Unglazed, porcelain cups (h. 7 cm/2 ¾ in.) with paperclay hands (almost life-size). *Photograph by the artist.*

are ideally suited to printing, also, with either ink and paint or slips and oxides. Both impressed and printed surface decoration are ideal for repeat production runs of tiles and panels.

The less formal, more abstract tiles are decorated in a more spontaneous fashion. The surface is first brushed with a layer of pure porcelain slip, either white or coloured. Subsequent layers of colour are built up by sponging or brushing slip onto selected areas. Resist techniques are used on some sections with wax, paper, tape, and a variety of mesh screens to assist in adding pattern and texture to parts of the surface.

Her work is dried slowly over several days between sheets of absorbent paper and weighted boards. Paperclay panels and tiles are once-fired to 1260°C (2300°F) in both oxidation and reduction atmosphere, and finished with various grades of carborundum paper after firing.

TRADITIONAL QUALITIES:

TRANSLUCENCY

The special translucent property of well-fired porcelain remains an essential ingredient in the work of a number of eminent ceramic artists in many parts of the world including **Arnold Annen** (Switzerland). Having worked with different clays and firing processes in Switzerland, France, Japan, Holland and Germany between 1970 and 1989, he returned to set up his studio in Basel. There he began to develop a unique technique for making distinctive, paper-thin porcelain bowls in the 1990s. This method demands a disciplined approach and an extremely high standard of craftsmanship. Initially, bowls were thrown with walls at least twice their final thickness. Accumulated slip was removed with steel ribs inside and out and then two hand-held gas burners were used to dry the piece until it became leatherhard. The burners were held opposite each other, one inside and one outside as the wheel revolved. A chuck is thrown with the same porcelain body and turned precisely to match the diameter of the bowl's rim. The bowl was inverted onto the chuck and gently tapped as the wheel rotated until it was properly centred before trimming. Sharpened metal strip tools were used to shave away successive layers from the outer surface of the bowl. Then the bowl was placed upright in another chuck so that the inside of the bowl could be worked on with sharp, kidney-shaped steel tools, thinning the wall still further. The abrasive action of the clay made it essential that tools were sharpened regularly as the work proceeded. The bowl was inverted once again for the foot-ring to be opened up and, with care, shaped approx-imately but left thick enough to withstand the stress of further handling. Annen checked the greatly reduced thickness of walls and base by shining a torch through them. At this stage they

Porcelain bowl, with extremely thin walls, by Arnold Annen (Switzerland), 1998. Wheel-thrown in Limoges TM10, decorated with trailed slip, d. 30.5 cm (12 in.), fired to 1250°C (2282°F)in a gas kiln. *Photograph by the artist.*

were little more than 2 mm (⅛ in.) thick. The rim was then refined with the same steel tools prior to decorating the outer surface of the bowl.

Annen re-centred the bowl upside down on the wheel to paint latex resist onto and around the foot and a little way up the side from the base. He held the bowl by the resist protected foot while he trailed narrow lines of latex diagonally across the form, working from the foot towards the rim, and force dried the latex with a gas burner. The emerging design was constantly checked and assessed. When satisfied, Annen took a large Chinese brush to apply separate, sweeping strokes of porcelain slip over the latex, using the gas burner to dry the slip instantly. The lines of latex were then peeled away and, with a fine nozzle, he trailed lines of slip selectively across the form and dried them immediately with the burner flame.

The extreme fragility of these bowls requires them to be fired upside down in a chuck made to fit from the same porcelain body. Annen makes his chucks with as much care as he gives to the bowls so that they will correctly support them in the kiln. Alumina is mixed with water and painted around the rim of the chuck to ensure that the bowl will release easily on removal from the kiln. The pieces were once-fired in a gas kiln to a maximum of 1260°C (2300°F) in a reducing atmosphere with spectacularly translucent results.

Annen uses a porcelain body from Limoges (TM 10) which is a popular choice among several of the European potters represented in this book. It took him four days of concentrated effort to complete each piece together with its supporting chuck. Due to the extreme thinness of the bowls it is impossible to rectify any mistakes and even the slightest air bubble will ruin the work. Everything must be done at exactly the right stage and this demands absolute concentration throughout the whole process. He fires his unglazed bowls in a gas kiln under reducing conditions in order to obtain a cold, white colour as the body has a

rather warmer tint when oxidised. He built his kiln well-insulated with ceramic fibre and controlled by computer so that he could fire quickly, taking only one and a half hours between 900°C (1652°F) and 1250°C (2282°F) and, thus, avoid risking deformation.

Recently, Annen has made a series of extremely thin, slip-cast bowl forms. Many layers of translucency are achieved when the piece is inverted on the wheel and selectively heated with an oxyacetylene burner. The concentrated flame causes flakes of porcelain to be detached and holes to appear in the wall. The translucent effects that this technique achieves can be breathtaking.

Translucency often has a bewitching effect on the observer and many other potters also make use of this exceptional quality, although it does require directional lighting if it is to be fully exploited. **Jeroen Bechtold** (Holland), for

Group of translucent bowls by Arnold Annen (Switzerland), 2000. Made in Limoges PC118B porcelain body, reduction fired to 1320°C (2408°F) in a gas kiln. *Photograph by the artist.*

example, carves away parts of the outside in varying layers from some of his pieces. Multiple glazes are applied and fired in oxidising conditions. Again, it is necessary for light to be shining into the pieces from behind or directly overhead if they are to be properly appreciated. **Arne Åse** (Norway) uses a different method to vary the thickness and thus the degree of translucency of his porcelain plates and bowl forms. He paints a design onto the raw pot with a shellac solution and allows it to dry before he thins the wall by carefully sponging away unprotected areas. His sensitive brushwork with the shellac resist helps him to achieve a richly textured surface whose delicate, translucent quality is revealed by the passage of light through the piece.

I use a similar method myself when working with Southern Ice Porcelain. Rather than using shellac, I prefer a water-based, acrylic medium to serve the same purpose. It has certain advantages for me, one of which is that brushes last longer and they can be more easily cleaned. This technique of painting successive layers between sponging and drying is particularly appropriate when the walls of a vessel have been

Porcelain vessel, by Horst Göbbels (Germany), 2001. Thrown and altered to oval section, with pierced design, h. 17 cm (6¾ in.). *Photograph by the artist.*

so thinly thrown that carving with normal tools would be impossible. During this process it is essential to remain sensitive to the degree of

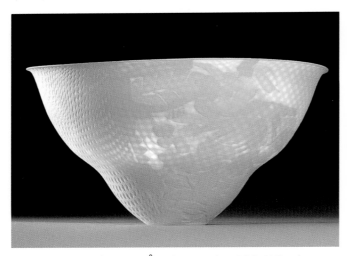

Porcelain bowl, by Arne Åse (Norway), 1993. Wheel-thrown, painted with shellac resist, and sponged to give different levels of translucency and surface relief, h. 30 cm, (11 ¾ in.), unglazed, fired in reduction to 1250°C (2282°F). *Photograph by Glenn Hagebu.*

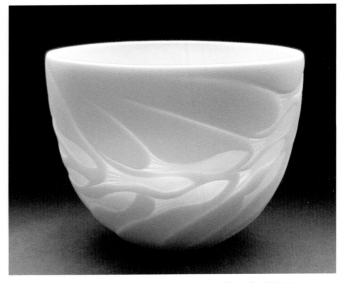

Porcelain bowl by Hanneke Verhey (Holland), 2002. Carved with shoal of fish design, 7 x 7 cm (2 ¾ x 2 ¾ in.). *Photograph by Frans Van Diepen.*

Porcelain bowl carved with fish, by Hanneke Verhey (Holland), 2002. Dimensions: 5 x 11 cm (2 x 4 ⅜ in.).
Photograph by Frans Van Diepen.

moisture that the piece can absorb without causing distortion. I use a hot air gun to ensure that the piece is completely dry before attempting subsequent brushwork. It can be a lengthy and delicate exercise achieving three or four different levels of translucency but, occasionally and under good lighting, the effort may be spectacularly rewarding. Like most porcelains, this body is revealed at its best when fired in a reducing atmosphere. The whiteness is much brighter and colder than the slightly creamy colour produced in an electric kiln. The risk of distortion during firing is greatly reduced when thrown vessels of circular section are placed upside down on a former made from the same material.

Horst Göbbels (Germany) also exploits the full potential of translucent porcelain and gives extra emphasis to its exquisite refinement by incorporating precisely pierced holes in some of his vessels and sculptural objects. In some cases, thinly rolled sheets of porcelain stand unwaveringly straight alone or in formal ranks behind one

another, minimally incised or pierced with strictly controlled designs. Additional linear elements are provided by coloured strings or wires which pass through the slab and appear to act as guy ropes holding the piece upright. The quiet, understated purity of these pieces achieves a sense of perfection that would be destroyed by unnecessary ornamentation. His vessel forms are treated with equal care and attention to detail.

Hanneke Verhey (Holland) is another artist to whom translucency is of paramount importance. Variation in the thickness of porcelain remaining in the walls of her exquisitely carved bowls requires light to enable us to fully appreciate her fluent designs. The small size of these objects invites handling and close observation and she wants people to pick them up and examine them closely. Verhey is inspired by the work of other artists, such as Hiroshige whose Japanese prints with fish she greatly admires, and by the graphic images of Escher. Personal experiences she has enjoyed such as snorkelling in Mexico and Belize and swimming among shoals of fish, or from working in her own kitchen garden are all brought to life in her work.

The bowls are wheel-thrown, trimmed and dried slowly. When they have dried completely, the decoration is outlined with a pencil before incising with a surgical knife. Verhey states that the first pencilled outline is the most difficult step she takes in the whole process of creating her designs. Initially, there is little indication how the final work will appear. When the first lines have been committed to the surface, the drawing proceeds with intense concentration. She works intuitively until figures and other elements which appear are resolved. She uses two different methods to incise: either she carves away the interior of her figures, or, as in a kind of cameo, their surroundings. Sometimes she applies both techniques in one and the same figure. Characteristically, she manages to create many variations and increasingly complicated patterns with great spontaneity and imagination around a single motif. The pieces are bisque fired to 1020°C (1868°F) and then polished with Wet 'n Dry silicon carbide paper. The final firing to 1260°C (2300°F) in a gas kiln is conducted in a reducing atmosphere. This achieves an extreme whiteness that cannot be attained in an electric kiln. Then they receive a final polish. The high degree of transparency in the relief carving in these pieces renders the use of colour or glaze unnecessary.

Angela Verdon (UK) began working with bone china in the 1970s and over the years she has devised her own, somewhat time-consuming methods in order to creatively exploit its translucent properties. Verdon is still very much concerned with luminosity and purity in her work and she executes much of it in a slip-cast porcelain body from Limoges. Recently, she returned to using bone china during a residency at the Royal Crown Derby Factory where she produced some extremely translucent tiles.

(Top) *Frog*, one of the hand-carved bone china tiles in the large screen at the Royal Crown Derby Factory, by Angela Verdon (UK), 2000. *Photograph by Stuart Blackwood.*
(Bottom) *Homage*, by Patty Wouters (Belgium). Translucent slip-cast bone china dish on a stand, 20 x 35 cm (7⅞ x 13¾ in.). 'By placing the porcelain dish up higher I want to pay homage to the material porcelain itself.' *Photograph by Katrin Daems.*

(Above) Porcelain form, by Curtis Benzle (USA). Inlaid Nerikomi and lit by incandescent light, 30.5 x 23 x 12.5 cm (12 x 9 x 5 in.), fired to cone 8 in an electric kiln. *Photograph by the artist.*

(Left) Porcelain vessel mounted on a stoneware pedestal, by Tim Gee (UK). Southern Ice Porcelain painted with shellac resist solution, washed back to create several levels of trans-lucency, 16 x 11 cm (6 ¼ x 4 ⅜ in.), fired to 1290°C (2354°F) in an electric kiln and polished with silicon carbide (Wet 'n Dry) paper after both bisque and final firings. *Photograph by the artist.*

SMOOTHNESS, WHITENESS AND PRECISION

One of the greatest attractions of the medium for those potters who choose to work in porcelain is its smooth grain and dense body. This invites a degree of precision in design and execution that would be difficult to achieve in a more granular clay. Clear, sharp profiles, positive shapes, crisply defined patterns and fine linear drawing seem to be completely appropriate to porcelain. Of course, strict control of the material, tools and processes is absolutely necessary by those who would work in this way and it will not suit any craftsman who prefers potting more freely and leaving more to chance. Often, it is a matter of personality. Ceramics, as in any other art form, reveals something of its maker's feelings and character. I must confess that much of the appeal of porcelain to me in my own work is the opportunity that it allows for preciseness. I like to be in control, to make things exact so that they fit as close as possible to a personal concept of perfection. Of course, I recognise that my ideal will not necessarily be the same as another would choose but I find great difficulty in working any other way. I can enjoy and admire asymmetry in the work of others but I am always searching to establish some kind of visual balance in my own. I feel sure that any conscious attempt to adjust my attitude or approach would appear contrived and fail dismally. This does not mean that precise forms lack sensitivity. Expressive qualities are not the sole prerogative of wild abandon!

A considerable degree of control is evident in the vessel forms of **Johan Broekema** (Holland). Sharply defined linear bands draw attention to the circular section of his wheel-thrown pieces. Using the wheel exclusively, he aims explicitly for ultimate perfection in his geometrical vessel shapes in some of which coloured slips contrast with the white porcelain body that is further exposed by incised lines of sgraffito. His work exhibits the same precise mastery of form when he uses other glazes such as the traditional celadons, tenmoku, oil-spots, or copper reds on his vessels and which often have narrow lines encircling them at strategic points to mark directional changes of profile. Geometric designs require exact placement of each element if they are to succeed. This degree of control does present the risk of producing a rather cold, clinical feeling which will not be attractive to everyone. However, such an approach is likely to be extremely successful

Porcelain bowl, by Johan Broekema (Holland), 2001. Linear banding inlaid with black slip having 20% body stain added to the porcelain body, 9 cm x 15 cm (3½ x 6 in.), semi-matt glaze composed of soda feldspar 75, wollastonite 12, magnesite 3, china clay 10, fired in a heavy reduction atmosphere to 1280°C (2336°F). *Photograph by the artist.*

when both form and surface treatment are composed in complete harmony.

Most potters will agree with **Caroline Whyman** (UK) when she says that, 'form, for me, is the most fundamental consideration for my ceramics. If the form is weak, I don't think that it can be redeemed by decoration. Finish is my next obsession, that is why I use porcelain because, for me, it demands care and attention to detail. Nuance is what I look for in form, and subtlety.' She often uses grid patterns in her decoration and can draw them, without measuring beforehand, by banding guidelines (vertical and horizontal) on to the pots with a blue or red stain used in colouring food. This shows up well on raw porcelain for any kind of decorating and it burns away in the bisque firing. 'It's great for trying out various ideas directly on the forms.'

Whyman uses a series of tools with tiny loops for carving into porcelain preparatory to inlaying coloured slips. She also uses porcelain stamps to impress dots for inlay rather than drill bits because it is much quicker. Other stamps have been made with carved designs to impress into

Group of porcelain vessels *Illusion* series, by Caroline Whyman (UK), 2001. Wheel-thrown and inlaid with black porcelain slip, glazed, h. 17–35 cm (6 ¾ x 13 ¾ in.). *Photograph by the artist.*

the clay. Her favoured slip is made from the porcelain body with the addition of 1% cobalt carbonate which is cheaper and produces less speckling than the oxide. This is a simple recipe but she always adds a deflocculant so that she has the advantage of a fluid slip without excess water wetting the leatherhard porcelain too much

as she works. 'This is especially important on plates with lots of decoration because they would just "pancake" from the effect of so much slip!' To save time, she applies the slip over the whole surface and lets it dry to a hard leatherhard condition before turning it away with a flexible metal kidney tool. She lines her wheel tray with a

Two porcelain vessels, by Caroline Whyman (UK), 2001. Wheel-thrown and inlaid with black porcelain slip, under satin matt turquoise glaze, h. 22 cm and 14 cm (8 ¾ x 5 ½ in.). *Photograph by the artist.*

plastic sheet to catch and save the trimmings to be used to make more coloured slip. This precaution also prevents her wheel tray from becoming contaminated. 'Occasionally, smudging occurs even when the pieces are quite dry, but I can deal with that more easily with Wet 'n Dry silicon carbide paper after bisque firing.'

Grids have always fascinated Whyman, 'they are *so* simple but offer *infinite* possibilities and I quickly found a connection between grid patterns and woven textiles. You either place something on the grid or below it; you either *add* decoration to the grid or leave it blank.' Much of her inspiration comes from geometric textiles and also from basket weaving, especially those from early civilisations. Similar patterns appear, she says, due to a basic grid framework that can be seen in work from South America, native North America, Maori carvings, African textiles, early Greek work, Indian/Asian weaving and Japanese textiles.

Through her own process of creating grids on the surfaces of three-dimensional forms, Whyman began to think about how these designs evolve from a simple division of halving, and quartering and that, as these divisions continue, they become smaller and more complex. What also became apparent was that, where these linear divisions lie over a swelling or diminishing form such as a vase, the proportion of the grid changes and reflects the form to keep the overall format of the grid in proportion. It is necessary that a grid based on squares keeps them in proportion if they are not to degenerate towards rectangles and thus lose its visual strength. She has become skilful in judging the correct distances between the lines and diminishing spaces. 'When I was working consistently, I would have very little need to measure these distances using anything other than my eyes!'

Dots in grids were a symbol of the universe for the Chinese. These can be seen as spiralled dots on their jade *bi* or *pi* as they used to be called. I think that I could continue working with these symbols indefinitely, trying to create harmony and balance. The space in and around the design plays a vital

Sternenkreis (Ring of Stars), by Ulli Böhmelmann (Germany), 1999. Sizes: 17–34 cm (6¾ x 13⅜ in.) *Photograph by the artist.*

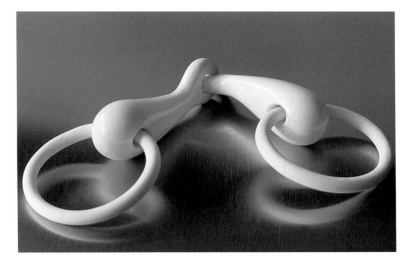

role in the dynamic of the overall appearance. When I feel that a design *really* works it is because there is a dynamic tension between the decorated and undecorated area.

The physical properties of porcelain in its plastic and leatherhard state does, undoubtedly, have a profound effect on the approach to working with it for many potters. It seems to encourage them to work with a high degree of precision – crisp, uncluttered profiles, sharply turned with a positive and critical attention to detail. Often for those who work in this way, it is a reflection of their own personality.

Neatness in one's character need not be inhibiting although it does contribute towards an ordered attitude to the material and any surface treatment. Clearly, there will be others whose nature will not permit them to work within such confines and they will approach porcelain making with greater freedom, as can be seen in later chapters of this book.

The extremely fine grain, whiteness and density of porcelain invites precise treatment in a way that would be utterly alien to coarser clay bodies. Cutting into the surface of sandy textured clays gives the potter a completely different feeling. My own work is mainly in porcelain but I find that my attitude immediately becomes looser and more vigorous when working in even a fairly smooth stoneware. Likewise, the work will appear more rugged than anything produced in porcelain. But it is that wonderful smooth, untainted property of a good porcelain body that appeals to me and many others most of all. It seems to invite the production of forms that display a quiet elegance in profile and presence.

(Above right) *Bridle* porcelain, by Gunhild Vatn (Norway), 2002. Slip-cast in plaster-moulds, 20 x 8 x 4 cm (7⅞ x 3⅛ x 1½ in.), fired at 1140°C (2084°F). *Photograph by Gunhild Vatn.*
(Bottom right) Burnished bone china form on a Cumbrian slate base, by Angela Verdon (UK), 2000. Dimensions: 50 x 30 cm (19½ x 11¾ in.). *Photograph by Stuart Blackwood.*

I would be working self-consciously and against my nature to attempt a more brutal approach. I must confess that, although there are times when I would rather abandon my perfectionist temperament, it is far easier for me to do so with other clays. Others will choose to comment differently on their personal response to this seductive medium.

Philip Cornelius (USA) explained how the white porcelain body is the ideal surface for his fine linear drawing in a series of pieces depicting aircraft. Diving/crashing airplanes are portrayed in various positions or situations in flight. He worked from models and charts in order to show as much detail as possible.

At the time, my son was an airline pilot, flying about the East Coast. He related to me some inside information about the harrowing experiences that he and his friends faced daily. The drawings were made directly as I could not use a pencil to even trace them in because the

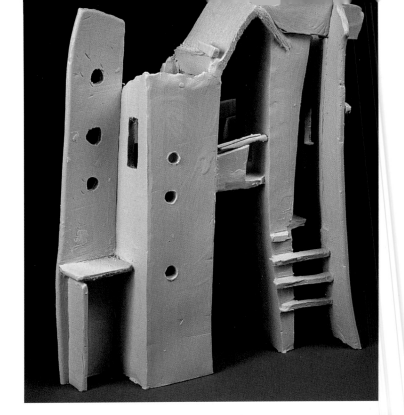

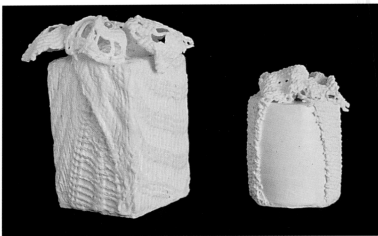

(Top) *White Ruins I*, by Toni Hambleton (Puerto Rico), 2002. Slab-built, porcelain sculpture fired to Orton cone 8 in an electric kiln, 28 x 20.5 x 13 cm (11 x 8 x 5 in.). *Photograph by Johnny Betancourt.*
(Middle) Gift packages by Perla Bardin (Argentina), 2002. Bone china, 20 x 15 cm (8 x 6 in.) and 30 x 20 cm (11¾ x 8 in.). 'First, I modelled a box with thin walls. After bisque firing I submerged the cloth in bone china slip, finishing the knot and hanging the package upside down to drain until dry. This kind of bone china is translucent at 1060°C (1940°F).' *Photograph by the artist.*
(Bottom) *Boxed Lunch*, by Philip Cornelius (USA), 1998. Porcelain with black engobe and drawing, 28 x 23 x 20 cm (11 x 9 x 8 in.). 'Charcoal is added to the kiln during the high firing at cone 8 and the firing continues to cone 10. The charcoal gives a wood-fired finish, however, with much more control'. *Photograph by the artist.*

lines would disappear in the firing and would confuse me making the drawing. *Clouds*, was drawn with a slip trailer and the flowing black underglaze is evident in the drawing. All of my pieces are bisque fired first and then an engobe-like composition may be sprayed onto the work. With over-spray the pieces take on a velvety look.

The wheel-thrown vessel forms by **Karin Bablok** (Germany) are often altered from their original section into asymmetric shapes. She retains the natural whiteness of the Limoges porcelain body and contrasts this with a black basalt glaze, painted deliberately and precisely as a counter-balance.

Like many porcelain artists **Toni Hambleton** (Puerto Rico) attempts to use the natural colour of the unglazed material to manipulate light through her pieces. It is this extreme whiteness that captures her imagination. She also uses porcelain slip over stoneware pieces to create that same white. 'My pieces are handbuilt from thin slabs cut to my whimsy to recreate my "memory buildings", "my ruins", where the pure white porcelain creates its own light and shadows.' She builds very white, serene spaces where any colour observed is the result of ambient light falling on and through her constructions.

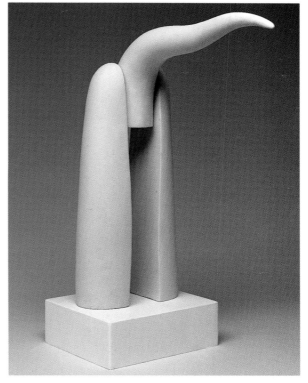

(Top) *Depending on Circumstances II*, by Ilona Romule (Latvia), 2001. Slip-cast, fired to 1280°C (2336°F), 18 x 35 cm (7 x 13 ¾ in.). *Photograph by Aigars Tukna.* (Above) Porcelain sculpture, by Ruth Duckworth (USA), 2000. Sculpture: h. 49.5 cm (19 ½ in.) on base: h. 7.5 cm (3 in.). *Photograph by James Prinz.*

CHAPTER TWO
FORM AND FORMING PROCESSES

THROWING AND TURNING PORCELAIN

It is a delight to watch any accomplished craftsman at work and to observe a skilled potter throwing on the wheel is particularly fascinating. The seemingly effortless rise and fall of the spinning lump of clay as it is coaxed towards the still centre and then opened up and raised so fluently. The stretching and swelling of the wet clay walls as they respond to the pressure of the potter's fingers to grow as if organic, magically into a new hollow form. This becomes a natural, intuitive process of making and one in which a feeling for the soft, plastic material flows through the potter's fingers as a sensitive expression of him or herself.

Porcelain is not the easiest of bodies with which to throw but it does have its special attraction. It does demand an acute sensitivity towards its condition at all stages of working. It can suddenly collapse if too much water is absorbed while throwing or if the thickness of the walls is irregular. Some potters illustrated in this book prefer to use slip rather than water as

(Opposite) *Wiggle Jar*, by John Tilton (USA). Wheel-thrown porcelain, matte crystalline glaze with tin oxide, 30.5 x 12.5 x 12.5 cm (12 x 5 x 5 in.). *Photograph by the artist.*

a lubricant. However, there is an element of risk attached to this practice if one allows slip to build up on the surface. It is wise to remove any surplus slip with a steel kidney or other tool from time to time during the throwing process.

An experienced thrower can produce large numbers of pots much more quickly than anyone who builds with slabs or coils. The wheel allowed me to make enough pieces to explore a variety of surface treatments during the period when I was a full-time teacher without the opportunity to devote long sessions to working on my own. Following several years developing thrown forms in earthenware and stoneware bodies my conversion to working almost exclusively with porcelain took place in the early 1970s when one of my students expressed a desire to formulate a porcelain body for a special project. I discovered a satisfying affinity with the nature of porcelain despite difficulties experienced with throwing it initially. Its smooth character and whiteness first appealed and then, as my ability to control it improved to the point where I could throw thinly enough to achieve a delicate translucency, I was completely seduced by it.

Careful preparation of the plastic porcelain body is essential before commencing to throw. Unless all air bubbles are eliminated and an

Pourer, by Janet DeBoos (Australia), 2002. Wheel-thrown porcelain vessel, h. 23 cm (9 in.), oxidation fired to 1260°C (2300°F). *Photograph by Greg Daly.*

even texture achieved, porcelain is much more difficult to throw fluently and efficiently than stoneware or earthenware clays which have similar deficiencies. This is because the more open texture and larger particle size of coarser clays provides them with greater wet strength. In the right condition, however, porcelain is a delight to throw. The clay creams smoothly, sensuously through the fingers in a way that can be best appreciated after a period of throwing with stoneware material. This is because the open, sandy texture of most stoneware bodies feels decidedly gritty in comparison with porcelain. Porcelain potters are aware that their material is, undoubtedly, far less tolerant of insensitive treatment at any stage of throwing

than coarser clays. Certainly, with porcelain, a deeper level of concentration is necessary. The thrower must be able to adjust pressure, movement and speed intuitively as the wheel revolves and should try to acquire a particular sensitivity to the changing condition of the clay. Porcelain can quickly become overworked and 'tired' and this makes it prone to collapse without warning. Some porcelain potters allow for the inevitable absorption of water during throwing by working with the clay in a slightly stiffer condition from the beginning because, unless they are kept sufficiently lubricated with water to prevent from them suddenly drying, the point may be reached where hands will stick to the clay and pull the piece out of shape.

When throwing, porcelain bodies can produce a good deal of slurry which should not be allowed to build up too thickly on a pot. It can be removed with a throwing rib or a modelling tool while the wheel is turning. Similarly, excess water must not be left to accumulate and pool inside as this can weaken the base and cause uneven drying. It is wise to apply sufficient pressure on the inside of the base to align the clay particles and reduce the risk of cracking. The way in which porcelain pots are released from the wheel can affect them later. Cutting through the base with an extra thin, stranded wire on a slowly revolving wheel helps to counteract the stress produced.

Wheel-thrown forms need not always remain round because it is a simple matter to alter the shape at any stage between wet and dry, to add or take away. Radical and dynamic changes can be made immediately after throwing the initial form although greater care may be necessary. For many ceramicists, throwing is merely the first step in the process of creation. Parts are thrown, altered, cut and reassembled in different ways to produce new and unusual forms.

Victor Greenaway, in Australia, throws a porcelain clay from Limoges that he has found most suitable for his personal technique. He wanted a clay that could be thrown and altered with little chance of cracking. More especially, he needed it to respond favourably to marks or grooves drawn in the wet clay immediately after throwing, without tearing or offering undue resistance. He believes that the strength of his work lies in the ability to work spontaneously and directly on each piece during a session on the potter's wheel.

> As a brush or chisel is the tool of a painter or sculptor, so too is the wheel mine. The dynamics are created through light and shade, modelled through the use of indentations and various surfaces and colours. The translucency of the porcelain contributes to this by passing light through thin linear markings and fine edges. As in a quick sketch or abstraction, the outcome relies on experience, intuition and confidence in the technique. Often, the result is uncertain and the work lost or discarded but the journey is an exciting one and constantly rewarding.

Fluent, unselfconscious throwing of vessel forms in porcelain demands considerable skill that can only be acquired through constant practice. Most practitioners set high standards for themselves and few are prepared to accept less than their concept of perfection. **John Tilton** (USA) is numbered among these. His pots demonstrate this consummate expertise. He admits to being a perfectionist, but not in the sense of being so faultless that the result is cold. He wants everything he does to have a certain quality of precision, 'but it also has to have spirit'. He searches constantly for excellence, relentlessly stretching the boundaries of his knowledge, understanding and skill. 'I am trying to push the pots, the glazes and the kiln further in order to make the purest statement that I can.'

When **Caroline Whyman** (UK) experiences an unusual number of problems with cracks forming in the base of thrown porcelain, both 'S' cracks and others in parallel series, she overcomes the problem by compressing the bases with a rib as she throws, and allows the pots to dry slowly and evenly. She says:

Porcelain bowls by Victor Greenaway (Australia), 2002. Multi-lipped bowl, yellow: w. 18 cm (7 ⅛ in.), h. 12 cm (4 ¾ in.), and spiral-lipped bowl with yellow interior: w. 26 (10 ¼ in.) x h. 15 cm (6 in.). *Photograph by Terence Bogue.*

Black dish, 11 x 18 cm (4 ⅜ x 7 in.), pierced ladle 9 x 29 cm (3 ½ x 11½ in.), jug 10.5 x 8.5 cm (4 ⅛ x 3 ⅜ in.), by Prue Venables (Australia), 2002. *Photograph by Terence Bogue.*

Porcelain bowl by Irit Abba (Israel), 2002. Wheel-thrown porcelain bowl altered while still wet or leatherhard, fired in oxidation to cone 8, h. 9 cm (3½ in.), d. 22 cm (8 ¾ in.). *Photograph by Yoram Lehman.*

I always lets all my work equalise in dampness, before I do any turning, by wrapping it up in a poly-thene sheet. This slows down the whole making process but ensures less cracks either in the base or the rims if I turn them when the tops are fairly dry and the bases damp. I throw by using slip instead of water, sometimes adding a minute amount of Fairy Liquid (dishwashing detergent soap) which makes a wetter lubricant and allows me to throw for longer. I also stretch the pots from the inside using wooden spoons modified to a Japanese egote shape. Turning and trimming is always done with very sharp metal tools and I take great pleasure in sharpening them on an oil stone each time I use them.

In their Nevada studios, **Tom Coleman** throws all the vessel forms for his wife, **Elaine**, to decorate with her fluent carving as well as his own pieces that are altered in various ways to adjust the circular section.

When **Alistair Whyte** (Australia) went to study in Japan soon after completing his ceramics diploma at the Bendigo Institute in Victoria, he had to make considerable adjustments to his throwing technique. Writing about his experiences in *Pottery in Australia* (Vol. 27, No. 4), he explained:

(Opposite) Two porcelain vases, by Alistair Whyte (Australia), 2002. Wheel-thrown, and painted with cobalt pigments. *Photograph by Terence Bogue.*

(Above) Three ribbed porcelain cups, by Jack Doherty (UK), 2002. H. 12 cm (4 ¾ in.). *Photograph by Sue Packer.*
(Right) Porcelain hand-thrown and altered translucent wine cups, by Tom Coleman (USA), 2002. Glazed with Elaine's White. H. 9 cm (3 ½ in.), w. 7.5 cm (3 in.), fired to cone 10 in reduction. *Photograph by the artist.*

All throwing of porcelain, apart from extremely large pots, is done off the hump. Many of the wheels used in Kyoto are fixed speed wheels and so the work is taken off the wheel while it is still spinning, and potters sit cross-legged in front of their wheels. The direction of the wheel spin is also opposite to Western potters, i.e. clockwise. Having initially learned to throw in Australia, most of these habits were too radical for me to change in a hurry, so I chose compromise and throw my own way using Japanese throwing techniques.

He goes on to emphasise the importance of making specific tools for a particular function in the throwing process.

When making a set of tools for, say, a saucer, the first tool made is the *tonbo* (or dragonfly) measure. This is made of bamboo and measures the inside depth and width of what is being made. It is to this measure that the throwing ribs are made. There are usually two, these being the *dango* (which is made from fine grained, softer wood) and the *hera* (usually made from *sakura* or *nashi* i.e. cherry or pear) which

is the finishing rib. The *sanfo is* the throwing rib, being about the thickness of a finger, and is used to draw the clay up to the correct height and thickness. The *hera is* carved back to a fine edge and is purely a final shaping and finishing tool.

Making a new set of tools for each item proved to be an excellent learning experience for Whyte. It was also an essential practice because his master's tools were designed for throwing with the wheel spinning in the opposite direction.

Bruce Cochrane (Canada) has used a number of different clay bodies mostly determined, he says, by concept and form. He tries to avoid allowing the material itself to dominate his ideas but feels that porcelain

Cruet Set and Stand, by Bruce Cochrane (Canada), 2002. Porcelain cruets, thrown and wood-fired. The stand is made from a coarse stoneware, salt-fired, 30.5 x 12.5 x 20 cm (12 in. x 5 in. x 8 in.). *Photograph by the artist.*

lends itself to an 'articulation of edge and surface tension' unlike any other clay body.

It is a versatile material which has helped me resolve many ideas about form and function. Its dense white background and strong interface with the glaze supports rich colour on a durable, functional surface. I am not so concerned with the potential for light transmission as my forms are not thinly potted. Fine Molochite (porcelain grog) is used to accommodate more complex forming techniques. When the skin of the form, the mark of the rib or the

Group of wheel-thrown, Southern Ice Porcelian by Joanna Howells (UK), 2002. Porcelain vessels, h. 15–40 cm (6–15¾ in.), decorated with applied slips that are combed and adjusted to the design. *Photograph by the artist.*

connecting seam needs to be revealed the pots are fired in wood or salt. Soft coloured, fat glaze coatings are achieved in high-fire reduction.

Tom Turner (USA) uses the wheel for making most of his pots that have evolved over more than 40 years of practice, observation and study. He believes that inspiration is drawn from historical vessels, the work of other potters and, 'occasionally, from deep within ourselves'. He is a potter who 'loves old and new pots along with the challenges, rewards and lifestyle of producing pots for a living'. His work deals with 'classical concerns in material, process and form. For me, a beautiful form is more important than a painted decoration whether it be a new pot or a 19th century jug'. He aims for

(Left) *Drift Ridge*, by Les Manning (Canada), 1998. Combinations of stoneware and porcelain bodies stacked together and wheel-thrown, altered, glazed and sandblasted, w. 27 cm (10 ½ in.), h.14 cm (5 ½ in.). *Photograph by Howard Owen.*

(Below) *Tanami Desert* series, large porcelain vessel, h. 41 cm (16 in.), designed and decorated by Pippin Drysdale (Australia), wheel-thrown for her by Warrick Palmateer, 2002. *Photograph by Adrian Lambert (Acorn Photos).*

his personal refinement of a few basic ideas concerning pottery and feels that 'function' is determined by the owner of his pots. He remarked that a teapot, for example, can serve any hot or cold liquid or exist merely for 'visual appreciation'.

Bone china is generally acknowledged to be very difficult, if not impossible, to throw because it lacks plasticity due to the low percentage of clay in the body. However, **Anne Hogg** (UK) used a throwable bone china for several years. It was prepared to a recipe developed by her husband, Chris. They live and work in a quiet Cornish village close to some of the finest china clay deposits in the world. The recipe for this plastic body is based on traditional ingredients as follows:

Bone ash	50
Super Standard Porcelain china clay (kaolin)	25
MF4 flux *	25
Westone-H white bentonite	2.5

*this item can be replaced by Cornish stone, or by a combination of 15% soda feldspar and 10% quartz.

SLIP-CASTING PORCELAIN AND BONE CHINA

Slip-casting multiples is the method of production mostly associated with industry but it is also used with great success by studio potters, in particular those who choose to work with those white clay bodies which are lacking in plasticity. Several artists have made imaginative use of this technique to cast large numbers of the same simple shape and placed them together in a particular arrangement or situation to create impressive large-scale imagery. But the prime concern of most potters is less likely to be mass production than the opportunity to prepare basic forms for further treatment such as by carving, piercing, individually decorating, altering or constructing in some other way. Porcelain lends itself as well to this process as does any fine-particle clay but it is especially appropriate for working with its close relation, bone china.

Walther Stürmer (Germany) started working as a potter, making stoneware vessels on the wheel, before taking on some architectural ceramic projects. He had considered porcelain to be a material that was 'too sterile and cold to appeal to a craftsman'. However, in 1967, Philip Rosenthal of the Rosenthal porcelain manufactory entrusted him with the technical management of a very ambitious venture. He had invited international well-known artists to create individual pieces 'in the spirit of the 20th century' for Rosenthal to produce in limited editions. Technical problems in attempting to reproduce the artists' creations were considerable and, at first, threatened the survival of the project.

In the course of his research, Stürmer visited Henry Moore in Much Hadham, met Victor Pasemore in London, Lucio Fontana in Milan, and Victor Vasarely in Annet-sur-Marne. Eventually, a total of 23 artists took part in the first phase and founded the 'Limited Art Editions' of Rosenthal that continue today.

In my own work, the rotational symmetry of pieces produced by the potter's wheel became too limiting. My new insight into porcelain became fascinating for me more and more. I wanted to explore it further and started to experiment on my own in 1978. So I worked hands-on with the material rather than creating models for

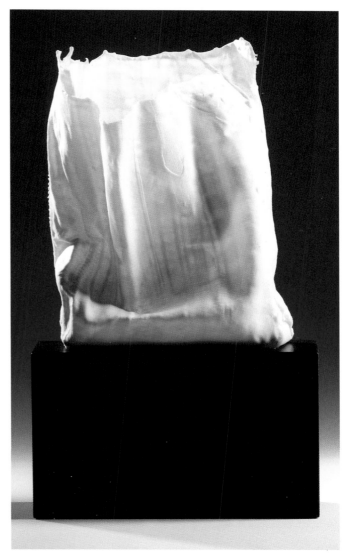

(Above) *Bitte Etwas Heller (Resigning Paper Bag)*, by Walther Stürmer (Germany), 2002. Textile bag dipped in porcelain slip, moulded, deformed in the kiln, h. 35 cm (13 ¾ in.) on a wooden base. *Photograph by Fotostudio Schuster, Munich.*

Jug and Folded Bowl, by Walther Stürmer (Germany). Porcelain, h. 22 cm (8 ⅝ in.) and d. 16 cm (6 ¼ in.) respectively. *Photograph by Fotostudio Schuster, Munich.*

reproduction. The process was difficult. The porcelain body does not have a good plasticity, it breaks easily and it is difficult to bring into a desired shape. Porcelain shrinks significantly during drying and firing. It softens at 1400°C (2552°F), changes shape and can tear easily. In the industrial production, all these characteristics create problems and must be eliminated. I do the opposite, I make them visible. I use them, I enforce these textures, I even provoke crevices, ruptures and distortion. As in no other material, the typical whiteness of porcelain gives appearance to a delicate play of light and shadows. Above all I cherish the dreamlike transparency of thin layers of porcelain.

Penny Smith (Australia) was trained originally as a furniture designer at the High Wycombe

Dialogue, slip-cast Limoges porcelain, by Penny Smith (Australia), 2002. Tallest: 44 x 8.5 x 12.5 cm (17 ¼ x 3 3/8 x 5 in.). *Photograph by Uffe Schultz.*

College of Art & Technology, Buckinghamshire (UK). This laid the foundation for future developments in her career. Those initial studies provided opportunities for Smith to understand the broader aspects of contemporary design and their application to daily life. A strong belief in the necessity of good design in everyday objects and a conviction of the positive role designers can play in industrial production have been key principles for the development of her ceramics. When Smith emigrated to Tasmania with her husband, John, in 1970, she found that there were fewer opportunities to apply her skills in furniture design so she began making sculptural forms in clay. However, her interest in mould making and multiple form production led Smith to work for a three-week period in a mould-making workshop at Stoke-on-Trent during 1979 where she learnt about designing for slip-casting and limited-scale production. This experience was to confirm the future direction of her ceramics.

In February 1995, Smith undertook a three-month programme as an Artist-in-Residence at the Arabia Foundation in Helsinki, Finland. She was the first Australian to be invited by Arabia to have this unique opportunity. The aim of her residency was to develop a series of vessels for her exhibition held at the Arabia Museum from 8 September to 8 October 1995. This series was based on a limited number of component forms or elements that explored the potential for flexibility within the processes of making. The methods and mechanics of making mass-produced ware particularly interested and challenged Smith within the framework of her residency.

The Arabia Foundation provided Smith not only with a studio to work in but, also, allowed her a free hand to design or make whatever she chose. All the materials such as clays, glazes, etc. were made available to her as well as the specialised knowledge and skills of the factory technicians in the Pro Arte workshops where limited editions are produced. Smith worked energetically to refine her mould-making and casting techniques. She found that working within a production team, rather than as a the solo artist working in her studio at home, challenging but, at the same time, she enjoyed the privileged access to all the facilities of the Arabia factory and expertise of technical staff. This residency proved valuable as she followed the work through from initial drawing to moulding, casting and construction.

Smith uses Limoges slip-casting powder for all her work because she finds it is the only porcelain casting material that allows her to cut and reassemble forms. It provides, also, the appropriate whiteness she requires and

Slip-cast Limoges porcelain, by Penny Smith (Australia), 2002. H. (tallest): 51 x 8.5 cm (16 ¼ x 3 ⅜ in.). *Photograph by Uffe Schultz.*

translucency when needed. All her pieces are wet-sanded at the bisque stage and polished smooth after glaze firing to 1200°C (2192°F). A clear glaze coats the inside of her pieces.

As curator of an exhibition of International Tableware Design in 1991, Smith wrote the following words in a catalogue:

> Any product, whether industrially-produced or handmade, exists as a result of human need, thereby reflecting the concerns of the society that desires it at the time of its production. Designers and manufacturers in general have learnt to respond to these needs by firstly creating the products and then promoting them as necessary and desirable. The confusion to the consumer about what is now acceptable as 'good' design is further complicated as industry attempts to cater to the demands of a multi-faceted society.

Bone china is renowned especially for its supreme whiteness and translucency. It differs from so-called 'true' porcelain both in its composition and in its relationship with glaze. Whereas, normally, the porcelain body and glaze fuse together as one at high temperatures, bone china is fired to maturity in the bisque firing around 1250°C (2282°F) and a 'skin' of glaze is fired on at a much lower temperature. Originally, its manufacture was confined almost exclusively to England and factories in Stoke-on-Trent and elsewhere made great quantities of wares in this material.

Industrially-produced English bone china is a medium that presents the studio potter with particular problems. Due to the necessarily high proportion of bone ash in a typical bone china body, it lacks the plasticity of porcelain and it is, therefore, mainly slip cast in plaster moulds. Models for casting moulds can be made in clay but plaster makes better original models. Solid lumps of plaster can be turned on a horizontal lathe to give a perfectly smooth surface or rectangular shapes can be cast between sheets of glass. Facets, twists and

A group of slip-cast and carved porcelain vessels, by Sandra Black (Australia), 2001. Made from Sealey's doll-casting porcelain in different colours. H. 6.5 –19 cm (2 ½ x 7 ½ in.), fired to cone 7 in an electric kiln.

other details are introduced by hand carving or planing the plaster model. Careful attention must be paid to the profile when modelling for a one-piece mould to ensure it will release the eventual slip-cast form. Multi-part moulds can also be used but seams are difficult to conceal unless the mould can be designed so that the seam runs along the edge of the model or where positive changes of direction occur. This is because seams will show up as raised lines on cast bone china after firing no matter how well they have been fettled away before

placing in the kiln. Newly made moulds should be allowed to dry naturally because they can crack if exposed to excessive heat.

The first contact that **Sandra Black (Australia)** had with bone china was at Canberra School of Art in 1983. She worked, initially, with a casting body fired to 1280°C (2336°F) but changed to using another which required a lower temperature because it offered a better response to colour and the advantage of cheaper fuel costs. Later, having resolved problems previously experienced with colour, she returned to using the higher firing bone china. She prepares her casting slip with great care and describes the procedure as follows:

1. Measure the water at 600 ml (21 fl.oz) to every kg (2.2 lb) of dry material.
2. Add deflocculent to water. Dispex, sodium silicate or soda ash are used singly, or in combination.
3. Mix dry ingredients together, add to the water and stir using a power drill with a paint mixer attachment to ensure even dispersal. At this point a little more deflocculent may be added to increase fluidity if the slip is too thick. Care is essential because if there is too much deflocculant it will have the reverse effect.
4. The slip is then sieved and, if required, ball milled for 2–6 hours. The slip is then tested by casting a small mould. Its condition is correct if it fulfils the following two parameters:

casting time between 5–10 minutes = 2–4 mm (½ –¹⁄₁₆ in.) in thickness.
it should drain cleanly away without shaking the mould.

The slip is stored in an airtight container and then left to settle for 24 hours before use. It must be thoroughly stirred (being careful not to trap air bubbles which causes pinholes to develop) before each cast is taken.

Vase with blue interior and bowl with blue exterior, by Sasha Wardell (UK), 2002. Layering and incising technique, h. 22 cm (8 ¾ in.) and 11 cm (4 ⅜ in.). *Photograph by the artist.*

Black's most recent choice for slip-casting is 'Sealey's doll-casting porcelain' from the USA that is normally fired to cone 6 but she takes it up to cone 7 for better vitrification and translucency. Her pieces are trimmed on the wheel after casting and guidelines marked out on the surface before carving with a surgical blade mounted in a cane holder.

Ready-made slips can be obtained from pottery suppliers for potters who find their preparation tedious. **Sasha Wardell** (UK) is one who feels that the material is difficult enough to cast and fire and she welcomes the opportunity to use prepared slips that help to simplify the process of working with bone china. She still finds it necessary to pass the slip through a 60s mesh sieve and to adjust its fluidity with a few drops of sodium Dispex deflocculant. Her pieces are cast for 1–2 minutes before draining the mould. Spare clay is then cut away and the cast left to stiffen overnight (in order to reduce the risk of distortion) before removing it from the mould.

Normally, it is important to ensure that the mould is clean and dry for casting but, if it is so very dry that the cast releases while draining excess slip, then it can be dampened slightly beforehand. In any case, casts will release at different rates according to the dryness of the mould and the atmospheric conditions at the time. On no account should attempts be made to dry the cast too quickly. Sandra Black stresses the need for patience at this stage because bone china has a notorious 'memory'. Sasha Wardell also speaks of this problem which she describes as the 'idiosyncratic nature of bone china' not only in coming to terms with its high shrinkage rate but also with its tendency to warp alarmingly. Wardell finds this 'both intriguing and frustrating' at the same time. She referred me to an article she wrote for *Ceramic Review* Vol. 111 (1988) in which she described this memory manifesting itself when a cast has been knocked or dented in the green state. This will be 'remembered', despite any attempt to repair the damage, and revert to its distorted form in the high firing. This is a feature of other thinly potted porcelain bodies but its effects are more exaggerated in bone china. It is a characteristic which Wardell believes 'could be exploited and therefore open up a whole new way of working with china, if the "surprise" element is desired'. However, she prefers to remain more fully in control in order to secure reliable results. She finds that bone china, possessing qualities of intense whiteness, translucency and strength, is a very seductive material to work with. 'It is a very "single-minded" clay, which forces the maker to work with clarity and precision. Its technical inflexibility and idiosyncratic making and firing characteristics might easily be a deterrent to investigation, but I consider these restrictions and limitations as a challenge to my creativity and working methods.'

Wardell's most recent work makes use of a method producing different layers within the casting. She explains that to achieve specific points of translucency in the work, she developed a 'layering and slicing' technique that created subtle facets on the outer surface of the pieces and involved slicing through 3 or 4 coats of different coloured slips to reveal underlying and increasingly transparent layers. Similar techniques exist in glass production, an inspiration in this area of her experimentation. Various combinations of coloured slips were tested to produce the most effective luminosity when overlapped and subsequently revealed. A gradual paring down using a sharp Stanley blade produced the best result on an unfired, bone dry piece. To obtain the most successful and effective 'slice' which did not result in indentation, the forms were required to be curved in profile. To allow for more individuality and variation within each piece, tests were carried out in drying and firing the forms, with or without 'setters' (a pre-cast former used to keep rims/edges in shape). Individual success depended on the openness of the shape, thickness of layering and irregularity of rim.

Pair of textured bowls (lines), by Sasha Wardell (UK), 2002. Water erosion technique, h. 18 cm (7 in.) and 12 cm (4 ¾ in.). *Photograph by the artist.*

She uses different coloured slips poured into the mould, one after the other, to build up a layering of 3 or 4 coats. When the piece is bone dry and has been removed from the mould, a sharp Stanley blade is used to gradually pare down the curved surface of the piece in random areas, revealing bit by bit the underlying colours until in some instances the last, or interior, layer is exposed. The incised pieces undergo a similar process as far as the layering is concerned. However, they are removed from the mould when they are still quite soft and a loop tool is used to cut or gouge through the layers. This has the same effect of revealing the underlying colours until the last layer is exposed. Great care must be taken to avoid going right through as the piece is particularly vulnerable at this stage.

Sasha Wardell's thinly cast forms are fired three times, firstly with a 'soft' firing to 1000°C (1832°F) after which the work is sanded with fine grade Wet 'n Dry paper. Originally, she omitted this preliminary stage but too many pieces were lost when being handled and cleaned up while still in the raw state. The next firing is taken to 1260°C (2300°F) and soaked at that temperature for

Tableware Set for Children, slip-cast porcelain by Hubert Kittel (Germany). Set comprises of: 3 pots, 2 cups, 1 bowl, 1 container, 1 rechaud / warmer (wood): 1 saucer, 1 breakfast plate, 1 bowl – warmer (wood). Lids: hard-paste porcelain, fired at 1400°C (2552°F), sprayed inglaze colours. *Photograph by Klaus E. Göltz, Halle.*

one and a half hours. This allows the body to mature and achieve perfect whiteness and translucency before decoration is applied. Finally, the work is fired to 1080°C (1976°F) to fix the coloured stains.

Sandra Black, on the other hand, uses an even lower bisque firing (to only 750°C/1382°F) before sanding the carved surface decoration of her particular bone china pieces. If they are taken to a temperature above 800°C (1472°F), the bisque ware becomes too hard. She has fired bone china in both electric and gas kilns but warns that a heavy reducing atmosphere can cause grey areas to appear. However, further firing in oxidation overcomes this problem. She has found that bone china will withstand rapid temperature changes in the initial part of the firing cycle and in the latter stages of cooling. 'I

have fired up to 720°C (1328°F) in one and a half hours for lustres and then opened the kiln at 600°C (1112°F) while cooling. One piece was fired three times in one day without cracking.' Such work is on a very small scale so pieces will accept these thermal stresses more easily. Her larger forms with various draped elements have also survived fast glaze firings to 1260°C (2300°F) in 3 ½ to 4 ½ hours without cracking.

Recipes

Black relies on two different recipes for making her bone china casting slips. The first of these was developed by Dr Owen Rye at Canberra School of Art. It is normally fired to cones 8–9 and consists of the following materials:

Group of vases, *Head First* by Johanna Hitzler (Germany), 2001. Porcelain slip-cast from identical moulds, cut, stacked and joined in various ways, copper glaze inside, h. 14 cm (5 ½ in.), fired to 1280°C (2336°F) in an electric kiln. *Photograph by Gunter Binsack, Leipzig.*

(B6 Body)	Eckalite No. 1 kaolin	30
	Bone ash (natural)	40
	Potash feldspar	22.8
	Silica	2.2

These ingredients are mixed with 600 ml (21 fl.oz) of water together with 2 g (0.07 oz) Dispex and 1 g (0.03 oz) of sodium silicate to each kilogram of dry material. In making her black stained bone china slip she adds 7% iron chromate, 7% black iron oxide and 3.5% cobalt carbonate to the mixture. However, it should be noted that these oxides act as powerful fluxes so the firing temperature may need to be lowered to around cones 4–5 according to the firing pattern adopted. As with all ceramic materials, great care should be exercised during their preparation and use. Danger from ingested dust and toxic elements can be avoided by wearing protective clothing such as masks and rubber gloves.

The second slip is a recipe devised by Mike Kusnik at the Western Australia Institute of Technology in Perth. It is fired to cones 6–7.

Cresta BB kaolin	40	mixed with water and
Bone ash (natural)	40	deflocculant in the same proportions
Nepheline syenite	20	as above.

Casting slip can be recycled but care should be taken to avoid contaminating the new batch. Sandra Black suggests adding no more than 20% scrap to any new mix of slip and recommends including 0.1% barium carbonate in order to neutralise sulphates which can cause peeling faults.

Slip-cast sections in either porcelain or bone china can be used in many different permutations to create some amazing new forms. **Johanna Hitzler** (Germany) has made a series of moulds that have adjustable sections which can be moved and rearranged in unusual

Arctic Light, by Angela Mellor (Australia), 2002. Bone china paperclay, large: h. 13 cm (5 ⅛ in.), small: h. 8 cm (3 ⅛ in.) medium: h. 11 cm (4 ⅜ in.), 1250°C (2282°F), oxidised. *Photograph by the artist.*

combinations of the different elements to produce slip-cast, sculptural vessel forms.

It was the ultimate whiteness, thinness and translucency of bone china that attracted **Angela Mellor** (UK/Australia) to experiment with slip-cast forms based on similar shapes that she had previously produced by slab building with porcelain. She finds that the tactile quality of bone china is very appealing and its marble-like surface has a warm sensuality about it. 'Slip-casting bone china allows me to make ultra thin shapes which are extremely translucent, pure and so white that ordinary porcelain seems almost grey in comparison. The supreme whiteness makes colours so much more vibrant.'

In earlier work with asymmetric forms Mellor did not employ the use of 'setters' to support the pieces in the kiln because she encouraged the forms to 'move', to become more fluid during the firing and thus closer in character to the organic forms of nature that inspire much of her work. Alumina is packed inside her pots and around the base to prevent them sticking to the shelf. In her latest work, she has dispensed with colour completely and now relies solely on the purity of the white bone china itself to convey her imagery. She describes her work as an investigation into the translucency of bone china and its potential for the transmission of light. She is deeply interested in the environment so landscapes, light, and coastal environments are reflected in her pieces. Photography has enabled her to captivate not only line and colour but also the unique mysterious quality of light.

The study of rocks, coral, shells and seaweed, has led to many ideas for design. Textures of these organic forms have been recreated from plaster moulds using bone china paperclay. Fragments of these have enabled me to introduce a delicate tracery of translucent texture into the work

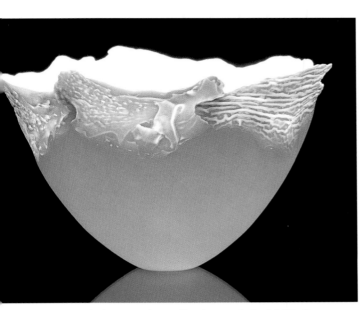

Ocean Light by Angela Mellor (Australia), 2002. Bone china with paperclay inlay, h. 12.5 (5 in.), 1250°C (2282°F), oxidised. *Photograph by the artist.*

reminiscent of organic forms found in nature.

The *Arctic Light* series is a continuation of the *Glacial Light* series begun in 2000, inspired by the stark beauty of Antarctica. This series explores the contrasts and variations of light through layers of textures found in nature, creating a dramatic effect when illuminated from above.

Most of my work is slip-cast in bone china and fired to 1250°C (2282°F) in an electric kiln. One-piece dropout moulds are used to avoid seam lines. Research over the past few years has involved working with bone china paperclay, which involves mixing paper pulp with the bone china casting slip. This very versatile medium has opened up many opportunities, allowing me to incorporate light and texture into the work (e.g. *Ocean Light*). A recent development has been to apply paper slip onto a textured plaster slab for a few minutes. It is then torn into strips and laid over a hump mould, each piece joined together with paper slip. The form is then removed from the mould before it dries and shrinks. The inside is then sealed with paperclay slip and left to dry inside a hollow mould. Forms can easily be manipulated while the paperclay is still damp to form more sculptural pieces, as can be seen in *Arctic Fold*.

Pavel Knapek (Czech Republic) produces amazing, well-defined relief panels using porcelain slip casts from paper patterns. Paper sheets are folded into sharp-edged relief horizontally on the bench. Sometimes the profiles are altered further or deformed before the model is painted to stiffen it and supported from underneath to make a plaster cast from the exposed upper section. When this first section of the mould is dry, a thin slice of porcelain (about 8mm/⅓ in. thick) is laid on top of the inverted mould with the original paper model still in place. Another cast is taken from this and made to interlock at one end to create a two-section plaster mould. When assembled together upright, porcelain slip is poured in to fill the narrow space inside the mould and a mirror image of the original paper model is made.

From time to time Knapek is asked to explain his work but he answers that it must speak for itself. He believes that once it is completed and has left his studio, any dialogue should be solely between the spectator and the sculpture. His pieces have no intended function other than reference to their own existence. He explains that he has been 'making porcelain relief sculptures since 1988. Forms for porcelain, forms for space, forms for light ... they are research about harmony. They are pure and of exalted fragility stretched to their utter limits. My largest pieces (80cm/31 in.) balance on the edge of possibility. Contraction during drying and firing is as much as 14%. All my work is fired in reduction to 1390°C (2534°F). I never use glaze.'

He marks out his idea with pencil on a sheet of paper to assist folding it into paper sculpture. The next phase consists of crushing the paper, breaking up the initial form in order to create a

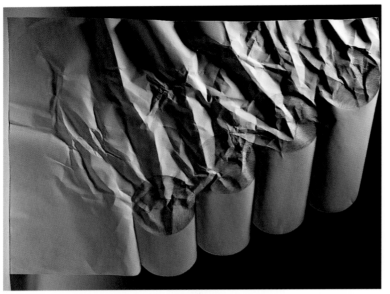

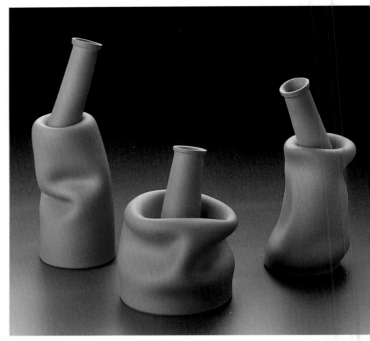

Three Drunken Bottles, by Hubert Kittel (Germany). Slip-cast bottles, deformed, coloured with cobalt solution, unglazed, surface polished hard-paste porcelain, fired to 1400°C (2552°F), h. 30 cm (11 ¾ in.). 'I designed a set of utilitarian, functional bottles for slip-casting and deformed them in the raw state to create a new sculptural, soft-shaped image. The homogeneous cobalt blue, soft matt surface seems to me an alienation: is this material porcelain or not?' *Photograph by Foto-Riedl, Selb.*

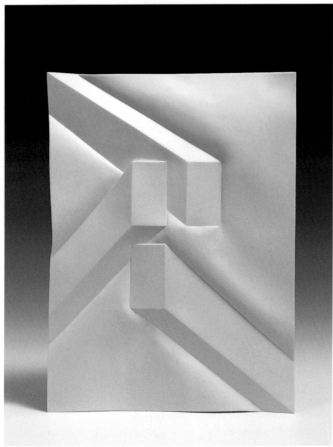

(Top) Porcelain relief sculpture, by Pavel Knapek (Czech Republic), 2002. Slip-cast and altered, unglazed, fired to 1390°C (2534°F). *Photograph by the artist.*
(Below) Porcelain relief sculpture, slip-cast and altered, unglazed, fired to 1390°C (2534°F). *Photograph by the artist.*

relief composition. Chance effects are accepted and incorporated into the whole because he feels that the combination of flat and crushed surfaces create their own purity of line and expression. These bas-reliefs are transplanted into porcelain to create his sculptures. He exploits the 'extraordinary fineness and astonishing malleability of porcelain. It captures the fleeting beauty of paper, its vulnerable fragility. This metamorphosis is preserved by the firing.'

Hubert Kittel (Germany) designed a set of utilitarian, functional bottles and cast them in plaster to reproduce the shapes. This allowed him to explore how the forms could be altered and deformed while wet to create a new sculptural, softer image. Another project was to produce a tableware set for children (see p.66) to be slip-cast in porcelain with 3 pots, 2 cups, 1 bowl, 1 container, 1 saucer, 1 breakfast plate, 1

Bone china form, by Remigijus Sederevicius (Lithuania), 1997. Slip-cast and mounted on a stoneware base, h. 60 cm (23 ½ in.), fired in an electric kiln. 'This piece was formed by submersing a balloon in porcelain or bone china slip to form a thin skin that is allowed to dry and then the balloon is deflated. The slip must be dense enough to make the piece. For forming layered pieces the slip should be thinner, but more viscous for a textured surface.' *Photograph by Gint Malderis.*

bowl and lids. This was in hard-paste porcelain (fired at 1400°C/2552°F) with sprayed in-glaze colours. This tableware program was originally designed as a learning set for his daughter: 'my own cup', 'my own pots' and so forth. He developed various sizes and handles, different solutions for locking the lid; and a special combination of porcelain and wood elements that would increase their durability. The whole program is intended to be adaptable to the special needs of a growing child (4–12 years). The range of colours is constantly changing. Many items are stackable. One pot is oven and fireproof, all pieces are dishwasher-proof (except the wood, of course). The design brief was to make the set compact, amusing and to appeal to a child, e.g. 'touch and use me'! This was produced as part of a commercial program between 1990–1995. Now it forms part of Kittel's own porcelain label and is manufactured as a craft design product.

Remigijus Sederevicius (Lithuania) uses a technique for casting porcelain or bone china forms that dispenses entirely with plaster moulds. He discovered that latex balloons are a perfect choice for his purpose because it is easy to control air pressure during the drying stage. This allows him to obtain extremely smooth inner and outer surfaces on quite large pieces. It is also possible to make different textures with various layers of slip and the use of other materials such as lace. Porcelain shapes are produced by submerging a balloon into dense or thick porcelain slip so that it adheres to the latex surface. Layers and textures can be built up in this way. This method works well with bone china, as it forms a very thin, transparent skin on pieces up to 40cm/16 in. in diameter.

LOW-FIRED PORCELAIN

Anne James (UK) uses porcelain in a low-fired, raku process without glazes. She mixes her own porcelain body and uses it for both throwing and slab building. Sometimes a small proportion of 'T' Material is added for larger slab bottle forms. When she rediscovered a tiny test of resin lustres that had been done some

Three slab-built porcelain vessels on black fired clay stands, by Anne James (UK), 2002. Tallest: h. 22 cm (8 ¾ in.). *Photograph by the artist.*

Four-slab built porcelain dishes with coloured slips and lustres by Anne James (UK), 2002. Large dish, l. 35 cm (13 ¾ in.) bisqued to 1000°C (1832°F) and then raku fired to 800°C (1472°F). *Photograph by the artist.*

years previously, she was prompted to explore the possibilities of their use on porcelain. Her work is mainly thrown and modified in various ways. Some pieces are simply beaten, others have parts cut out and are rejoined. The base may be replaced with a slab while others have a shoulder and neck added as a separately thrown piece. All are sprayed with coloured slips and burnished. Tools tend to be teaspoons, pebbles, boxwood tools and a little pad of foam or cotton wool wrapped with thin soft plastic to

finish off. Bowls are thrown, skimmed and pushed into ovals or squares, often leaving a curved base which stands in a ring. Some recent dishes are made by the cut and join method in which slabs are rolled out and allowed to stiffen a little. Small V-shaped cuts are made and the edges slightly overlapped and joined together with gentle pressure from a little wooden roller. The forms are governed by the width and placing of these cuts. The pieces are propped up with small blocks of soft foam until they are self-supporting.

A variety of resin lustres are applied to the burnished, bisque-fired surface and painted directly with for printing, either as texture or cut to create simple patterns. Latex resist is often painted on, and the lustre sponged or painted in the gaps. Two or three different lustres may be applied on separate areas of the piece. Firing is carried out in a top-loading electric kiln to about 850°C (1562°F) and then treated in the same way as raku. Pieces are removed hot from the kiln before smoking in sawdust. For the bowls, she uses a

Slab-built porcelain vessel with coloured slips and lustres by Anne James (UK), 2002. Raku-fired and smoked in sawdust, on slate stand, h. 25 cm (10 in.). *Photograph by the artist.*

shallow metal box which has a layer of sawdust with a hollow made to accommodate the bowl form. The bowl is set into the sawdust so that the back is covered, but the top surface is free. A little sawdust is usually scattered on to the inside and then the piece is quenched. This gives a very black outside and a varied smoky or speckled upper surface.

When the piece is dry, the pattern and colour are assessed and the process continues. James' bowls and dishes are sometimes fired five or six times adding more lustres each time, so that a multi-layered image emerges to reveal different appearances depending on the light. They vary considerably due to the thickness of application and the order in which colours are applied. She has found that vessel and bottle forms are more difficult to multi-fire by this process, because they are more prone to cracking. Finally, the back of the bowl is lightly waxed but the lustred areas are not waxed as it kills the light refraction and flattens out the colours.

Patty Wouters (Belgium) also uses low-firing techniques with porcelain because it is a white and very responsive clay. She finds it more sensual to work with than stoneware or earthenware; therefore the production process is particularly pleasant. She accepts that there is a greater risk during production due to its fragility which can cause deformation in the kiln but says that the possibility of 'breathtaking results' makes the effort worthwhile. It was a deliberate choice to use primitive firing methods because the fire itself contributes much to the end result through direct contact with her ceramics. She expresses fascination with the way in which each firing produces different and occasionally, surprising effects.

Wouters throws vessels in porcelain (mostly Harry Fraser P1149) and applies layers of terra sigillata to them. After a high bisque firing (1050°–1100°C/1922°–2012°F) a low saggar firing is conducted to between 600°–900°C

(1112°–1652°F). She uses porcelain for this technique because the subtle colours develop so well and over a wider range. She believes that the combination of porcelain and terra sigillata in the saggar makes it appear to be almost translucent ('like pâte de verre'). Although it is more difficult to burnish porcelain (as it will break more easily when thinly thrown), her results are generally better than using the same method with burnished stoneware.

There is a considerable degree of symbolism in most of the work by Wouters. One example of this can be seen in her *Rocking Pot*. Here, a small, rectangular plate attached vertically to the lid is engraved with a wave pattern that seems to vibrate when seen against the light. She says that the graphic lines allude

to 'communication-waves of good vibrations that can be sent into the world by rocking the pot' and remind her of a trip to Ladakh where she visited several Tibetan monasteries. There, she watched monks writing prayers on white, almost transparent fabric in the most beautiful calligraphy. These sheets are hung outside where they catch the wind so that their prayers and good wishes fly out into the world.

ARCHITECTURAL APPLICATIONS FOR PORCELAIN

The large wall installations by **Ole Lislerud** (Norway) provide convincing evidence of the confident expertise with which modern studio potters have exorcised those peculiar problems, real or imagined, in handling porcelain. To be able to make, manipulate, decorate and successfully fire a flat sheet of porcelain no more than 3 mm/$\frac{1}{16}$ in. thick and with a surface area up to 1 m/3.3 ft long by 80 cm/31 in. wide is no mean feat. But to complete an architectural commission for the Supreme Court building in Oslo, which entailed the production of 250 m² (2691 ft²) of equally thin porcelain slabs inscribed with the full text of the Norwegian Constitution, was a remarkable achievement. Lislerud was awarded that commission when he won an open competition for the work in 1992. His winning design consisted of two tall columns each 32 m/104 ft high by 4 m/13 ft wide and curved as a section of a circle. The columns are covered with porcelain slabs, 30 cm (12 in.) X 65 cm (25 in.) X 3 mm ($\frac{1}{16}$ in.), upon which he displayed calligraphic inscriptions using a technique he has developed, similar to making a lithographic print.

The methods used to make the components for constructing his sculptural installations were developed during a ten-year period of intensive experiment and systematic research. Casting

Rocking Antenna Vessel, by Patty Wouters (Belgium). Wheel-thrown porcelain, bisque-fired to 1080°C (1976°F) and then soaked in iron sulphate to obtain the earth colours in final saggar firing with combustible materials. D. 30 cm (11 ¾ in.). The white slip-cast porcelain sheet is carved and fired to 1250°C (2282°F). *Photograph by Katrin Daems.*

Graffiti Wall – God is Woman at the University of Oslo /Domus Theologica, by Ole Lislerud (Norway). Porcelain, high-fired to 1400°C (2552°F), produced at Porsgrund Porcelain factory in Norway. Total size: 16 x 3 m (52.5 x 9.8 ft), *Photograph by Glenn Hagbru (Architect: Terje Hope).*

plaster on polished marble slabs produces extremely smooth boards 2.5 cm (1 in.) thick. These plasterboards are then used to cast porcelain by pouring slip on them from one position while they are inclined at a sufficient angle for the slip to flow evenly. The size of the plasterboards matches that of the shelves in Lislerud's kiln. The procedure of actually casting thin slabs of porcelain is the most difficult part of the whole process of manufacture because small mistakes can create big problems. The most common faults resulting from incorrect casting are: cracking, warping and distortion with corners curling to destroy the flatness. Tilting the plasterboard while pouring slip from the top edge helps to avoid subsequent cracking. Lislerud discovered that pouring slip in a more random way shows up the drying process as cracks appear along the joins and overlaps as the porcelain dries rapidly in contact with the plaster. Hence the need to ensure an uninterrupted flow of slip to cover the board. Wooden battens are placed around the edges of the plasterboard to contain the slip to a depth of 3 mm (⅛ in.). The battens are not fixed to the board because he finds that they will maintain their position without moving while the slip is poured. After ten minutes the slip has dried sufficiently for the battens to be removed. A thin-bladed knife slices between the batten and the porcelain and also under the slab to loosen it. 'If this is not done carefully it will definitely warp.' Ten minutes later the slab is pulled gently away from the plaster, first one end and then lifting from the other. The newly loosened slabs are then placed on paper-lined plasterboard (as used for ceilings and partitions in the building trade. Fantastic for drying porcelain and keeping it flat!) of the same size and left to dry.

When trying to speed the production of his

Detail of *Graffiti Wall* by Ole Lislerud (Norway). *Photograph by Glenn Hagbru.*

porcelain slabs, Lislerud abandoned the normal drying procedure and found that he could transport the newly cast slabs directly into the kiln. By applying a thin coating of aluminium oxide dust to the leatherhard slabs before turning them over onto the 'builders' plasterboard' they would slide easily onto the kiln shelves. 'These slabs turned out to be completely flat and, because they were leatherhard and only 3 mm (⅛ in.) thick, none were broken when stacking and sliding into position.' On the other hand, completely dry slabs are sometimes 'so fragile that they can crack just by looking at them!' These large tiles are fired with great care and allowed to cool down for as long as possible. However, as always in porcelain, success will depend on a thorough understanding of basic techniques and on the essential skill and knowledge that can only be acquired through practical experience.

By carving into the plaster slab before pouring slip, precise, surface relief marks and patterns can be produced on the cast porcelain tile. Another technique is to incise through a very thin layer of coloured porcelain (e.g. black) slip applied to the surface of the plaster. A different coloured slip (e.g. yellow) is then painted over those incised marks before the final thickness of porcelain is poured. The first layer of thin slip tends to stick partially to the plaster ('which can produce very interesting visual effects') when the slab is released while a thicker layer of slip gives a more even colour. Multiple layers with different colours can be applied and scraped through to form quite complex designs. Lislerud is able, also, to change the scale and character of his calligraphy by 'writing' with a slip trailer, drawing directly on to the plaster with either coloured slips or specially formulated glazes prior to casting the porcelain slab. These designs trailed on to plaster will release completely with the cast slip. If necessary, he will leave such compositions to dry and be cast hours or even days later.

Lislerud's most recent work has evolved through processing and developing his designs on a personal computer. This has enabled him to transform images drawn on clay and transfer them to glass or textiles by silkscreen printing. The same technique was used to compose a curtain for a theatre at a Performing Arts Center. Here the original drawing was on a porcelain plaque 30 x 30 cm (12 x 12 in.). The digital photo was then transformed to 25 x 8 m (27 x 9 ft) before printing by computer on textile fabric. But it is his large architectural wall pieces that are most impressive. He believes that ceramic art has become an important source of inspiration among architects nuance and this has encouraged artists to move with ever more confidence into architecture projects.

The *Graffiti Wall* by Lislerud is situated in the main entrance at the Faculty of Divinity, University of Oslo. It was completed in September 2000 and the composition, developed on a computer, covers approximately 45 m² (484 ft²) of high fired (cone 14) porcelain tiles displaying texts and graffiti collected over a 3-year period, collected from such diverse places as the Berlin Wall, and texts from famous poets to the toilets at Oslo University. The *Graffiti Wall* includes an LCD monitor with continuous updates on lectures and information from the university administration. A personal computer is incorporated also in the wall to allow students to access the internet or send e-mail messages.

Digital photography enabled Lislerud to take examples from some of his previous work to combine with new material. He feels that an analogy with musical composition is relevant here. Similar calligraphic elements that appeared in his earlier pieces have been re-used and adapted to suit this new installation, thus creating extra visual depth and interest. By working this way, his imagery has developed to offer multi-faceted layers of information.

Decals and photo transfers are familiar techniques, but computer technology is the most important factor that has improved this practice and helped Lislerud to resolve ideas much faster. Digital photography and graphical programs such as Adobe PhotoShop have opened up new avenues to explore concepts for work on a larger scale. Working to a grid and module system together with architects also ensures a system of construction that functions smoothly.

The Graffiti Wall project was his first large-scale ceramic project using a computer. Sketches, drawings and images were scanned into the computer and manipulated to arrive at the final composition. Selected elements were transformed into decals to be combined with brushwork and airbrush painting. All the tiles were multi-fired to give the appearance of complex graffiti.

Large-scale wall sculptures in porcelain are by no means the sole prerogative of European ceramicists and at least one American, **Dale Zheutlin,** has completed a number of important architectural commissions in this medium. Designing for specific sites involves collaborating closely with architects, interior designers, art consultants and clients representing public agencies and large corporations. However, she says that it is important for the artist to retain creative control. She described her experiences in this kind of work in an article for *Ceramics Monthly* (June 1993) and I am indebted to her and to the magazine for allowing me to quote some of the salient features involved. She was awarded a financial grant in 1986 and this allowed her to experiment and develop the necessary technology to accomplish the kind of large-scale projects that interested her.

Handling oversized slabs before they are fired presents a problem. They are difficult to turn without stretching or bending, so I dry them on boards covered with plastic and newspaper.

Twin Spans, porcelain wall panel by Dale Zheutlin, 1991. Dimensions: 450 x 180 cm (15 x 6 in.), fired in oxidation. Commissioned by the Delaware River and Bay Authority, Wilmington. 'The image is abstracted from the Delaware River Bridge.' *Photograph by Andrew Bordwin.*

City Panel from *The Scott Collection*, commission for the Royal Victoria Infirmary, Newcastle-Upon-Tyne, by Paul Scott, 1998. Painted underglaze with screen-printed inglaze decals on HF porcelain, 1.8 x 0.65 m (6 x 2.1 ft). *Photograph by Keith Paisley.*

Working directly on the floor, I change the top layer of newspaper every six hours. The clay is weighed down with boards for the first 24 hours, then air dried.

In order to avoid firing difficulties, Zheutlin found that it was necessary to work out her design in segments to be fired together on site.

I started with slabs 2.5 cm (1 in.) thick and no more than 46 x 62 cm (18 X 24 in.) overall, because that was the maximum size that could fit into my 72 cm (28 in.), octagonal kiln. These segments were fired on edge, four at a time, then regrouped as wall units. I now have a top loader, rectangular electric kiln, which offers flexibility in experimentation and a degree of economy, plus it will fire larger slabs.

As her work evolved, Zheutlin changed from concentrating on 'flat, planar surfaces without colour to more dimensional construction with colour developed from a variety of glazes and stains. I began to cut the slabs, then put them back together by overlapping, tilting, intersecting and reassembling.'

Experiments and glaze tests were conducted with the help of an assistant to establish a palette of 32 colours. Taking into account a 5% shrinkage rate, the slabs were rolled out and allowed to stiffen before laying them on the floor in preparation for carving, incising, the application of stains and glazes, and to be cut into manageable sections. They were left covered and weighted until dry and then stored in vertical racks. 'After firing, the sections were assembled on armatures so that a template could be made to serve as a hanging guide. I always try to do a trial hanging in my studio, although this is not always possible for very large projects.'

Smaller tiles have long been used to cover extremely large and often complex architectural structures but porcelain is a less familiar material for this purpose than either earthenware or stoneware. One of the most amazing uses of stoneware tiles is that of clothing the multiple arching roof of the Sydney Opera House. Porcelain is being increasingly used for more decorative purposes despite its inherent difficulties. **Paul Scott** (UK), for example, uses combinations of porcelain tiles to create panels and murals rather like a painter might use a white surface for drawing and painting. He prepares a mixture of ceramic stains suspended in water and proceeds to draw directly on to the porcelain bisque with a pen. This method produces fine

(Above) *Porcelain Wall Panel*, by Tamsin Watkins-Jones (UK). Small barium blue glazed tiles, inlaid with metal oxides, loosely laced together with copper wire. The knots used are the same as those used on the Han dynasty jade burial suits, which inspired the panels. Dimensions: 55 cm x 45 cm (22 x 17 ¾ in.). *Photograph by Jonathan Gooding. (Courtesy of Mr. & Mrs. N. MacGregor).*

(Right) Porcelain tile panel, by Russell Coates (UK), 2000. Hand-made tiles decorated with enamels and underglaze blue stains, based on a 'North African' theme for the Medina Restaurant on the P&O liner 'Aurora'. Dimensions: 170 x 90 cm (67 x 35 ½ in.) *Photograph by Peter Lowry.*

linear drawings which he supplements with thin washes of similar ceramic 'inks'.

Tiles are used in another way by **Tamsin Watkins-Jones** (UK). She ties them together with wire and suspends them from a rigid bar as a wall hanging. She has only recently begun to explore the possibilities of this method but finds the combination of the copper wire knots and blue tiles exciting. She feels that the inlaid metallic oxides become wire-like in appearance

during the firing, melting into the surface of the barium glaze and creating a very rich surface quality. When handled, these panels have a wonderful weight and sound to them, they flex and chink like exotic pieces of armour.

Recently, **Russell Coates** (UK) completed a contract to make a series of tiled wall panels for the new P&O cruise ship Aurora being built in Germany. Each tile, following a North African theme, was individually made by hand from rolled porcelain slabs. The tiles were painted with enamels on a clear glaze that allows the

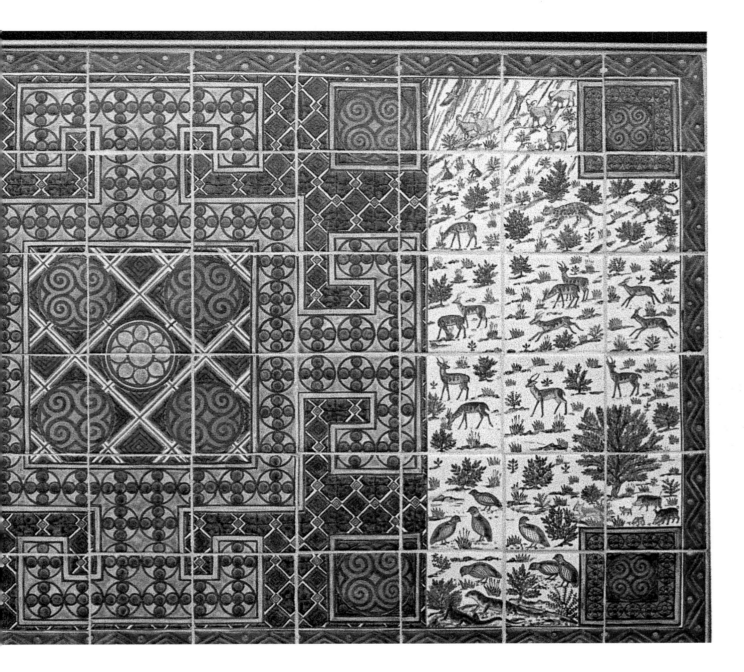

creamy white porcelain body to show through. Mounted on aluminium, the panels were edged with brass. The whole project took 13 months of concentrated effort to produce.

Angela Verdon (UK) undertook a residency at the Royal Crown Derby Porcelain Factory as part of the 'Year of the Artist' scheme in 2000. While there, she used their china body to create a large-scale, translucent screen of individual, hand-carved bone china tiles mounted in a wooden frame. This is now situated in the main entrance foyer at the Company's office. She acknowledges the considerable assistance she received from the factory workforce to ensure success in this project. Despite the inevitable difficulties encountered, this was a 'memorable experience spanning nine months, from which I learnt a great deal and discovered new enthusiasms and challenges'. These sentiments were reinforced for her when one of the skilled employees who had worked in the factory for more than 40 years, remarked that 'there is still something new to discover about this material, some new quality to appreciate and a different approach to be taken'.

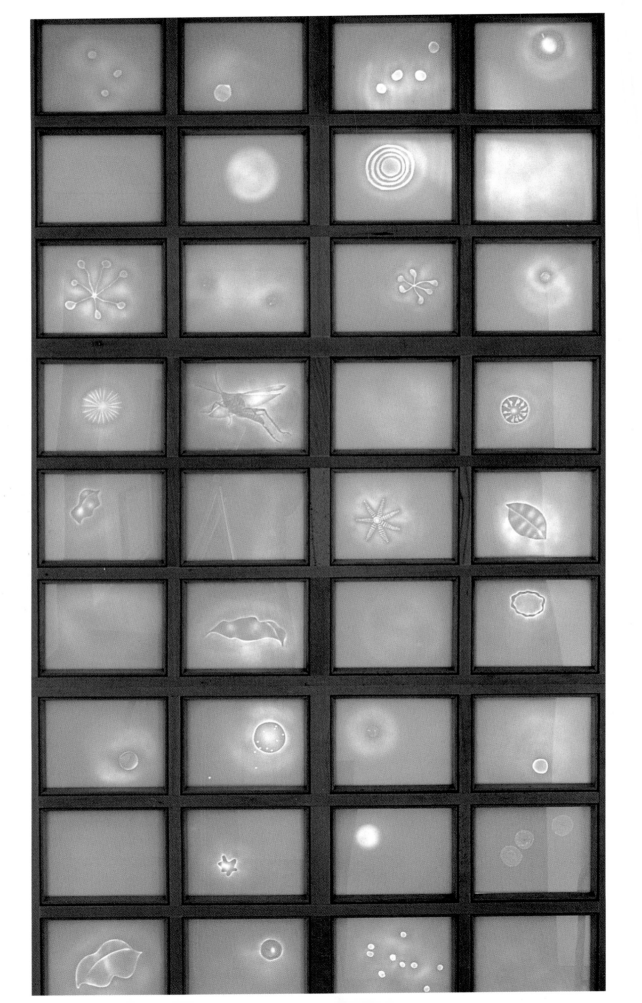

(Above) Porcelain tile panel, by Arne Åse (Norway), 1998. Painted with shellac resist and sponged to give the texture, 40 x 60 cm (15 ¾ x 23 ½ in.), unglazed, fired in reduction to 1250°C (2282°F). *Photograph by Glenn Hagebu.*

(Above) Wall panel lit by fluorescent light, by Curtis Benzle (USA). Made from inlaid porcelain tiles, fired to cone 8, mounted on plexiglass in an aluminium frame, h. 2.4 m (8 ft). *Photograph by the artist.*

(Opposite) Part of a large bone china screen by Angela Verdon (UK), 2000. It is made up of individual, hand-carved tiles, mounted in a beech wood frame for the main foyer at the Royal Crown Derby Porcelain Factory.
Photograph by Stuart Blackwood.

Verdon draws marks and images directly on the clay cast and carves them out or around, leaving certain parts prominently raised and surrounded by very thin areas. 'I want to draw the eye in and towards an image by the light and colour in a subtle way to create a sense of calm stillness in the piece.' The concept of 'less is more' is what she strives to achieve in these works, to move away from what she feels is her almost obsessive attention to carving detail and to 'really simplify'.

The architectural panels by **Curtis Benzle** (USA) begin with a very thin slab (1mm/¹⁄₁₆ in.) of porcelain that is painted onto a cloth as slip. On top of that slab he places either nerikomi slices or paints with coloured slips. Further work is done on the surface when the slab has dried to a leatherhard state and additional detail inlaid. It is then cut up into tiles that range from 1.2–2.5 cm (½ to 1 in.) in size. After firing, the tiles are reassembled and attached to a glass or Plexiglass according to the final dimensions and location of the finished piece.

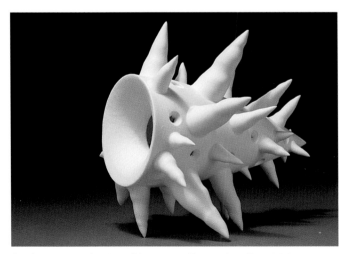

CHAPTER THREE

SOURCES OF INSPIRATION AND MEANS OF EXPRESSION

SCULPTURAL APPLICATIONS

Potters have long exploited the marvellous versatility of porcelain for fashioning intricate, smoothly finished shapes from the whimsical to the more provocative and esoteric of three-dimensional expressions

Porcelain lends itself to working in such extremely fine detail that it has been used for modelling figures, animals, plants etc. for centuries. Victorian dolls often had porcelain heads so delicately modelled and coloured as to appear almost lifelike. Modern potters also have enjoyed this facility to imitate or recreate nature in porcelain. When increasing numbers began to rediscover porcelain in the second half of the 20th century, it seemed appropriate that they should work in small scale. This was due in part to the perceived technical difficulties and partly in deference to it. The material was so different from the coarse, heavy looking stonewares which had dominated the field of studio ceramics after the Second World War that it demanded a new approach. It could be easily pinched into paper-thin pieces and then manipulated and twisted into shapes that resembled natural forms whose delicate appearance belied their fired strength. From the 1960s onward natural forms such as flowers, fungi, birds, fish, and a cavalcade of fantasy creatures have been produced in great numbers. Most are little more than shallow, decorative items of no artistic significance destined to join the multitude of twee kitsch objects from previous generations.

(Left) *Stone Valley Dyad*, by Marc Leuthold (USA), 2002. Unglazed, coloured and carved porcelain, h. 18 cm (7 in.). *Photograph by Eva Heyd.*

Stichtyomitra, by Arnold Annen (Switzerland), 1999. Porcelain sculpture made in Limoges porcelain (PC118B body), d. 20 cm (8 in.), h. 20 cm (8 in.), reduction fired to 1320°C (2408°F) in a gas kiln. *Photograph by the artist.*

Flowers Forever, by Perla Bardin (Argentina), 2002. Bone china, h. 30 cm (11 ¾ in.), w. 40 cm (15 ¾ in.). This special kind of bone china is very thin and transparent at 1060°C (1940°F). *Photograph by the artist.*

A number of distinguished English potters, attracted to porcelain by its fine working properties, proceeded to exploit it with imagination and distinctive flair. Foremost among them were Peter Simpson and Mary Rogers. Although their work was inspired by, or made reference to, organic forms, it rose far above the mere imitation of nature. Simpson's work in the mid-1970s evoked ripe fruits and seed pods with smooth spherical forms split apart to reveal interiors tightly packed with wafer-thin sheets. This contrast between simple exterior and crowded contents was an exploration not only of the aesthetics of form but also of the very nature of porcelain itself. Similarly, Mary Rogers pinch-built a series of small bowls with walls so thin that they could be coaxed into folds and layers to orchestrate the quality of light passing through them rather like the petals of a poppy flower. They were as much

a response to the plastic purity and translucency of the material and the process of making as they were a comment on the natural world. These expressions prompted many imitators, especially among students many of whom produced clusters of frilly, fungoid objects often lacking in understanding, sensitivity or purpose. Other potters chose to combine the contrasting character of heavily grogged stoneware bodies and that of porcelain within one object. Peter Beard (UK) developed a memorable series of pieces incorporating delicately pinched, conglomerate 'growths' of translucent, glazed porcelain erupting from geometrically-shaped black stoneware in a way that gave added emphasis to their respective natures.

Maggie Barnes (UK) worked initially in stoneware but, as her interest focused onto particular areas of the natural world which she found especially inspiring, she realised that only porcelain could provide the means that would enable her to express her feelings about them. 'The material both disciplines and rewards the maker, it is a demanding and seductive clay, responding better to coaxing than to a more forceful approach.'

Her fascination with natural objects began early in life.

Since a small child wandering around the beaches and waterways of the East Coast with my father, who was a passionate fisherman, I have gathered objects from the natural world. The child's habit of collecting 'treasures' to hoard at home stayed with me, grew into adulthood with me, delights me still, and is the foundation from which creativity is fed to this day. I was fortunate to have a teacher in those formative years who encouraged me to explore the natural world of my childhood environment, to make drawings and to use words to record my findings. He remained my dear friend until he died and took pleasure in watching my obsession evolve until it found its natural expression in clay

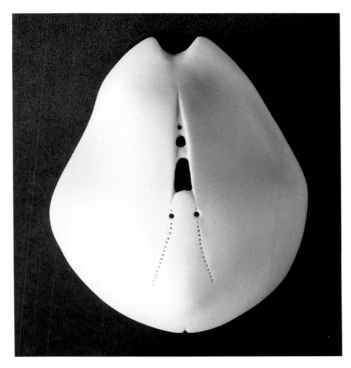

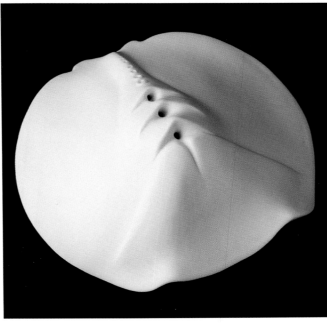

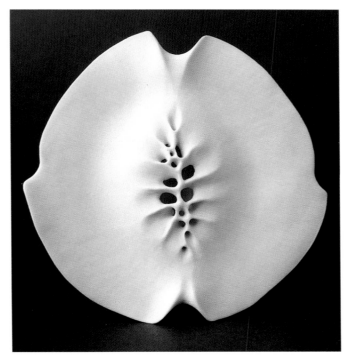

(Above Left) *Skull Form* by Maggie Barnes, 2002. Porcelain, handbuilt, carved and pierced, unglazed, burnished and polished, h. 5 cm (2 in.), l. 12 cm (4 ¾ in.), w. 9 cm (3 ½ in.), light reduction fired to 1260°C (2300°F).
(Below Left) *Marine Form with Spine*, by Maggie Barnes, 2001. Carved and pierced, unglazed, burnished and polished porcelain, handbuilt with modelled additions, reduction fired to 1260°C (2300°F), h. 5.5 cm, d. 11 cm (2 ⅛ in.), 2001. *(Collection Professor Anne Lintott.)*
(Above) *Marine Form*, by Maggie Barnes (UK). Unglazed, polished porcelain, handbuilt, carved, pierced and burnished, reduction fired to 1260°C (2300°F), 10 cm x 10.5 cm (4 x 4 ⅛ in.), 1995. *(Milner-Barnes Collection).*
Photographs by Jerry Hardman-Jones.

many years later. It has never been my intention to 'copy' nature but to somehow capture and express, through the medium of porcelain, some of that initial wonder and pleasure experienced with eyes and fingers when the 'found object' is first encountered. When someone says 'it feels like a ... or if reminds me of...' as they turn the porcelain piece in their hands, then I know that part of my own delight has been communicated and shared. It does not matter too much whether we are reminded of the same things or not; the fact that these are echoes of the natural sources which inspired the piece is enough. There is then a kind of dialogue between the maker and those who encounter the work.

I find I am currently absorbed by what I think of as the legacies of life, objects and structures which remain and survive, sometimes obscured in life, but which are revealed by exposure to time and the elements. Skeletal remains become objects of aesthetic merit and delight when literally 'stripped to the bone'. Bird skulls are a particular

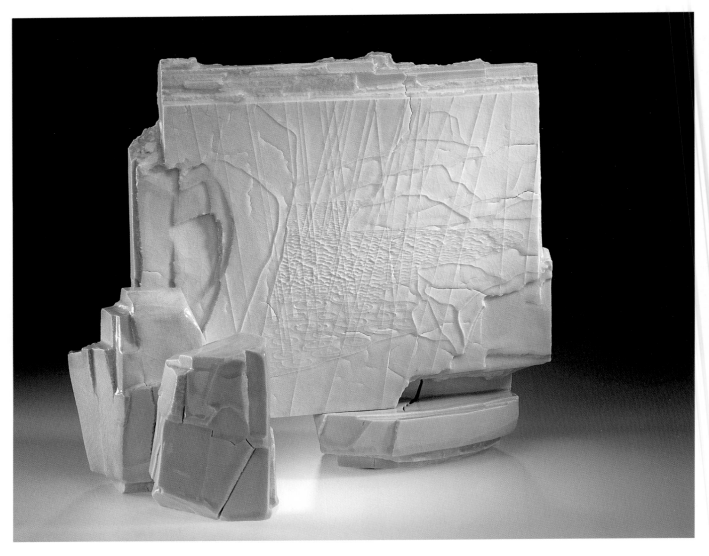

example of this — perfectly balanced sculptural objects — exposed by death and existing, altered, beyond it. Porcelain remains, for me, the ideal material through which to express these ideas.

A series, *Marine Forms,* developed as a result of Barnes' explorations and these were made with two thinly rolled slabs of porcelain which were allowed to stiffen slightly in a curved mould and then joined at the rim to create a slim, hollow form. When leatherhard, the rims are reshaped with a scalpel to define the form and these edges are pared away with a stainless steel blade to thin them further. The main body of the piece is then carved and pierced on one or both sides and the openings gently cleaned up and smoothed with a very fine, damp brush.

Sometimes the carving extends into and over the rims, altering the form and producing a less symmetrical shape. Pinching and/or paddling with a small wooden spoon helps to extend the narrow edge where the two rims meet before they are refined until they become wafer thin and translucent when fired. These pieces are textured by sponging and brushing thick slip onto selected areas, creating contrasting surfaces and adding tactile and visual interest. Following bisque firing, the pieces are polished with carborundum paper and the process repeated after the final firing. In these small sculptures that fit within the palm of one's hand, Barnes has managed to capture the *essence* of the found objects which inspired them.

Wayne Higby (USA) is a ceramic artist and

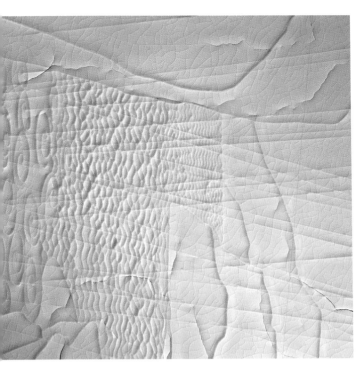

(Left) *Lake Powell Memory – Rain*, by Wayne Higby (USA), 1996. Porcelain sculpture fired in a reduction atmosphere to cone 11, h. 45 cm (17 ¾ in.), w. 48.5 cm (19 ½ in.), d. 30.5 cm (12 ¼ in.). (Collection of Barry & Irene Fisher). *Photograph by Brian Delesbee.*
(Above) *Lake Powell Memory – Rain* (detail).

teacher who is drawn to landscape for inspiration in his own work.

Earth and fire, light, time, space – my work is a meditation on the relationship between human mind and material existence. Clay and glaze offer a sensual means for entering the contemplative. Scaled to the body, the work presents contained space that opens to vast panorama. It offers an invitation to an out of body experience. It is not about landscape. As in traditional Chinese art, nature is a path to awareness and knowledge.

I make in order to find a zone of quiet coherence – a place full of silent, empty space where finite and infinite, intimate and immense intersect ... the material and immaterial oscillate giving birth to poetry.

My current efforts in porcelain are in response to travel and work in the People's Republic of China and to an ongoing commitment to keeping

the adventure in the studio alive. For many years, my central interests have not changed although the work has. Today, I'm thinking more about architecture, but essentially I am concerned with landscape imagery as a focal point of meditation. Space, both real and implied, is of utmost importance. I strive to establish a zone of quiet coherence – a place full of silent, empty space where finite and infinite, intimate and immense intersect ... the material and immaterial oscillate. In combination they become the alchemical philosopher's stone. Perhaps, psyche and matter are the same.

Jenny Beavan (UK) states that her objective through her ceramics is to portray aspects of the journey taken by 'healthy' water, making sure that every process seeks challenges and offers surprise at all stages.

Whilst thinking 'water' I attempt to understand its nature, and the cycle water takes to advantage both its own well-being, and ultimately our own health. Porcelain feels such an appropriate material to explore and express the life and cycle of 'healthy' water. It possesses the properties of densest stone, and yet has qualities of fragility, translucency and fluidity. It has a pure, fine and uncontaminated quality, whilst possessing a playful memory, seen through its natural movement and versatility. It also follows a journey of change by pure performance – it is always unpredictable and can resist, crack and slump quite naturally. There is such a powerful mix of inner strengths in this material.

In acceptance of the natural phenomena of the material, I seek to portray the versatility and power of both porcelain and water; they share the same 'free spirit', determining their own life force/equilibrium by defying unnatural pressures to be tamed. Decomposition and renewal are key elements to the evolution of this new work. Suggestive themes such as 'percolation', 'energy',

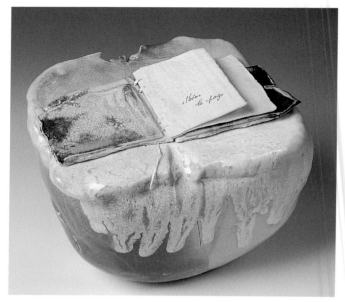

Bloc Note, by Agathe Larpent-Ruffe (France), 1996. Porcelain 'stone', 20 x 20 cm (8 x 8 in.), paper 'book' 10 x 12 cm (4 x 4 ¾ in.). *Photograph by Francois Xzavier Emery.*

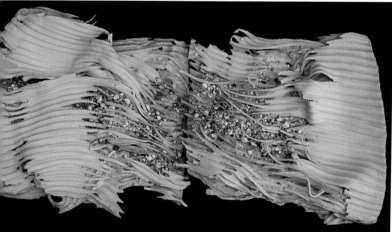

(Top) *Earth Vessel*, by Jenny Beavan (UK). Shigaraki clay, rice straw with river beach and volcanic sands, porcelain, glaze (dry), feldspar (dry) and glass, 47 x 34 cm (18 ½ x 13 ⅜ in.), firing: electric kiln 1280°C (2336°F). (Made in Japan, 1999). A solid lump of porcelain is wrapped around the Shigaraki clay mix. Using a cutting wire a section is removed from the mass to leave a 'u' shape, which overnight collapsed into the resulting shape. This was a direct consequence to the amount of water present. 'The Earth gave birth to biological life in the first place, but that biological life has helped in turn to sustain the geological life of the planet. We as human beings are capable of changing some of Earth's geological activities, – the flow of rivers, and erosion of land, – the workings of the atmosphere and oceans. This we can do safely only if we understand fully how Earth works, and learn to live in a sustainable way on the planet. If we treat water with reverence we will recognise that it has many powers – to inspire, to heal, to give life, and to take away life'. *Photograph by the artist.*
(Above) *Under-current*, by Jenny Beavan (UK), 2001. Porcelain, glaze in wet and powdered form, glass, beach sands, w. 55 cm (22 in.), d. 30 cm (11 ¾ in.), worked from a solid lump of porcelain. *Photograph by the artist.*

and 'flow' are aspects which involve my interest in geological formations, natural phenomena and connections made to all aspects of the natural world and its survival.

In all of my making processes, I aim to achieve a balance between freedom of expression and consideration of order. Involving, for instance, the building of a random form. This form then presents suggestions about its chaotic structure. Transformation by imposing action necessitates spontaneous decision-making, trust and willingness within a kind of relationship, in order to explore and create a new inner form, whilst retaining elements of a former existence.

At every stage there is a sense of mystery and every revelation has the potential to enlighten, giving opportunity to discover more about ourselves, and the world in which we live.

The porcelain sculptures by **Agathe Larpent-Ruffe** (France) evoke a variety of emotions. Some call to mind aspects of geology or landscape. She creates stone-like pieces that appear dense, solid, immobile objects over which enamel glazes seem to move and flow and, sometimes, other materials such as paper are incorporated

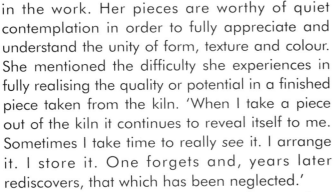

Porcelain sculpture, by Agathe Larpent-Ruffe,1995.
Dimensions: 30 x 25 cm (11 ¾ x 9 ¾ in.). *Photograph by Francois Xzavier Emery.*

Porcelain sculpture, by Sueharu Fukami (Japan), 2000.
Slip-cast under pressure, glazed, pale blue celadon glaze,
reduction fired in a liquid petroleum gas kiln, 132 x 27 cm
(52 x 10 ½ in.). *Photograph by Takashi Hatakeyama.*

in the work. Her pieces are worthy of quiet contemplation in order to fully appreciate and understand the unity of form, texture and colour. She mentioned the difficulty she experiences in fully realising the quality or potential in a finished piece taken from the kiln. 'When I take a piece out of the kiln it continues to reveal itself to me. Sometimes I take time to really see it. I arrange it. I store it. One forgets and, years later rediscovers, that which has been neglected.'

The vocabulary of visual art often involves organisation or adjustments in the relationship of opposites such as light to dark, rough to smooth, pattern to plain, colour to non-colour (i.e. to black, white or neutral tones), 'hot' to 'cold' colours, line to mass, positive to negative, open to closed, inner to outer, tall to short, wide to narrow, horizontal to vertical, etc. We are usually more aware of these elements of design when viewing sculpture or two-dimensional art because 'function', in the sense of domestic application, is no longer part of the equation. On that basis, any three-dimensional sculptural object in ceramic should be judged to stand or fall on its own criteria because the material used in its manufacture has no bearing on its acceptance or rejection. However, the position of ceramic sculpture in the world of 'fine' as opposed to 'decorative' art, irrespective of scale or method of manufacture, is subject to continuing debate.

It was at an exhibition of contemporary Japanese ceramics several years ago in the Victoria and Albert Museum, London, that I first saw examples of abstract porcelain sculpture by **Sueharu Fukami**. The technical and aesthetic perfection of his pieces is truly astonishing. It would be difficult to match the sheer beauty and refinement of these elegant, slip-cast works. Through the interplay of sculpted concave and convex surfaces with their sharp points and crisply defined edges, Fukami makes forms that each, delicately balanced on a tiny base, appears almost weightless as if about to swoop and soar effortlessly into space. A simple celadon glaze, reduction-fired by liquid propane gas, completes their immaculate finish. These pieces are among the most satisfying demonstrations of the potential that porcelain materials and techniques can offer in the creation of expressive sculptural forms.

Beate Kuhn (Germany) is well-known for her imaginative sculptural vessel and animal forms constructed from multiple wheel-thrown sections which are assembled and fired to 1340°–1360°C (2444°–2480°F) in a gas kiln. She displays a mastery of technique that few can rival. As many as 50 separate pieces may be used to build one of her amusing cats but, despite the complexity of their construction, the artist has managed to capture the 'essence' of the animal with a touch of humour. Even the smallest features such as the eyes, ears and paws are made on the wheel. Sympathetic observation has enabled her to translate her feelings for the animal and for her chosen medium in a way that pays tribute to both. Although they are instantly recognisable, these objects are in no sense realistic models of cats. Apart from the natural softening effect of the glaze, no attempt has been made to disguise the individual segments which make up the form. Porcelain contributes a sumptuous quality to these very personal expressions that cannot be equalled by other clays. Some recent porcelain work by Kuhn consists of multiple arrangements of individually thrown cylinders and shallow bowls cut open, altered, joined or reassembled and unified to assume a completely new identity. She uses these elements rather like a composer assembles together separate notes and arranges them to make music.

Continuous exploration and re-examination of a recurring theme, whether it be of a particular form, an aspect of design, or an abstract concept is a fruitful exercise for anyone who responds to the necessary discipline involved. Jeroen Bechtold (Holland) is fascinated by vestiges of history that stimulate creative thought. *The Reconstruction of the Holy Grail* is concerned with the remains of something that exists only in legend.

Slip-casting is the main technique used by

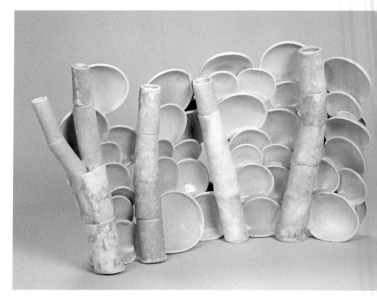

(Top) *Porcelain Cat*, by Beate Kuhn, 1993. Handbuilt from individually thrown segments and fired in a reducing atmosphere to 1360°C (2480°F). *Photograph by Bernd Göbbels.*

(Bottom) *New Music*, by Beate Kuhn (Germany), 2001. Porcelain wheel-thrown plates and cylinders joined together under multiple feldspathic glazes, reduction fired in a gas kiln to cone 6a, h. 30 cm (11 ¾ in.). *Photograph by Peter Schmidt.*

82nd Reconstruction of the Remains of the Holy Grail, by Jeroen Bechtold (Holland), 1992. Porcelain sculpture made from slipcast and press-moulded elements, with multiple glazes and firing under oxidising conditions. The interior of the form is covered with a 22 ct gold lustre, 48.5 x 48 cm (19 x 18 ¾ in.). *Photograph by Rene Gerritsen.*

one to become the main form that was cut and folded open. This action helped to determine the final appearance. Parts were cut away from other casts and joined onto the first to increase its size and visual impact. This freed him from the limitations of slip-casting. Some of the remaining sections of clay were used as temporary 'architectural' supports for the opened form. Similarly, further supports are required while in the kiln to prevent distortion. These must be made from the same material to equalise shrinkage. Smaller casts were made of figures and decorative items that were sprigged on to the main form as the work proceeded.

Final adjustments were carried out when the piece was leatherhard and able to stand without physical support. Then the inside was sanded until perfectly smooth. The piece was fired four or more times with successive layers of glaze ('I use glaze purely as a medium to apply pigments and stains') and the interior coated with a clear glaze. Finally, a further firing with gold, platinum or mother of pearl lustres enriched the inner surfaces. Rather like a seashell whose rough exterior contrasts with its smooth inner face, these pieces evoke a feeling of preciousness, but with an added sense of mystery.

The horrific attacks on the twin towers of the World Trade Center in New York made an indelible impression on millions of people worldwide. Bechtold, also, was deeply moved to respond through the production of a series of translucent, slip-cast tower forms. This time, however, little glaze was used. Instead, the colour is derived from the porcelain itself, from the differences in thickness and, where obvious colour is used, it develops from ceramic stains mixed with the clay.

Bechtold because it allows him to easily control the wall thickness. He finds that casting is also best for the cut and assemble method he uses because the clay particles are not forced into alignment as they are when throwing and this reduces the risk of cracking. Originally, he graduated from art school intending to work as an industrial designer and was thus drawn to the casting process. He believes that 'it is better to be master of only one technique than to be average in many'.

Bechtold filled several moulds with porcelain slip which were left to stand for half an hour or more, depending on the humidity in his studio. After draining the moulds, the pots were left to dry naturally for a few hours. When he removed them from the moulds he selected

If smoothness is required, I polish the surface. If glaze is required, I use a simple, clear porcelain glaze, but extremely thinly.

Translucency of the works is important and

Row in Blue-White, by Jeroen Bechtold (Holland), 2001. Blue porcelain, inlay in slip-cast, white porcelain, 7.5 x 7.5 x 47 cm (3 x 3 x 18 ½ in.). *Photograph by the artist.*

for that I use multiple layers of porcelain in different ways. Multiple casting techniques make it possible for me to achieve differences in thickness of the wall. I use the time between casting of the layers as a means of expression. Experience tells me when to apply a new layer on top of the previous one, thus allowing fresh patterns to appear. The time between layers depends on the humidity conditions in my studio. Another

technique is an extremely simple one in which I cast one layer and cut diamonds and squares into it to take out every other one before casting again. This produces different levels of translucency and some results of the exercise can be seen in the rows of towers.

The emotional response to natural phenomena or to aspects of the human condition has been

well-documented in my previous books. It will remain a constant source of inspiration for countless generations of potters but there are many others whose approach is more of an intellectual exercise which results in an abstract arrangement of shapes possessing no obvious points of reference. The Dutch potter, **Wil Broekema** (Holland), for example, works almost exclusively with precise geometric shapes made from thin, perfectly finished sheets of porcelain. A recurring theme is concerned with the subject of 'balance', physical, visual and aesthetic. Porcelain is the ideal material for her to use because, she says, it has a dense grain structure that allows her to make ultra thin sheets that are relatively strong and which become translucent when backlit. Linear elements, incised or in relief are drawn on the clay to complement the formal composition. The addition of wires and glass beads in some of Broekema's sculptures increases the impression

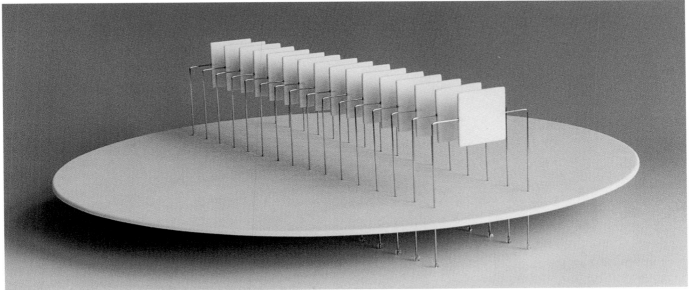

(Top) *Three Towers*, by Elisabeth Schaffer (Germany), 1999. Inlaid porcelain columns, slab-built and mounted on iron bases. Originally called 'Manhattan' but altered following the attack on The World Trade Center in New York on 11th September 2001. *Photograph by Antje Anders.*

(Above) *Untitled*, by Wil Broekema (Holland), 1999. Limoges porcelain with steel wire, 30 cm (11 ¾ in.), fired to 1240°C (2264°F) in an electric kiln. *Photograph by the artist.*

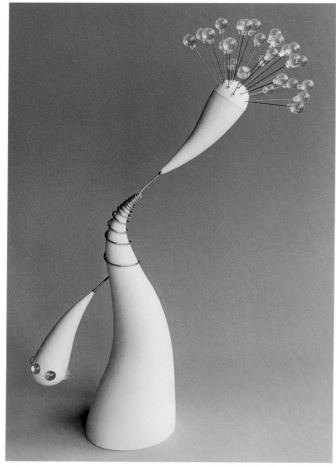

Untitled, by Wil Broekema (Holland), 2000. Limoges porcelain with brass wire and glass marbles, h. 25 cm (9 ⅞ in.), fired to 1240°C (2264°F) in an electric kiln.
Photograph by the artist.

is first fired to 960°C (1760°F) and then thoroughly sanded smooth before refiring up to 1240°C (2264°F) in an electric kiln with an oxidising atmosphere. After the firing the individual elements separately, they are assembled and joined together with adhesives. Coloured lines and other selected areas are glazed with a mixture of frit and body stains. Her finished pieces have an air of cool, reserved, understated elegance about them.

> These sheets are like little landscapes in which everything can happen. With little moulded forms, steel or brass wire and glass marbles I create my own little universe. I try to obtain a visual balance in my objects. In the recent sculptures I try to express movement ('movement turned to stone'). And terms like 'growth' and 'wind' come to mind. Another fascination is in creating volumes with repetitive elements on one line. With many little porcelain sheets in a row you can create a volume like a cloud, tree or another geometric volume.

Some ceramic artists are using other materials such as clear plastic rods and boards, steel or brass wire, nylon threads, glass beads, metal objects and even feathers to complete a sculptural image. **Jo-Anne Caron** (Belgium) often adds feathers to a series of pyramid forms that have interested her for several years. These objects are slip-cast in moulds taken from paper models because she requires sharp, well-defined edges. The upper part of the pyramid is added to a base later with hole pierced through it when leatherhard to release air. The work is fired extremely slowly over two days and she allows a further three days to cool down completely.

Ceramics is a wonderfully versatile medium but the nature of clay is such that the size of any form made and fired in one piece has to be quite small when compared to objects fashioned from wood or metal. Greater scale can only be achieved by making and assembling a number

of three-dimensional drawings in space. Feeling that some of her pieces seemed too severe she decided to introduce limited colour in an attempt to 'make them more dynamic' and light-hearted. Her paramount concern is to achieve 'harmony in form, composition and colour'.

Broekema rolls her slabs of porcelain by hand and cuts them into various geometric shapes. Her sculptures are always untitled, she explained, so that the spectator can use their own imagination to interpret them however they wish. All her objects are made from Limoges porcelain. The slabs are hand-rolled with moulds used for casting the cone and ball forms.

Surface reliefs are made by pressing cardboard 'stamps' into the thin sheets. The work

Flying Pyramid, handbuilt porcelain fired to 1230°C (2246°F), with added feathers, w. 26 cm (10 ¼ in.), h. 30 cm (11 ¾ in.), by Jo-Anne Caron (Belgium), 2002. *Photograph by the artist.*

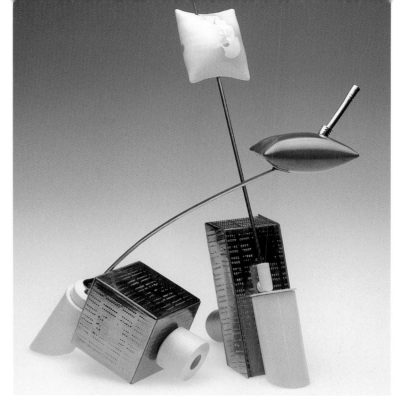

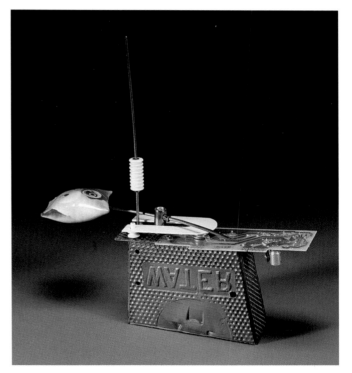

(Top) *Two Flying Ts*, by Margaret Realica (USA), 1999. Porcelain, thrown and altered, including boxes impressed on computer boards, bronze rod, steel rod, Hanovia lustres airbrushed, 30.5 x 7.5 x 8.3 cm (12 x 19 x 3 ¼ in.). (Bottom) *Computerized T*, by Margaret Realica (USA), 1999. Porcelain, thrown, impressed on water drain, computer board, steel rod, 31.5 x 34 x 18 cm (12 ½ x 13 ½ x 7 in.). *Photographs by Ira Schrank.*

of separate components. The possibilities then become infinite. The process of making and handling, the need to ensure the clay is completely dry before firing and, finally, the capacity of the kiln all impose restrictions on scale. Therefore, the impact of much sculptural work in ceramics is diminished due to its small size. If we do not know the true scale of some of the porcelain assemblages by **Margaret Realica** (USA) and illustrated in this book, for example, we can imagine them to be several metres high. We are aided in this respect by seeing them as photographs rather than the objects themselves. They could, indeed, serve as maquettes for more substantial constructions. Realica was born in England but now lives and works in California. 'Deconstruction and reconstruction' is a recurring theme in much of her work. She has drawn on personal experiences in making some of her composite sculptures including images of bombed out buildings explored as a child. Giving an explanatory title to such works may help one to understand something of their origin and of the artist's intent. However, the objects are powerful enough to stand and be judged in their own right despite their small scale. She says that 'a piece of art should be able to stand alone, stripped of any verbal intervention. It should appeal to the eye, mind and spirit. Words should not be necessary.'

> My thinking and vision revolve around nature, the machine, the environment, human conditions, and experiences past and present. I work with the broken and the whole of these, the conflicts and incongruities, a world where the differences between the organic and the mechanical have broken down. The challenge is still within the theme of opposites like past and present, but working towards a harmony of the two and reaching for the unexpected.

The work is of porcelain, thrown on the wheel and altered. The slabs used for the boxes are deconstructed from thrown cylinder forms and can be with or without impressed images. Two high-fire glazes, an opaque and a gloss, are sprayed on and fired to cone 7. Finished pieces are airbrushed with multiple layers of metallic lustres fired to varying degrees depending on the colour and effect desired. Work is assembled and cemented with rods, plexiglass and electrical parts.

In Realica's current *Tea Pot* series, she uses porcelain together with these other materials to compose compelling images in three-dimensions. Unlike her earlier sculptures that were pictured in the first edition of *Contemporary Porcelain*, Realica has become more concerned with reconstruction. The teapot, which was the stimulus, has now completely transcended its original form. Now, she is thinking more conceptually and simplifying the pieces. Realica explained that the pillow-like form of thrown porcelain that appears in her sculptures was derived originally from a dream about tea, hence the association with a pillow

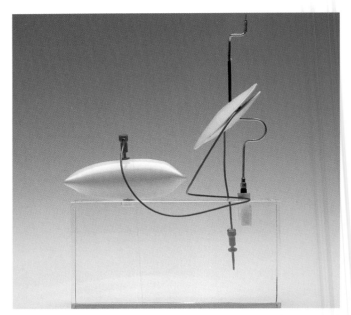

Unplugged, by Margaret Realica (USA), 2001. Thrown and altered porcelain, plexiglass, wire, 19 x 26.5 cm (7 ½ x 10 ½ in.). *Photograph by Ira Schrank.*

and obvious reference to a tea bag.

These unique objects, with their machine-like appearance, are somewhat disconcerting in that they seem to suggest some kind of mechanical function totally unconnected with clay. They should, of course, be viewed purely as individual compositions existing in their own right, where the elements of mass, volume, space, texture and line all contribute to the whole. She explains how this work evolved from the concept of 'teapot', a familiar domestic vessel constructed from a number of identifiable elements.

> The roots are of the teapot. The concepts are of energy, light, and water. It is a collection of images and thoughts. I play with opposites, deconstructing and reconstructing components of the mechanical and the organic. My aim is to have a coexistence of the two represented in one integrated form. Mixed media has been introduced in the recent pieces, and I am working for a balance between porcelain and today's mechanisation.

Incredibly, every single piece of Realica's work in porcelain is, initially, thrown on the wheel.

Group of porcelain sculptures by Ruth Duckworth (USA), 2000. *Photograph by James Prinz.*

Even the slabs are made from thrown cylinders. These are allowed to set slightly and the walls are further compressed with a rubber kidney tool while the wheel rotates. When the cylinders have stiffened to the point where they are no longer sticky to touch but still fairly soft they are removed from the wheel, cut open with a surgical knife and rolled out flat. 'Rolling out thrown pieces produces finer slabs that warp much less and can hold their shape.' She finds that fewer stress cracks occur in slabs made this way and then combined with other thrown pieces. 'The procedure may seem a little lengthy but I find it actually saves time and it gives me a more polished, machined-like finish.' She feels that the action of pulling up the clay when throwing is more suited to the way she works rather than the heavier compression obtained by normal slab rolling.

In some of her porcelain sculptures, especially those based on the notional idea of teapots, Realica demonstrates the range of her technical skill by introducing convincing reproductions of machined metal objects like screws, threaded tubes and nut and bolts. The illusion is strengthened further by airbrushed metallic lustres. Her pieces are burnished with rubber when leatherhard and with a stone when dry. Bisqued to 1060°C (1940°F). Some parts are then glazed with either an opaque matt white or a bright white, lithium glaze and fired in an electric kiln to between 1260°C (2300°F) and 1300°C (2372°F). Finished pieces are airbrushed with multiple layers of metallic lustres fired to varying temperatures, according to the colour and effect required, and then assembled and cemented with rods, plexiglass, and electrical parts.

The unusual porcelain sculptures by **Ruth Duckworth** (USA) cannot be easily classified. They grow out of a rich ceramic tradition but

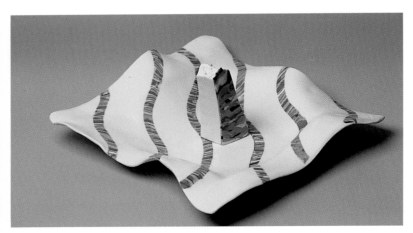

Kaleidoscope I, by Annika Teder (Estonia), 1998. Hand-built porcelain slab with coloured porcelain inlay and a solid porcelain object with coloured inlay in the middle, h. 10 cm (4 in.), w. 27 cm (10 ½ in.), fired to 1380°C (2516°F). 'When I look through a kaleidoscope I see there constantly changing colours and ornaments. This process is like an everlasting dialogue between clay and me. I try to find balance between casualty and order, when I put together the structure of a form with the coloured pattern. My work has been changeable like the sea — from wavy porcelain slabs to groggy sculpture forms. Each time I work with coloured porcelain layers and mix them, something new will appear, never the same pictures like in the kaleidoscope'. *Photograph by Ylo Josing.*

they stand alone being unlike other ceramic expressions from either the past or the present. Their subtlety and coolness owes something, perhaps, to her European background. Having fled Nazi Germany in 1936, she first studied sculpture, working mainly in wood and stone, in London. That previous experience as a sculptor was to stand her in good stead when she later made the transition into working with clay. In 1964 she moved to America to take up a teaching post at the University of Chicago and she has lived and worked in that city ever since. She managed to purchase an old factory building in 1982 and this was converted into a home with plenty of space for a large studio. This allowed her to work on a much larger scale. Several important architectural commissions soon followed and some of these have

been illustrated in my previous books. However, it is her smaller pieces in unglazed white or black porcelain which, for the purposes of my current research, are worthy of particular attention. Some pieces suggest plant growth or bones (especially vertebrae or ball and socket joints) and they would succeed equally if executed in bronze or polished brass. However, the smooth white surface of porcelain responds particularly well to the soft modelling action of light falling across it. Duckworth manages to distil the very essence of morphological experience and sensation into these undemonstrative abstract sculptures.

Altering the physical properties of porcelain by mixing it with other materials has often provided a rich source of inspiration in itself.

Order and unpredictability come together in some of **Mary White's** sculptural work. In the early 1980s, she began to make organic forms in porcelain using the material rather like torn paper to be assembled in layers. Her ideas come from 'layers of rock on the seashore, shells, waves

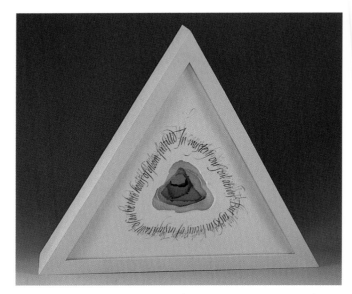

Porcelain sculpture by Mary White (Germany). Layered design with calligraphy surrounding a mirror in the centre, wooden frame, 35 x 35 x 35 cm (13 ¾ x 13 ¾ x 13 ¾ in.), fired to 1250°C (2282°F) in an electric kiln. *Photograph by the artist.*

rippling over sand, and colours in the sea and sky. I like geometric forms which need skill in making and also freer organic forms which require imagination and even accident for their freshness. Sometimes, I can manage to combine these in one piece.' She returns again and again to the concept of 'craters'. She began making flanged bowls with cratered centres. These were followed by globe forms set into open-sided pyramids revealing craters which had coloured glass or mirrors at the bottom. 'Mystery fascinates me. I like to give people surprises. They see a simple shape, hold it in their hands and find something that involves them, perhaps a mirror that reflects their eye, or remove a lid from a box to find something unexpected inside.' The formality of a square or triangular frame draws attention to the irregular, cratered centre. We are invited to look into and past several separate, thin layers leading to the colour and reflections deep inside. A beautifully lettered inscription encircles the crater. All her work is made from the well-known David Leach Porcelain Body (which she colours with body stains to provide herself with a palette of almost 30 different shades) and fired to 1250°C (2282°F) in a small electric kiln.

Porcelain is an important constituent of the special body mixtures prepared by a number of ceramic sculptors who, rather than use porcelain alone, choose to combine it with white or stained stonewares for one reason or another. Although this practice loses certain of those qualities we might reasonably expect to find in pure porcelain, its addition to other bodies can make a significant contribution to the character and appearance of a piece. Similarly, porcelain elements are often used to contrast with or be supported by larger sections made from a coarse or grogged stoneware clay.

Peter Beard (UK) is another abstract artist whose white bone china sculptures are mounted upon a base or plinth constructed from stoneware clay. He explained how he manipulates wet bone

Feather form, by Peter Beard (UK). Bone china, sandblasted, stoneware base, h. 30 cm (11 ¾ in.). *Photograph by the artist.*

china into rough shapes, then shaves and scrapes them into basic forms when leatherhard. They are allowed to dry before carefully sanding to refine the final shape. A small hole is drilled in the bottom of each piece to allow mounting on to a supporting base after firing. A damp sponge is used to remove sanding marks when the piece has completely dried and then it is low bisque

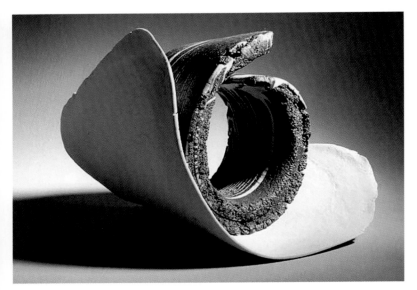

Untitled porcelain sculpture, by Aline Favre (France), 2001. Dimensions: 35 x 30 cm (13 ¾ x 11 ¾ in.).

Photograph by Jean-François Claustre.

Glas Maol: Cloud Pillar, by Tony Franks (UK), 2001. Bone china, 58 x 45 cm (22 ¾ x 17 ¾ in.), fired twice to 1200°C (2192°F), then 1220°–1230°C (2228°–2246°F). Sandblasted, polished and coloured after bisque firing.

Photograph by Shannon Tofts.

fired to 600°C (1112°F) in an electric kiln. A design is drawn in pencil and masked with latex at this stage. The object is sandblasted when the latex has dried removing the unprotected surface to the desired depth. Latex masking is removed and the piece is bisque fired again to 1000°C (1832°F), and then sanded with Wet 'n Dry silicon carbide paper and/or flexible diamond abrasive paper to make a super smooth surface. The bone china form is placed in a clay box (saggar) half-filled with very clean alumina hydrate before adding more of this material, well-packed, and a weighted lid positioned so the contents are kept in place. The alumina hydrate allows the piece to shrink but keeps it from warping (a serious problem with bone china used in this way). After firing, the alumina is brushed off and a final rub down with diamond paper gives a soft sheen. A stainless steel rod is glued into the hole in the base and then fixed in the stoneware plinth, which has a dark glaze and has also been fired to 1280°C (2336°F) in the electric kiln.

Aline Favre (Switzerland) also combines porcelain with stoneware elements in her sculptural expressions, so that the two clays are either in harmony or in opposition to each other. She explains how she tries to set up a 'dialogue'

between them in which the white, pure and delicate porcelain is confronted by other coarser heavily textured materials like raw or black stonewares. 'Their specific languages allow me to play with and to fit them together into space. Oppositions are made of light and heavy, delicate and raw, white and black. Fire reveals their particularities mixing tightness, collapse, tearing.'

Tony Franks (UK) makes quite large sculptural pieces from bone china that defy tradition. Every piece is bone china, fired twice to 1200°C (2192°F), then 1220°–1230°C (2228°–2246°F). After bisque, they are sandblasted, polished and coloured. Sometimes they undergo a third firing to 1220°–1230°C (2228°–2246°F) in order to develop the colours he requires. He explained that his current work records a dialogue with landscape, particularly the Scottish Highlands and Islands.

The nakedness of this land has something bold, stern and solitary about it; sparse, melancholy and lonely, but not despairing. Physical links between the reality and the image are established by mixing with the bone china and basalt clays organic matter from

(Top) *Architecture* series, by Maria Bofill (Spain), 2002. Porcelain with Molochite, handbuilt with slabs and coils, bisqued at 980°C (1796°F) in an electric kiln, brushed transparent glaze (1280°C/2336°F) fired in gas kiln in reduction, 13 x 26 cm (5 x 10 ¼ in.). *Photograph by the artist.*
(Bottom) *Architecture* series, by Maria Bofill (Spain), 2002. Porcelain, paper porcelain, handbuilt with slabs, bisqued at 980°C (1796°F) in an electric kiln, brushed transparent glaze, (1280°C/2336°F), fired in gas kiln in reduction, 5.5 x 23 cm (2 ⅛ x 9 in.). *Photograph by the artist.*

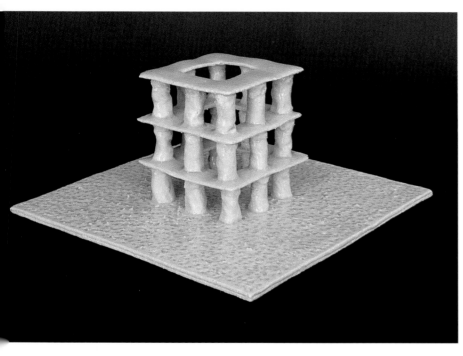

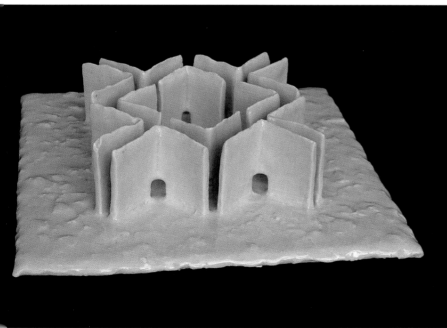

specific sites, leaves and moss, heather, grass and ferns. On firing, fossil memories of these materials remain, sometimes being exposed through sandblasting, cutting and grinding. The way the work is made reflects in accelerated fashion the way the land is made; the processes of pressure and time, heat and frost, accumulation and degradation; texture exposing by erosion fossilised memories of a moment; but above all an awareness of the geological concerns of deep time, slow shift, constant renewal, and the fundamental relationship between structure and surface, geology and landscape, climate and energy. The familiarity and continual wonder of these special places trapped between earth and sky.

Maria Bofill (Spain) creates objects 'without function; it is a search fluctuating between the classical and the contemporary. She is particularly interested in goblets, columns and capitals and often starts work with a clear idea of the form in mind but this may undergo modification during the creative process. She is always working on several pieces at the same time. She describes the making process:

It is similar to the creation of an architectural structure: placing and removing the parts, examining and combining the different elements until a satisfactory shape is achieved. This may be the original idea or not. Problems arising during the work with porcelain often give me new ideas for further pieces. Porcelain is a material which makes me feel at ease when working. It allows me to obtain results that are perfect for my objectives but I also appreciate any small deformations that may appear during the firing.

Bofill continues to explore her series of 'architecture' or 'labyrinths' sculptures, because it allows her to challenge perspective and suggest 'a dialogue between the world outside and the emptiness within'. The labyrinths represent a reflection on the passage of time, and pictures of urban or imaginary landscapes realised as small-scale Mediterranean settings. They can be seen as pure fantasy or as actual projects taken from her 'richly personal world'. Glazed work is fired in a gas kiln with a reducing atmosphere to 1280°C (2336°F), while those pieces which are decorated with engobes are fired in an electric kiln in oxidation to 1240°C (2264°F).

Porcelain is being increasingly used to make panels and wall sculptures some of which are quite substantial. Often, they are made up of a number of smaller elements for ease of handling and to avoid problems in drying and firing which can result in cracks appearing, but large panels can be made in one piece when

Box of Photographs, by Sylvia Hyman (USA), 2001. Transfer-printed porcelain in a stoneware box, 23 x 18.5 x 11.5 cm (9 x 7 ¼ x 4 ½ in.). *Photograph by John Cummins.*

the body recipe includes a proportion of bisqued porcelain ground into small particles as a grog to open up and to give support to the plastic material while working. Shrinkage and drying difficulties are thereby reduced.

Sculptural pieces by **Sylvia Hyman** (USA) are handbuilt from slabs of porcelain, bisque fired to cone 06 (approx. 1000°C/1832°F) and sanded until absolutely smooth. They are mostly left unglazed with only small areas of glaze for accents and fired again to cones 5–6 (approx. 1190°–1215°C/2174–2219°F) before spraying onglaze enamels directly on to unglazed areas (with some parts masked to remain white) and refiring, finally, at low temperature. New developments in Hyman's work include printed surfaces on some of the scrolls and surface hitherto left plain. These are described in more detail in Chapter Four.

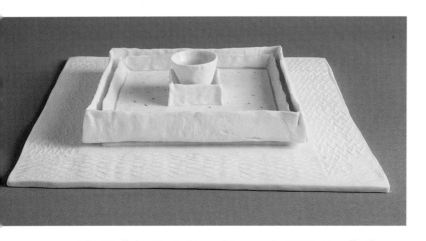

The Well, by Marta Nagy (Hungary), 2000. Handbuilt porcelain sculpture with glaze and lustre, 4 x 34 x 34 cm (1 ½ x 13 ½ x 13 ½ in.), fired to 1380°C (2516°F). *Photograph by István Füzi.*

Three Coloured Spheres, by Malgorzata Dyrda-Kujawska (Poland), 1992. Unglazed porcelain, plus glazed, coloured cones of porcelain, h. 48 cm (19 in.), fired in a factory kiln on a quartz sand pillow, 1380°C (2516°F). *Photograph by Czeslaw Chwiszczuk.*

Unusual and exciting porcelain sculptural pieces, possessing elements with the kind of rhythmic geometry often found in natural forms, have been developed by **Peter Masters** (Australia). These pieces, which have no other function but to occupy space while delighting the eye, are executed with a high degree of mathematical precision that gives them a strong, tactile appeal. Despite the strict organisation necessary to achieve the precise placement of the individually applied clay balls or spikes, Masters works intuitively, relying solely upon the accuracy of his eye to judge the exact relationship of each to the others within the overall pattern. The spiral movements created with these additions energise the forms and call to mind similar in nature such as cacti and sunflower seedheads without being in any sense imitative. He explained his concept of these forms as having a basic volume resembling, perhaps, a turnip or a bean, but he

'attempted to transcend any association with recognisable species. Thus the environments in which these forms might exist may be earthly, but certainly not domesticated. However, a viewer may still feel that these forms are not of this world, and this is perfectly acceptable, because their origins could indeed be cosmic.'

The basic spheres and ovoids are either wheel-thrown (for pieces smaller than 50 cm /19 ¾ in. in diameter) or coiled, to produce a domed 'onion' shape with thick walls that are turned when leatherhard and refined to fit the precise curvature required for each piece. The spikes are made separately by rolling between forefinger and thumb, grading their sizes and spacing according to where they are to be arranged on the main form, becoming smaller and more tightly packed towards the top and bottom. The repetition of so many small units produces an appearance of considerable complexity.

Masters created many 'growth' forms incorporating patterned surfaces which evolved intuitively. He has always been fascinated by the sea and sea life and by growth patterns in nature, and he is 'awed by gigantic vegetables like marrows and squash'. He describes the forms he makes as:

consisting of a spherical shell with a relatively short, tapered extension referred to as the 'ovoid' (resembling perhaps the subterranean part of a turnip) and a singular projection, either extending into free space or rejoining the ovoid. Having only two contact points with the supporting surface, they are very dynamic, primary forms with visual rotational instability. They vary in size from about 20–60 cm (8–24 in.) in diameter. The ovoids have a high relief surface pattern of balls or spikes. Thus, there is a very active secondary movement. With some patterns, incorporating holes or additional inserts in the balls or spikes, a tertiary movement takes place. The forms are high-fired and sodium vapour glazed giving them very luminous, and contrasting, matt surfaces with brightness or colour. The main hues are yellows, greens, blues, browns and pinks on a white porcelain ground.

Recently, Masters has experimented with more open forms and using coloured glass sheet slumped over the opening. This is intended to be part of the piece and required exhaustive tests with different annealing or cooling programmes to make the combination succeed.

Marc Leuthold (USA) described how, for 15 years he has created fluted wheels, discs, and conical forms. In these forms, carved radii emanating from a focal point are the basis for a multi-referential abstract language.

Spherical models of the universe have influenced these circular forms. The 18th-century German philosopher Jakob Bohme created geometric

(Top) *Sphere Protrusion*, by Peter Masters, 2001. Porcelain sculpture, d. 32 cm (12 ½ in.). The strong, rhythmic raised pattern is built up from individually applied elements. (Bottom) Bowl form with slumped red glass, by Peter Masters (Australia), 2002. D. 38 cm (15 in.). *Photographs by the artist.*

circular diagrams to communicate ideas about the cosmos. Similarly my sculpture seeks to express the macrocosm through the microcosm.

The circular format is dense with symbolic meaning in every culture. Pi discs, smooth circular forms with a circular void in the center, were

Turkish Yellow Wheel, by Marc Leuthold (USA), 2002. Unglazed, coloured and carved porcelain, h. 15 cm (6 in.).
Photograph by Eva Heyd.

placed on bodies at burials in Neolithic China. The Pi discs were believed to provide access to eternal life. The Gothic Rose window served a related function in Medieval Europe. Abstract expressionist painter, Jay DeFeo created her masterwork, *The Rose*, from 1958–66. *The Rose* is essentially a high relief painting made of heavy paint and other materials with 3-D linear elements emanating from a central focal point. Similarly, I suspect I am drawn to the unity, power, and purity of circular radiating forms. Viewers may recognize classic forms – the solar disc, the mechanical cog, or radiating forms in nature, waves of wind and water; however, in the circular forms that I create, I strive for an abstraction that cannot be easily explained and that produces a restless oscillation of associations.

Some of the most recent sculptures are a

departure from the circular forms. They are smooth, biomorphic forms. These 'receptors' are reminiscent of ears and other sensory organs. Occasionally placed alongside the wheels to form 'dyads,' they invite the viewer to question their apparent magnetism.

Leuthold also pays tribute to family influences on his work. His parents, having studied weaving and design in Zurich under the tutelage of Johannes Itten, left Europe after the Second World War to start a new life in the USA. Leuthold has used the repeated movement of a carving knife to create reticulated sculptural objects. Since 1993, he has experimented with installations because he wanted to incorporate issues and other interests more overtly within the context of the work.

Rhythmic or repeated components added to or subtracted from particular forms can produce spectacular visual results. **Barbara Chrząszcz** (Poland), for example, has created a large sculptural object through the repetition and multiplication of handmade elements projecting outwards from a tall stoneware cylinder mounted on a rotating metal stand. She likes to work in porcelain because it allows her the opportunity to exploit its delicacy and pure whiteness in minimalist expression. 'The whole work has a rotary movement resembling Buddhist prayer books whose every turn brings about a prayer, a wish or a simple thought.'

The multiplication of units of similar shape but varying in size contribute to the imaginative porcelain sculptural objects by **Lara Scobie** (UK). Her forms are intricately constructed by building up complex layers of thinly rolled clay. Small strips are torn from thin sheets of porcelain and then pressed into an Indian printing block, of which she has a small collection, so that the resulting textured piece was incorporated into the design. Ropes and scrolls of clay are added to the assemblage, each unit helping to create a three-dimensional composition rich in texture, pattern and visual interest. These wonderfully evocative sculptures are bisque fired to 1000°C (1832°F) before oxides and underglaze stains are applied in broad washes of colour with a large brush. Sponging some of the colour away subsequently left deposits to pick out and give emphasis to the

Infinity, by Barbara Chrząszcz (Poland). Unglazed, handmade porcelain elements inserted into cylinder of grogged clay covered with a cobalt/iron/manganese slip, h. 180 cm (71 in.), fired to 1380°C (2516°F) in a tunnel gas kiln. *Photograph by Czeslaw Chwiszczuk.*

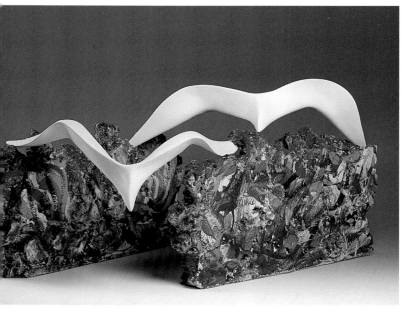

impressed textures. Several layers of colour were built up in this process. Finally, a large brush dipped into a transparent glaze is swept over the form and fired to 1300°C (2372°F).

The suppleness and plasticity allows me to stretch and bend each tiny element, and to build up many layers of delicately patterned clay. The works are my interpretations of various objects both real and imaginary while incorporating relative symbols into the design to give the piece a unique identity and a true sense of worth and meaning.

(Above Left) *Fly* by Annika Teder (Estonia), 1999. Each bird is modelled from one porcelain slab and polished, fired at 1380°C (2516°F), the waves – handbuilt solid grog painted with coloured porcelain, fired at 1260°C (2300°F), 30 x 60 cm (11 ¾ x 23 ½ in.). 'My work has been changeable like the sea. I've been working with very different clays. Each time the clay I start working with is a challenge for me. It's a dialogue between clay and me. Each clay has its character and I need to find my way to approach it. My forms are created out of a relationship between the contrast of stability and instability and their intense balance. I set the structure of grog against the white pure surface of porcelain. The image of sea, waves – causality against order – the birds.' *Photograph by Ylo Josing.*

(Left) *Basket,* by Lara Scobie, 1993. Constructed by building up layers of thinly rolled porcelain. Texture is produced by pressing the clay into old Indian printing blocks. Colour is inlaid into the textures by brushing oxides and underglaze stains into it and then sponging away to leave a residue in the depressions.

(Above) *Cluster,* by Andrea Hylands (Australia), 1999. Bone china, soft slab construction, slip-cast spheres individually pierced, and assembled after firing, h. 35 cm (13 ¾ in.). (Private collection, Amsterdam). *Photograph by Andrew Barchem.*

In the most recent work by **Andrea Hylands** (Australia) she uses a range of media that often combines ceramic work with painting and 'transformational media'. She no longer uses colour as a form of expression but relies on the whiteness of the material to define a sculptural form.

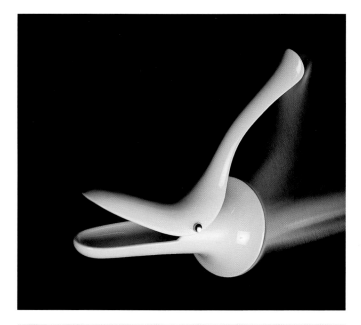

The work is related to the physical environment and the relationship between people and nature, investigating the landscape's fragility and concern for the living world. The egg, as a symbol, has been important in my work. Bone china is the whitest of ceramic materials and is therefore compatible with the way I work. I use combinations of slip-casting, press-moulding, soft slabs and handbuilding techniques. The slip I use for casting is prepared from the plastic bone china body to which I mix quantities of water and Dispex only.

I have made numerous large plaster batts applied with an assortment of textures that I am able to transfer onto the plastic porcelain and use in various ways. This process is either by manipulating the soft clay slab by pressing, or by pouring slip onto a plaster batt. These textures enable me to provide information and expression about the physical aspects of the landscape.

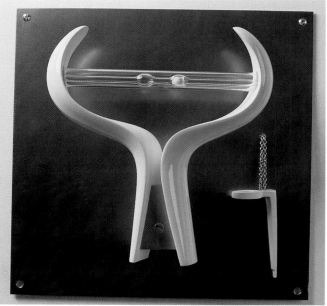

(Top) *Speculum*, by Gunhild Vatn (Norway), 1999. Slip-cast porcelain (from the installation *Still Life*), 18 x 15 cm (7 x 6 in.), fired to 1230°C (2246°F).
(Bottom) *Keys*, by Gunhild Vatn (Norway), 2001. Porcelain, glass, brass, steel, 30 x 30 cm (11 ¾ x 11 ¾ in.). Slip-cast in plaster-moulds, fired at 1140°C (2084°F).
Photograph by Steinar Myhre.

Hylands fires her pieces in an electric kiln to around 1250°C (2282°F) and, at the end of the firing cycle, the kiln is soaked for about 30 minutes. Glaze is rarely used but she polishes the bone china or porcelain with fine Wet 'n Dry sandpaper after the final firing.

Gunhild Vatn (Norway) makes precisely articulated porcelain forms that have no need of colour. She says that beauty and the grotesque exist together in her works. Some of her forms are based on medical and gynaecological tools, and instruments for female circumcision. She feels that the gruesome activities signified by such tools is in stark contrast to the fragility and beauty of their porcelain equivalents. Her sculptural objects range from copies or imitations of instruments to pure abstractions, in unusual transformations. Visual associations have an impact on the total experience of the works, and these reflect a deeper artistic idea with the aim of provoking a confrontation with pain that is legitimised by culture. Through her work, she tries to stimulate and disturb the viewers' thoughts and feelings. By cultivating a technically perfect industrial style of expression, she is able to contrast this with aspects of human vulnerability so that form and material are balanced between disgust and fascination.

Vatn explains that the use of materials and their contextual setting are essential to the story told by her objects. Porcelain, for example, is prized as an aesthetic and exclusive substance. It is also a strong and hygienic material with the necessary properties for bathroom and sanitary applications.

Our associations with the material accentuate something close and intimate within the sensual expression of form that I seek. In combination with other materials such as velvet or stainless steel, I wish to combine a clinical element while alluding to something ritualistic.

My interest focuses on the individual's interaction with culture, religion and rites. My intention is to bewilder and play on ambiguity with the objects that are both aesthetic and urgently uncomfortable. *Cutting the Rose*, from 1997, was a key element in my artistic development. Its theme is female circumcision. By creating the instruments for such surgery, in clinical porcelain, I aim to solicit reflection and trigger physical sensations. My intention is to arouse empathy in the viewer creating identification with the pain itself. The work touches on a number of themes, including women's liberation, cultural imperialism and religious conflicts. This can be interpreted as a commentary on how, with a degree of arrogance and aloofness, we respond to other people's suffering without really understanding their pain. This is a theme that emerged in Norway in the past few years after reports that female circumcision is still practised in certain Muslim circles. These themes have also been pivotal in my later work.

Vatn has based some of her work on the *speculum*, a gynaecological instrument, in a sculptural expression.

Its apparent function provides numerous associations. Meaning and symbolic value can be diversely interpreted, creating an ambiguity, but visually it arouses sensations because such instruments are made for body contact. Among such feelings are vulnerability, pain and humiliation. I think that this 'motif' is significant as a metaphor for some of my concerns, and it was utilised in the installation *Still Life* from 1999.

Richard Shaw (USA) has worked in ceramics, a medium that has been his main source of expression, since the mid-1960s. Many pieces have been produced that are either containers or refer to containers. This gives him a format to work from within the tradition of functional ceramics, European and worldwide.

Shaw's unique porcelain objects are skilfully assembled when leatherhard from various slip cast, press-moulded, handbuilt and thrown elements that often imitate a wide range of found objects. The transfer-printed parts that he uses to make up his forms are disturbingly realistic

C.P.'s Paintbox, by Richard Shaw (USA), 2001. Porcelain, 11.5 x 33 x 29 cm (4 ¼ x 13 x 11 ½ in.). *Photograph by Anthony Cunha.*

112

representations of familiar domestic items such as jars, tins, books, chairs, twigs and other pieces of wood. He says that he fell in love with porcelain for its whiteness, purity and translucency. Not only does porcelain represent value and elegance for him, but it also supports the use of natural colour, an essential requirement for an artist dealing with representation. Shaw has enjoyed working on porcelain's white surface since he was first drawn to its beauty, plasticity and adaptability. Although, he soon realised the material required a great deal of hard work and patience. We can gain an insight into his obsession with still life compositions in the following:

I like the simple and common objects that have poetry and magic in them. The still life with its absent arranger moves me. When I was at Sevres, I would go to the Louvre and take slides of parts of paintings. For example, what was on the table by the duke's left hand, but leaving out the duke. Some of the objects may have been symbolic at that time, however, the absence of their message makes them even more powerful to me. I would like my work to give people what these *parts* of paintings give to me. Part of that feeling is the immediate desire to return to one's studio to make something as beautiful.

I have been working in this mode of realism since 1976. My earlier work dealt with illusion, so I believe it was a logical transition to my present work which has been traditionally referred to as trompe l'œil. I use the still life to suggest an arrangement by an absent person – male or female, of the common objects they use in daily life, which they have left for a moment, frozen in time. The figures are also about containers; still lives and objects that have been anthropomorphized into people frozen in action or repose. I hope that my pieces offer function, humour, surprise, beauty and universality.

(Opposite) *China Cove*, by Richard Shaw (USA), 2000. Porcelain sculpture with over-glaze transfers, 38 x 23 cm (15 x 9 in.). *Photograph by Charles Kennard.*

Describing his technique, Shaw says that ceramic decals (transfers) offer several advantages that can't be obtained with hand decoration. Most obvious is the ability to make two or more copies of a particular design. Another is the possibility of drawing on paper, reproducing it through a printing process, and applying it to the work as a decal instead of drawing directly on to the piece. Reproduction of photos and found two-dimensional material can also be utilised through ceramic decals. For low-fired works, it is necessary to apply glaze over the colour to fix it, however, the high temperature used to mature the porcelain body makes washes and layers of colour adhere to

(Above) *Struggling Form*, by Harumi Nakashima (Japan), 2002. Handbuilt porcelain, 55 x 38 cm (22 x 15 in.), fired to 1230°C (2246°F). *Photograph by Taku Saiki.*

(Left) *Subterranean District 0201*, by Hideo Matsumoto (Japan), 2002. Porcelain, bone ash glaze, ceramic pigment, fired at 1240°C (2264°F), 50 x 30 cm (19 ½ x 11 ¾ in.).
Photograph by Yo Nagata.
(Below Left) *White Ruins V*, by Toni Hambleton (Puerto Rico), 2002. Slab-built, porcelain sculpture fired to Orton cone 8 in an electric kiln, 20.5 x 15 cm (8 x 6 in.).
Photograph by Johnny Betancourt.
(Below Right) *White Ruins II*, by Toni Hambleton (Puerto Rico), 2002. Slab-built, porcelain sculpture fired to Orton cone 8 in an electric kiln, 20 x 5 cm (8 x 2 in.). *Photograph by Johnny Betancourt.*

the body in a more painterly fashion. All the work is constructed in glazed porcelain.

The impressive and unusually rhythmic, sculptural works by **Harumi Nakashima** (Japan) are decorated with blue (transfer) spots in a white glaze that help to emphasise and define the forms. Larger dots appear stretched across expanding areas, becoming more tightly packed where parts are restricted. He does not make preliminary designs for his complex pieces on paper, but prefers to build them up directly by hand working with the plastic porcelain. He says that this is because he is attracted by the feel of the clay itself and the technique by which the material is transformed into ceramics. He likes to be deeply

involved with the clay at every stage from wet to dry and he is content to accept that the entire process through to the fired ceramic is a demanding experience, 'Sometimes we rebel against each other or, with others, work together as one.' He often calls his sculptures *Struggling Forms* and this term seems to sum up the actual creative activity. He describes his work as 'a cool mirror which sees through my inner struggle and reflects my true self'. Each sculpture is built up completely before Nakashima cuts into it and removes long strips of clay to open it up and allow the interior to make its own contribution to the total image.

Some of the powerful, sculptural images, similar to the form illustrated (see p.113), were created by **Hideo Matsumoto** (Japan) as part of his *Subterranean* series. They appear almost like fragments of conglomerate rocks. He explained that he became interested in what he describes as 'the subterranean layers' observed within the surfaces of some 12th-century Chinese ceramics. Each piece of his work is made from white, slip-cast porcelain in plaster moulds combined with finely cut porcelain elements and pieces covered by black slip.

THE HUMAN FIGURE

Porcelain is an ideal material for preserving the finest details in figurative sculpture. Some of the most exquisite and evocative figures are those designed by **Imre Schrammel** (Hungary) for production in limited editions at the Herend Porcelain Factory in Budapest. Schrammel is sensitive to the ever-increasing pace of modern life and to the disposable attitudes of society. 'What we make in the morning we throw away by night time.' These thoughts made him pause to reflect more on values of the past. Early pottery figures seen in museums first attracted his interest but the real inspiration for this delightful series of figures came from his visit to Venice during the annual Carnival. He described the feelings that prompted his new work in a brochure for the factory in November 1997.

> More than a decade has passed since I saw, among the Asian masterpieces of the Arts Museum in Kyoto, a coloured pottery figure, in height hardly more than one-and-a-half times the span of my hand, standing alone in the middle of a glass case. The paint was gone where soil acids had eaten it away here and there. The figure, from the Tang period, represents a lady at court.
>
> Ten years is a long time but I could not forget the figure, although it had been surrounded by many other marvellous pieces of which I had hazier memories.
>
> I thought of that court lady again as I started modelling figures at Herend. How fine it would be to create something as lasting as that, something able to speak over the centuries as that pottery figure had spoken to me. I know pottery and porcelain do not command the respect in Europe that they do in the East. Not

ABC, porcelain figure, by Imre Schrammel (Hungary), 1999. Modelled and slip-cast, h. 97 cm (38 in.). *Photograph by Kornél Kovacs and Józef Varga.*

Japanese Girl, by Imre Schrammel (Hungary), 1999. Porcelain figure, modelled and slip-cast, h. 37 cm (14 ½).
Photograph by Kornél Kovacs and Józef Varga.

even figures by Johann Joachim Kandler or Franz Anton Bustelli are displayed in the inner sanctums of fine art, although they are works of the same calibre as their distant Tang dynasty relatives. Could I produce porcelain figures I would not blush to see in the same room with the works of immortal masters? I was setting myself a very high standard, for apart from the more distant models, Herend Porcelain

(Left) *Carnival Group*, modelled and slip-cast porcelain, h. 43 cm (17 in.), by Imre Schrammel (Hungary), 1999.
Photograph by Kornél Kovacs and Józef Varga.

today requires it. The Herend manufactory, as it passes its 175th anniversary, conserves exceptional knowledge of craft skills that must not be wasted on work of a lower standard. If I have had the good fortune to realise my ideas through these world famous craftsmen and craftswomen, like a composer having his work performed by a superlative orchestra, I can only, in all humility, submit to them of my best.

I was helped in this by the whirl of the Venetian Carnival, which I could not even imagine in any other medium than porcelain. Each and every figure seemed imbued with mystery. No one could tell whether the costume concealed a man or a woman, a fresh young face or a wrinkled old one. Legends, fairy-tales and mythological beasts come alive in them, conjuring up in us anew the childhood submerged behind our civilized, overheated imaginations.

Suddenly, I thought of porcelain, of 'white gold'. That too is enigmatic, it shines like a precious stone presenting the world in a different, deceptively dazzling light. In my fancy, the sight of the sun's disc, glowing through the mist, and the dim radiance of Venetian splendour were manifested at once in porcelain. I could not resist the challenge. I was drawn to evoke in this noble material the waking dream of Venice's magic. I imagined that Herend lads and lasses had dressed in Herend-patterned costumes and were strolling there in St Mark's Square. Tourists in their thousands were taking their picture and filming them, and they, meanwhile, were turning into porcelain ... into sparkling, opalescent 'white gold'.

The human figure is an important element, also, in the sculptural work of **Sárka Radová** from the Czech Republic. Realising that she would never manage to work freely on a potter's wheel, she applied her energy to ceramic sculpture. Her figurative compositions have been described as 'a representation of ideas and fantasy projected on the reality of life

Four Heads, by Sárka Radová (Czech Republic), 1995. Porcelain sculpture, h. 65 cm (25 ½ in.). *Photograph by M. Polák.*

... symbolically diffused with the future, a never-ending movement of transformation and understanding'. A particularly successful piece, *Generation III* shows a group of figures supporting each other and reaching upwards to where the topmost four, who are modelled in greater detail, look to the future.

Anna Malicka-Zamorska (Poland) also bases much of her work on figures and she says that whatever she makes in porcelain is like 'a game, telling fairy tales about heroes in my life, people and animals'. Casting her sculptures in plaster moulds enables her to multiply the images and refine them. She has no interest in technology beyond that which suits her purpose

and is fortunate to work in a factory where 'slip-casting porcelain runs from a tap and kilns are working day and night' so she can concentrate all her energies towards her art.

The history of European porcelain, its associations with concepts of beauty, of wealth, of power, the themes of the early figurines; all provide resonance and tension in terms of the relationship between subject matter and material.

Although **Michael Flynn** (UK/Germany) had made a series of porcelain figures in the early 1980s, it was only in 1996 that he became fully aware of the inherent properties of this material.

At that time he was given several bags of porcelain by the Institut für Kunstlerische

(Left) *Generation III*, by Sarka Radova (Czech Republic). Porcelain sculpture, h. 85 cm (33 ½ in.).
Photograph by M. Polák.

(Above) *Machos*, by Anna Malicka-Zamorska (Poland), 1998. Porcelain and grogged clay with bronze masks and plumes, h. 102 cm (40 ½ in.), reduction fired to 1380°C (2516°F).
Photograph by Czeslaw Chwiszczuk.

(Below) *Angels*, by Anna Malicka-Zamorska (Poland), 2000. Slip-cast, paper porcelain with helmets in grogged clay stained by oxides (iron/manganese/cobalt), reduction fired to 1380°C (2516°F). *Photograph by Czeslaw Chwiszczuk.*

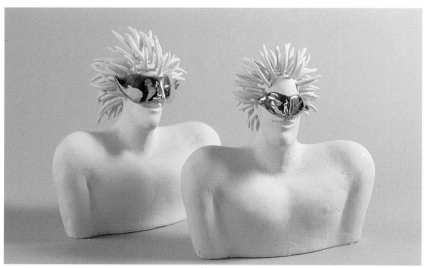

(Above) *They*, by Anna Malicka-Zamorska (Poland), 2001. Slip-cast porcelain, unglazed, h. 36 cm (14 ¼ in.) reduction fired to 1380°C (2516°F) with mask glazed with gold lustre at 800°C (1472°F). *Photograph by Czeslaw Chwiszczuk.*
(Right) *Dancer with Fish*, by Michael Flynn (UK/Germany), 2001. Handmade in 'Westerwalder' porcelain, glazed, painted with oxides, h. 42 cm (16 ½ in.) *Photograph by the artist.*
(Below Right) Porcelain figure sculpture, by Ruth Duckworth (USA). H. 42 cm (16 ½ in.). *Photograph by Saverio Truglia.*

Keramik in Hohr-Grenzhausen in Germany and invited to participate in an exhibition of salt-glaze porcelain at Rosenthal in Hamburg. He quickly became excited by the possibility of extending his ideas through the use of porcelain with all its associations. The formal and aesthetic qualities of porcelain soon began to assert themselves, to lend the images a brightness, a liveliness, a clarity that refreshed longer standing themes in his repertoire and provided new directions formally and intellectually.

Porcelain has become a major focus in my work. I have experimented with several different bodies. Each, of course, has its own specific qualities. I have worked at several major porcelain factories including Meissen in Germany and Walbrzyk in Poland. Both of these are fired so high, 1450°C (2642°F) and 1380°C (2516°F) respectively, that I am limited to using onglaze colours. I also find their whiteness somewhat stark. The fragility of the Meissen body, when it is leatherhard and dry, necessitates the addition of paper fibres. Often I prefer to work with Limoges or Royal Copenhagen or Valentine's Special Porcelain which are

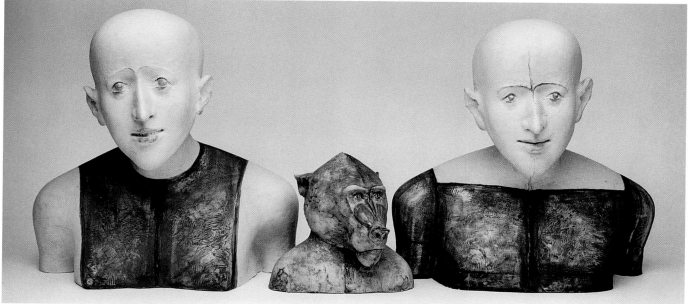

(Top) *Drumbeat*, by Michael Flynn (UK/Germany), 1999. Handmade in David Leach Porcelain, glazed, painted with oxides, h. 45 cm (17 ¾ in.). *Photograph by the artist.*

(Bottom) *Paar mit Affe (Couple with Ape)*, by Volkmar Kühn (Germany), 1992. Modelled porcelain, 38 cm x 85 cm (15 x 33 ½ in.). *Photograph by Christophe Beer.*

creamier in tone and on which I can use my own glazes. My favourite glaze is one using Wollastonite from Nigel Wood's book, *Chinese Glazes*. I use it as a celadon sometimes but also get good results from the electric kiln. Colours are usually stains and oxides, sometimes on glaze enamels. I fire between 1243°C (2269°F) and 1320°C (2408°F) depending on the body.

All of Flynn's figures are hollow, and are constructed from roughly cylindrical elements. The walls are very thin and the pieces are often joined together with wet clay when they are bone dry. He has discovered that, with some

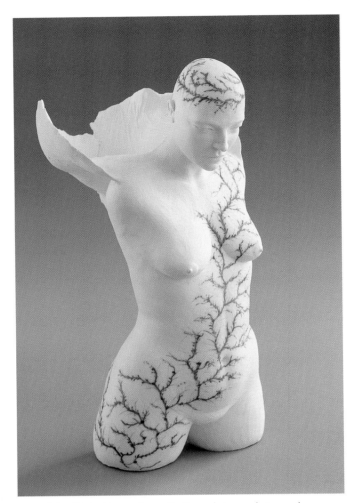

Angel, by Dalit Tayar (Israel). Porcelain sculpture, thrown and altered, painted with cobalt pigment, h. 20 cm (8 in.). *Photograph by Leonid Padrut.*

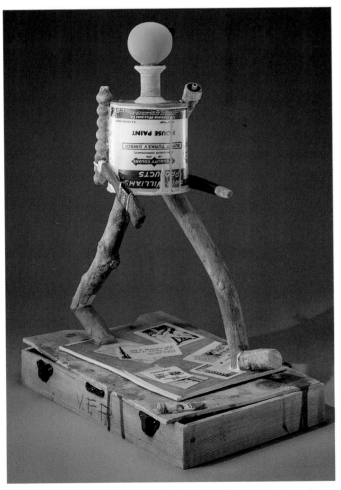

Paint Pot Walker, by Richard Shaw (USA), 2000. Porcelain with over-glaze transfers, 7.5 x 35.5 cm (19 x 14 x in.). *Photograph by Charles Kennard.*

porcelains, the individual sections to be assembled need to be leatherhard or may require the addition of paper or cotton fibres for extra strength. Any cracking that develops in drying is usually left visible, unless it is structurally threatening. 'I feel that such cracks, like my fingermarks, are evidence of how the piece has come into being and lend weight to its existence.'

The beautifully modelled figures by **Dalit Tayar** (Israel) are assembled entirely from wheel-thrown sections which are then altered and carved to complete the forms. They may be quite small in scale but they have the power of much larger sculptures. Sometimes, her figures appear trapped in rock or peer out from

Angel, by Dalit Tayar (Israel). Wheel-thrown porcelain, h. 35 cm (13 ¾ in.), and in stoneware, h. 50 cm (19 ¾ in.). *Photograph by Jackie Sorrero.*

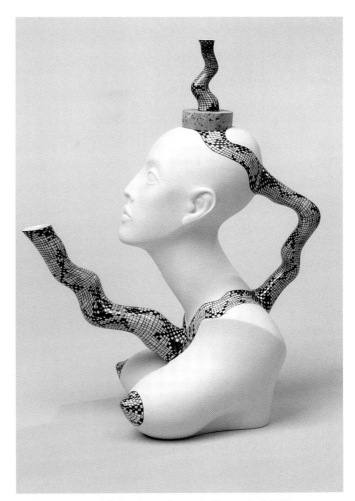

Bald But Beautiful, by Ilona Romule (Latvia), 1999. Porcelain teapot fired to 1280°C (2336°F), followed by china painting and gold lustre to 790°C (1454°F), 27 x 12 cm (10 ⅝ x 4 ¾ in.). Photograph by Aigars Tukna.

confined spaces. They provoke thought as to the circumstances in which they find themselves. Her figures are made from cylinder-shaped sections that are thrown on the wheel. The thin, even and plastic quality of thrown porcelain enables her to cut, alter and piece them together like a three-dimensional jigsaw puzzle. Extra clay is added and modelled by hand and, later, she uses dental tools to carve the finer details. The work is assembled very shortly after it is thrown. 'It's a sticky task but worthwhile in order to avoid warping and cracking during firing. I use porcelain mainly for its colour and fineness which allows me to carve out very small intricate details.'

Ilona Romule (Latvia) finds it difficult to explain how her figures materialise and are transformed in porcelain from her feelings and experiences of daily life.

> I only use my technical skills and the possibilities offered to me by the material and then a three-dimensional story appears. Porcelain provides the language for this story. The primary function of figurative porcelain is not a pot, or a bowl, or a cup. I expect viewers to see not just containers for liquid but a receptacle of ideas, emotions, pain, sexuality. The topic is an old one: the relationship between a man and a woman.

Another artist in this field, who has made a considerable impact with her sensitively

Clowns, by Kati Zorn (Germany), 1994. From a series of modelled and slip-cast porcelain figures, h. 19–23 cm (7 ½ –9 in.). *Photograph by Ulrich Fischer.*

Bull from the Sea, by Rudy Autio (USA), 1983. Handbuilt porcelain sculpture, 86 x 61 cm (34 x 24 in.). *Photograph by the artist.*

modelled and often humorous porcelain figures, is **Kati Zorn** (Germany) now working independently in her own studio at Cursdorf. Her delightful figures, whether mythological or based on animals, portray a range of human emotions and are often shown in surprising contexts. Technically excellent, these unique pieces explore contemporary issues in an unusual way. As a teenager, Kati dreamt of becoming a fashion designer or a potter but through her training as a porcelain artist and designer at Porzellan-manufaktur Lichte and in Meissen she has been able to make a successful fusion of the two professions.

VESSEL FORM

The most familiar pots, perhaps, are containers for domestic use that are circular in section. Such forms often have the greatest physical strength. For many years, most of my own work has been thrown on the wheel. My vessel forms evolved, firstly, as a direct response to the material, porcelain, which seems to suit my 'perfectionist' nature and, secondly, through my

(Above, left) White cup, oval tea strainer, container for tea strainer, white jug, by Prue Venables (Australia), 2001. Overall dimensions of group: 15 x 22 x 23 cm (6 x 8 ¾ x 9 in.). *Photograph by Terence Bogue.*

(Above, right) Porcelain tea set, by Patsy Hely (Australia), 2001. Found items, wood (teapot lid), powder-coated aluminium (saucer). 'One of a series of sets which incorporate old porcelain objects with new. The bread and butter plate is Noritake, the cup of unknown origin. They were selected because the porcelain used is particularly lovely. I then made a teapot and jug to match. The wooden lid is turned red-gum (by Paul Tiernan), the aluminium saucer is from a series of old aluminium spun objects that I had powder coated.' *Photograph by Rod Bucholz.*

preference for simplicity and crisp, clear profiles. These uncomplicated shapes provide me with three-dimensional 'canvases' to express ideas and feelings while remaining sensitive to the relationship between form and surface treatment. I enjoy making bowls, especially those that spring from a small base, swelling out and upwards in a natural, unbroken curve or flaring dramatically towards a wide rim. The bowl was probably the first vessel form to be made in clay. It has been produced in an enormous variety of shapes throughout history. Certainly, for thousands of years it has been one of the most useful of all pottery vessels. It is an *open* form whose inner and outer surfaces invite visual and tactile appreciation. The bowl also lends itself to considerable artistic invention. Square, rectangular, oblong or oval are all common examples of symmetrical shapes while, for some potters, asymmetry offers them a more stimulating aesthetic challenge.

The Australian potter, **Prue Venables**, enjoys making small, functional vessels which provide her with constant challenges and excitement. All her work is thrown and turned and then gently bent into a new shape while still soft. The porcelain retains a memory of all changes, so movements must be confident and direct. Much of her work has developed through an interest in altering simple thrown shapes. Their bases are removed and the side walls bent into new contours. Bases are added when the forms have stiffened sufficiently to handle without distortion. She tries to introduce a 'sprung tension' to the piece while retaining the softness of the throwing. The bending is often severe enough to cause cracking if the timing is not accurately judged. She finds that porcelain tolerates such movement only when precisely ready. If this pressure is applied too early in the drying stages it can collapse, while

Cup and saucer – *Crystal Pink Series*, by Judi Dyelle (Canada), 2000. Wheel-thrown, high-fire porcelain, fired in propane gas kiln to cone 10 (1305°C/2381°F) in reduction, crystalline glaze. Cup: h. 7.5 cm (3 in.), w. 9.5 cm (3 ¾ in.). Saucer: d. 16 cm (6 ¼ in.). *Photograph by Stan Funk.*

seems simple and yet is capable of gently holding and reflecting so much ceremony and personal connection. The finished object stands innocently – as if oblivious to the complexities of its history, of making and firing processes.

The translucency of porcelain, the light dancing on the sprung tension of a rim, the softly melting body inviting touch, even the frustration of failure – all this and more continue to invite me.

Venables' forms are hand-thrown, and then gently bent into a new shape while still soft. The porcelain retains a memory of all changes, so movements must be confident and simple, their timing precise. Later, new hand rolled bases are added and the slow drying begins. A high temperature reduction firing brings a soft, luminous,

adjustments made to the form too late lead to cracking. In her most recent work, an apparent simplicity conceals the laborious making process. She continues to use thrown clay as a building material rather than a finishing point, and pots are altered when still wet. Venables enjoys what she describes as 'the contradictory nature of these pieces where the sprung tension of the throwing remains clear, but the origins of forms are uncertain'. She expresses a particular interest in the making of functional objects and the fact that her work contains references to 18th and 19th century English industrial pottery as well as to more contemporary and familiar, metal and plastic vessels.

A search for simplicity and quietness, an essential stillness, motivates my work.

The making of functional pots, the exploration of objects to be held and used, alongside a search for new and innovative forms, provides a lifetime of challenge and excitement. A beautiful cup

Porcelain teapot with forged iron handle, by Joanna Howells (UK), 2001. Wheel-thrown with Southern Ice Porcelain and decorated with applied slips that are combed and adjusted to the design, h. 21 cm (8 ¼ in.). *Photograph by the artist.*

translucent quality to the material.

The delightful porcelain pots by **Joanna Howells** (UK) are thrown and altered while still soft, in order to escape the circular section imposed by the wheel, by means of stretching the clay and impressing the surface. She applies a slip and draws through it with a variety of combs and tools, including her fingers. In this way each piece embodies a few moments of free expression that make it unique. She treats her smaller domestic work with the same care as she does the larger sculptural pieces.

I have never felt that the epithets 'domestic' and 'functional' debar pottery from qualities usually associated with art. The approach is bold and free, the surfaces lively. Yet, after firing, the results are subtle, quiet, serene. While porcelain was traditionally potted very thin to emphasise its delicacy and translucency, I like my pots to have more generous lips and handles, magnanimous volumes and sensuous surfaces, while retaining elegant form. Porcelain not only does all that without compromising its customary qualities, but it can also do the unexpected, such as combining quite happily with demotic iron handles.

As for influences, these are perhaps too many to disentangle. They often suggest themselves after the event. On a conscious level I detect the influences of the Chinese Sung dynasty, at least in my early career, and ancient Cycladic sculpture in more recent times. Perhaps as important is the natural world of the South Wales coastline where I now live – the effects of wind on cliff and wave on shore, the state of permanent flux.

For **Bruce Cochrane** (Canada) functional utility continues to serve as the foundation for most of his ideas. His designs are influenced by the study of historical ceramics, natural objects and architecture, but he finds that 'useful pottery and its intimate connection with the daily rituals of life, has the potential for a rich aesthetic experience'.

Xing cups and saucers, by Joanna Howells (UK), 2001. Wheel-thrown and altered, Southern Ice Porcelain, h. 10 cm (4 in.). *Photograph by the artist.*

Teapot, by Bruce Cochrane (Canada), 2002. Porcelain, thrown and altered, sandblasted at the bisque stage, salt-fired, 25.5 x 15 cm (10 x 6 x 12 in.). *Photograph by the artist.*

The pots I make, no matter how simple or complex, are meant to be experienced on a physical and visual level. The way an object carries, lifts, cradles, pours and contains are properties which I strive to make engaging for the user, offering more than just convenience.

I explore and develop ideas through working

in multiples. Concentrating my efforts on a specific series of forms allows me to define and clarify my thoughts as well as to solve problems in a sequential order.

Emmanuel Cooper (UK) also refers to vessel forms for continuing inspiration, in particular, a series of teapots, jugs, bowls, vases and lidded boxes, all of which are related to domestic function and to the traditional role of the potter as artisan. Cooper stresses the idea that a vessel should be an object of interest in its own

(Top) *Metropolis I*, bowl by Emmanuel Cooper. Porcelain, thrown and turned with yellow glaze and gold leaf, h. 12 cm (4 ¾ in.), d. 26 cm x high, 2002. *Photograph by Michael Harvey.*
(Middle) *Highway 1*, bowl by Emmanuel Cooper, 2002. Porcelain, thrown and turned with white stain matt glaze over slip, h. 2.5 cm (1 in.), d. 19 cm (7 ½ in.). *Photograph by Michael Harvey.*
(Below) *Place to Concentrate*, by Pavel Knapek (Czech Republic), 1997. Slip-cast porcelain sculpture, 45 x 56 x 56 cm (17 ¾ x 22 x 22 in.). Photograph by the artist.

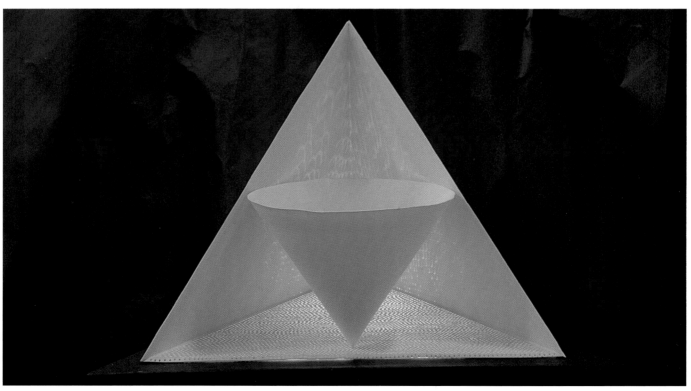

Deep Bowl, *Southwest* series, by Robin Hopper (Canada), 2002. Porcelain with terra sigillata and bronze pigment brushwork, once fired to cone 9 in oxidation, subsequent firing with trailed chrome red glaze fired at cone 06, h. 20.5 cm (8 in.), d. 20.5 cm (8 in.). *Photograph by Janet Dwyer.*

Porcelain bowl, by Ursula Scheid (Germany), 2002. Wheel-thrown, painted with triangular pattern in black slip over tape resist, glazed, d. 16.5 cm (6 ½ in.). *Photograph by the artist.*

right in addition to any purpose it may serve as a container. He is attracted to porcelain whether it is used alone or opened up with fine alumina hydrate because it allows him to produce a variety of intense colours that would not be possible in stoneware.

Recently I have been working on thrown, cone or funnel-like forms in porcelain, where equal consideration is given to the inner and outer space. Hence the forms are meant to hover between enclosed and open forms, and so invite inspection on the inside and the outside. The profile of the piece is crucial, as is the balance between the fairly narrow foot and the rim. Again, there is an attempt to create a harmonious tension, if there is such a thing. The foot must be neither too wide, or the piece sinks into the table, or too narrow when it looks too unstable. Inspiration comes from old fashioned lampshades, often used in offices, made in metal, sometimes enamel, but also in plastic.

The pots are made from Potclays 'Green' porcelain with about 5% alumina sand wedged in. This gives the body slightly more tooth, which is

slightly easier to throw. The alumina also makes it less translucent, but as I want whiteness this does not greatly concern me. In any case, it is a fairly opaque porcelain body, but one with which I am familiar.

Glazes and surface are important. In contrast to my stoneware, where I like experimenting with textured, volcanic surfaces, the porcelain is more traditional in being refined and delicate. Plain, deep white tin glazes are among my favourites, though I often use a clear glaze over the tin glaze to achieve greater depth. I like to use a yolk yellow glaze stain speckled with spots of blue or green, but get frustrated when the yellow looks washed out or is too opaque. Other colours under review are a viridian green and an inky blue. The use of a slip containing vanadium pentoxide can give interesting results. Under a semi-matt glaze it will produce a speckled, slightly broken surface, which is sufficiently subversive for my anarchic streak.

All are biscuit fired to 980°C (1796°F), glazed by either painting or pouring, and fired to 1260°C (2300°F) in an electric kiln.

Both **Karl** and **Ursula Scheid** (Germany) continue to make uncomplicated vessel forms

Lips Bowls, by François Ruegg (Switzerland), 2002. Group of five slip-cast porcelain pieces on black steel stand, glazes, and overglazes, firing to cone 9 and cone 018 respectively, 10 x 92 x 22 cm (4 x 12 ½ x 8 ¾ in.). 'An ovoid shape suggested a mouth to me, and its edges were transformed into lips. Stretching the shape, I produced various expressions, underlined with the colour of lipstick. On the shelf, a group of objects smile to you.' *Photograph by Magali Koenig.*

Translucent porcelain bowl, by Arnold Annen (Switzerland), 2000. D. 17 cm (6 ¾ in.), reduction fired in a gas kiln to 1320°C (2408°F). *Photograph by the artist.*

Tamsin Watkins-Jones (UK) refers to the beauty and pleasure she finds in a pot that has a fineness of form especially when clothed in a glaze of extraordinary depth and quality.

The relationship of quiet and restrained forms to the simple marks placed on them, for example, a fine vertical line of oxide that divides a form in two, a broad diagonal brushstroke that does the same, or a blush of copper on a soft, milky white crackle glaze. How these marks enhance the interest of the pot when held and turned in the hand. I try to obtain a balance between the different areas within a piece to produce a pot that is satisfying and complete. I am interested in exploring the unique ceramic qualities that arise from a slow-firing process, exploring the character of glaze on porcelain, a consequence of the deep interface between the two after such a firing.

that provide them with clean surfaces for embellishment with sharply defined patterns in dark slips. Their forms and applied designs are always carefully considered and meticulously executed.

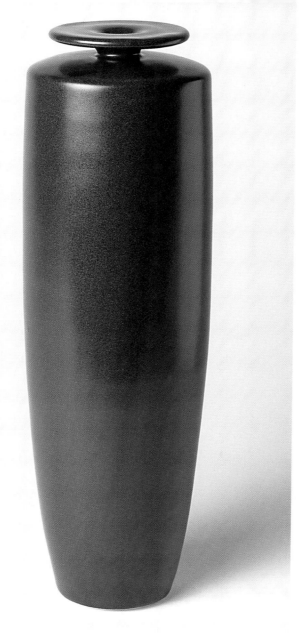

(Above) Thrown and turned bottle, by Tamsin Watkins-Jones (UK). Black satin glaze, h. 31 cm (12 ¼ in.). This form is thrown in two sections; up to the shoulder in one, the shoulder and lip in the second. They are joined when leatherhard and after turning. The joining edge is bevelled. Slow firing and very slight reduction allow dusty browns and greys to develop in the black glaze. *Photograph by Jonathan Gooding.*

(Top Right) *Bottle with Dancing Flower*, by Scott Malcolm, 2002. Porcelain, wheel-thrown and incised under celadon glaze, reduction fired to cone 12, h. 11 cm (4 ¼ in.). *Photograph by Peter Lee.*

(Bottom Right) Covered Jar, by John Tilton (USA). Wheel-thrown porcelain, matte crystalline glaze with copper, 25.5 x 15 x 15 cm (10 x 6 x 6 in.). *Photograph by the artist.*

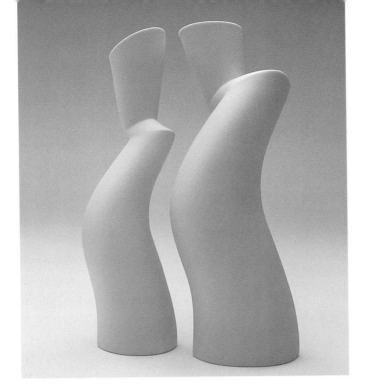

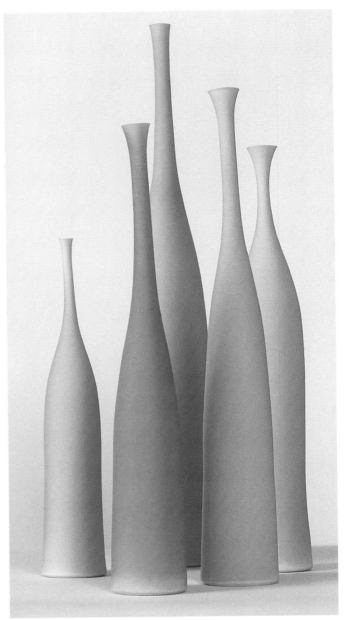

(Top) Slip-cast Limoges porcelain, by Penny Smith (Australia), 2002. H. (tallest) 33 x 7 x 8 cm (13 x 2 ¾ x 3 ⅛ in.). *Photograph by Uffe Schultz.*

(Bottom) Wood-fired porcelain vessel, by Catharine Hiersoux (USA), 2002. Carved surface, d. 46 cm (18 in.). *Photograph by the artist.*

(Right) *Acqua Bottles*, by Sophie Cook (UK), 2002. Wheel-thrown porcelain, h. 40–60 cm (15 ¾ –23 ½ in.). *Photograph by the artist.*

THE VESSEL AS SCULPTURE

Some potters use the facility of the wheel only to make shapes which are then altered away from the circular cross-section or cut and reassemble them into new forms. Often, this leaves little evidence of the throwing process visible in the finished piece. **Sarah-Jane Selwood** (UK) established her Edinburgh studio in 1992. Her pots are wheel-thrown, cut and reconstructed, in a Limoges porcelain and high fired in reduction to 1280°C (2336°F), glazed or hand-diamond

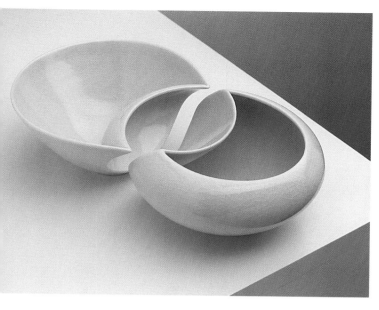

and perfection of a form is challenged by its disruption and reconstruction. From the simple curve of the original form new volumes and lines emerge changing the internal and external space of the vessel instilling within it a suspended movement – a tension – a memory. These reconstructed pieces possess a precise, quiet, undemonstrative elegance with their clear, delicate crackled glazes.

The vessel forms by **Karin Bablok** (Germany) clearly offer the option to be used as containers but they also exhibit sculptural characteristics. All her unique pieces are thrown on the wheel, initially, and then altered by gently beating with a wooden paddle to obtain flattened areas and sharp edges well away from the normal

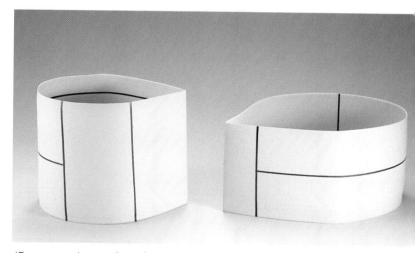

'Ergänzung' porcelain, by Karin Bablok (Germany), 2002. Wheel-thrown and altered, painted with basalt glaze, h. 30 cm (11 ¾ in.) fired in reduction atmosphere 1280°–1300°C (2336°–2372°F). Both pieces have at least one flat side so that they can be combined in different ways to become one form. *Photograph by Joachim Riches.*

(Top) *Double Transposition*, by Sarah-Jane Selwood (UK), 2001. H. 14 cm (5 ½ in.), d. 11 cm (4 ⅜ in.), thrown porcelain (Limoges). Pair of complimentary forms are precisely cut, sections exchanged and rejoined to create intersection, bisque fired 1000°C (1832°F). Ice Crackle glaze fired to 1280°C (2336°F) in reduction. *Photograph by Shannon Tofts.*
(Bottom) *Fugue* by Sarah-Jane Selwood, 2001. Thrown porcelain (Limoges), h. 10 cm (4 in.), d. 13 cm (5 in.). The form is precisely cut multiple times, sections inverted and rejoined, bisque fired 1000°C (1832°F). Ice Crackle glaze fired to 1280°C (2336°F) in reduction. *Photograph by Shannon Tofts.*

cylindrical profile produced on the wheel.

Ceramicists frequently take a vessel form as their starting point to develop ideas. In some instances, the functional aspect of the form as a container remains, in others it may have completely disappeared. **Paula Murray** (Canada) chose to work in porcelain because

polished. In her vessels Selwood explores the tensions of rhythm, line and space. The simplicity she believes that it symbolises purity, heights of sophistication, strength and fragility. She handbuilds vessels using casting slip in a plaster mould.

> By incorporating fine sheets of fibre-glass used in wooden boat restoration called 'surface veil', I am able to set up stress lines as the work dries and is altered in this process. Over the years, I have developed considerable skills in this stress management. Wonderful patterns emerge and tension is created depending on the thickness of the clay, the placement and the direction of the fibres in the lay-up of the piece, and the speed of the drying process. As the work on each piece proceeds, through several firing, finishing and glazing stages the voice of each form is expressed.

Murray's vessels are fired in stages, unglazed to 1260°C (2300°F) in an electric kiln using saggars to support the forms. She devotes many hours to each piece, refining the surface before submitting them to the rigours of low-temperature salt firing. The tactile dimension of the work with the surface 'sometimes akin to coral at other times water washed rocks' are important to her. After applying terra sigillata slips and glazes with an airbrush to the vitrified porcelain, the pieces are delicately placed touching each other, filling the kiln to enhance the flame patterns and texture imparted by the reducing, salted atmosphere. Small bowls containing salt and metallic oxides are placed amongst the pots. During the 8-hour firing the kiln is usually salted twice above the burners. She sees her role in this process as the conductor of an orchestra, attempting to express something beautiful with the energy of these ingredients.

The whiteness of porcelain holds attractions for those potters who do not necessarily wish to fire it to its traditional and more usual high-maturing temperature. Firing porcelain bodies in sawdust at relatively low temperatures well under 1000°C (1832°F) (after an initial bisque

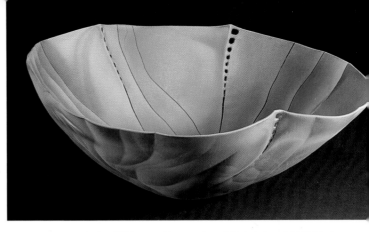

(Top) *Fragmenting Earth* vessel form, by Paula Murray (Canada), 2002. Unglazed porcelain with terra sigillata fired to 1260°C (2300°F), followed by a second firing with salt and metallic oxides, 53 x 8 x 23 cm (21 x 20 x 9 in.). (Bottom) *Bridging Space* vessel form, by Paula Murray, 2002. Unglazed porcelain with terra sigillata fired to 1260°C (2300°F) followed by a second firing with salt and metallic oxides, 43 x 101 x 97 cm (17 x 40 x 38 in.). *Photograph by the artist.*

firing around 1040°C/1904°F) appeals to some because certain colour effects and surface flashing from smoke and the reaction with metallic salts can be obtained. A fair amount is inevitably left to chance in this process and the ware is usually only decorative due to its comparative fragility.

Porcelain provides a bright white ground for **Elisabeth Schaffer** (Germany) to inlay coloured

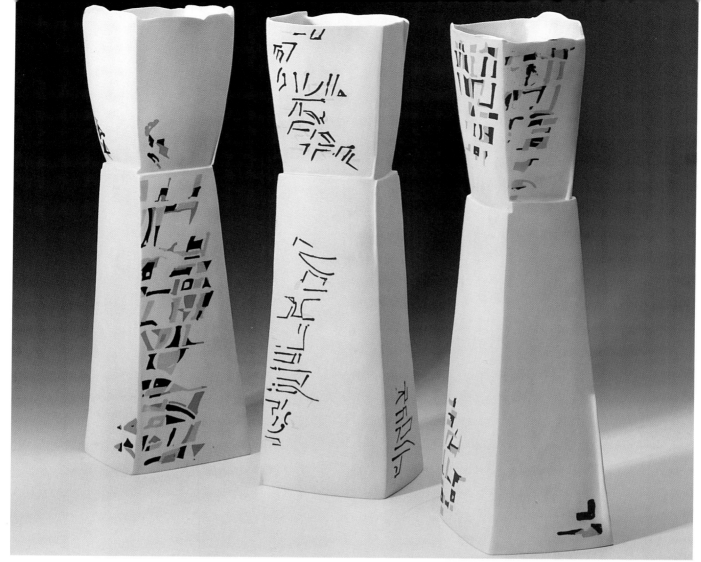

(Above) *Three Vases*, by Elisabeth Schaffer (Germany), 1999. Porcelain slabs made from slip poured on to plaster with coloured porcelain elements inlaid, h. 42 cm (16 ½ in.). 'A thin layer of white liquid porcelain painted on a plain plaster slab acts as a resist on to which coloured slips are freely added before a fresh layer of white porcelain is poured on top to ensure complete integration of the colour within the slab.' *Photograph by Antje Anders.*

(Right) Incised porcelain lizard teapot, by Elaine Coleman (USA), 2002. Green celadon glaze, h. 27 cm (10½ in.), l. 30.5 cm (12 in.), fired to cone 10 in reduction. *Photograph by the artist.*

slips rather like hieroglyphic fragments on tall vessel forms. She builds these from slabs made by painting a thin layer of white porcelain slip on a plain plaster slab that acts as a 'resist' on to which coloured slips are freely added. Then, a fresh layer of white porcelain is poured on top to

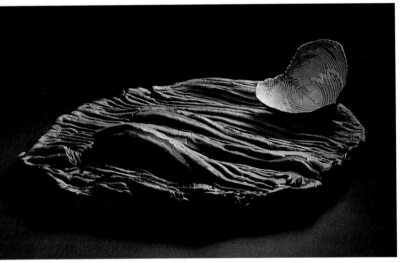

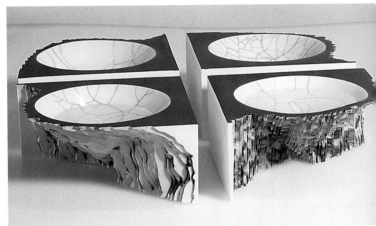

(Top) Group of porcelain slab dishes, by Jack Doherty (UK), 2002. Largest: 45 x 45 cm (17¾ x 17¾ in.). *Photograph by Sue Packer.*

(Bottom) Survival, by Dorothy Feibleman (UK), 2002. Porcelain form, 90 x 85 cm (35 ½ x 33 ½ in.). *Photograph by Osaki Studio.*

(Top) *Wingcups*, by Hubert Kittel (Germany). Slip-cast hard-paste porcelain elements with underglaze and on-glaze decoration, blue slip and transfers. The feet are glued into position. H. 14 cm (5 ½ in.), fired to 1400°C (2552°F). *Photograph by Gunter Binsack.*

(Above) *In Extinction*, by Wolfgang Vegas (Venezuela), 2000. Porcelain, slip-cast in 'transformable mould', oxides, engobes, glazes, 7.5 x 35 x 35 cm (3 x 13 ¾ x 13 ¾ in.), electric firing, 1280°C (2336°F). *Photograph by Gilles Boss.*

ensure complete integration of the colour within the slab.

The unusual teapot by **Elaine Coleman** (USA) has been altered from the original wheel-thrown section to an almost organic shape that is given further emphasis by fluent carving that encompasses the form. The flowing lines are echoed by the leaning strap handle. Another familiar domestic utensil has been given new

life in the work of **Hubert Kittel** (Germany) who has attached wings to his slip-cast cups and elevated them on three-legged stands in place of saucers. Similarly, bowls and platters can take many forms as can be seen in the works illustrated by **Wolfgang Vegas** (Venezuela), **François Ruegg** (Switzerland) and **Jack Doherty** (UK). The intricately patterned bowl by **Dorothy**

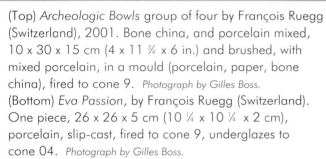

(Top) *Archeologic Bowls* group of four by François Ruegg (Switzerland), 2001. Bone china, and porcelain mixed, 10 x 30 x 15 cm (4 x 11 ¾ x 6 in.) and brushed, with mixed porcelain, in a mould (porcelain, paper, bone china), fired to cone 9. *Photograph by Gilles Boss.*
(Bottom) *Eva Passion*, by François Ruegg (Switzerland). One piece, 26 x 26 x 5 cm (10 ¼ x 10 ¼ x 2 cm), porcelain, slip-cast, fired to cone 9, underglazes to cone 04. *Photograph by Gilles Boss.*

Feibleman (UK) that she calls *Survival* appears to be floating on a restless sea. Quite simple vessels take on a new, corporate identity when grouped together as in the still-life sculptures by **Elsa Rady** (USA) and **Gwyn Hansen Piggot** (Australia). Objects assembled in this way rely on the relationship of the physical elements, the shadows cast across them and on the 'empty'

(Top) *Still Life with Yellow Cups*, by Gwyn Pigott (Australia), 2002. Limoges porcelain, 6 pieces, w. 37 cm (14 ½ in.), h. 25 cm (10 in.). *Photograph by Brian Hand.*
(Bottom) *Still Life No: 42*, by Elsa Rady (USA). Porcelain on painted aluminium shelf, 35.5 x 61 cm (14 x 24 in.).
Photograph by Paul Sanders. Courtesy of Jay and Rachael Tarses.

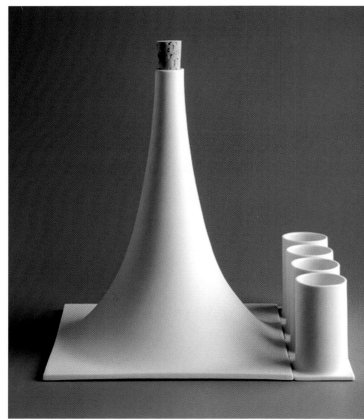

Carafe with Goblets, slip-cast to a design by Frank Claesen for the Piet Stockmans Studio Collection in 1999. Photograph by G. Ramaekers.

(Top) Eggcup, by Johanna Hitzler (Germany), 1999. Porcelain, stainless steel, black cellular rubber, 13 x 3.2 x 8 cm (5 x ⅜ x 3 ⅛ in.), fired to 1280°C (2336°F) in an electric kiln. (Above) Three Vases, by Johanna Hitzler, 2001. Slip-cast porcelain with copper-glazed interior, h. 33 cm (13 in.), fired to 1280°C (2336°F) in an electric kiln.
Photographs by Gunter Binsack, Leipzig.

spaces between to create a successful image.

Johanna Hitzler (Germany) creates a wide and varied range of vessel forms from one or two quite simple plaster moulds. She makes the sections of the mould so that they are flexible enough to be manipulated and pushed into different configurations. These slip-cast elements can be cut, altered, stacked and joined together in a bewildering series of compositions. She is convinced that she could not have pre-designed many of the shapes that have been developed in this way. She continues to find the process fascinating and is excited by the prospect of discovering new combinations in the evolution of vessel forms.

Piet Stockmans (Belgium) runs a highly efficient workshop producing many hundreds of slip-cast pieces each year. The *Carafe with Goblets* set was slip-cast to a design by Frank Claesen for the Piet Stockmans Studio Collection

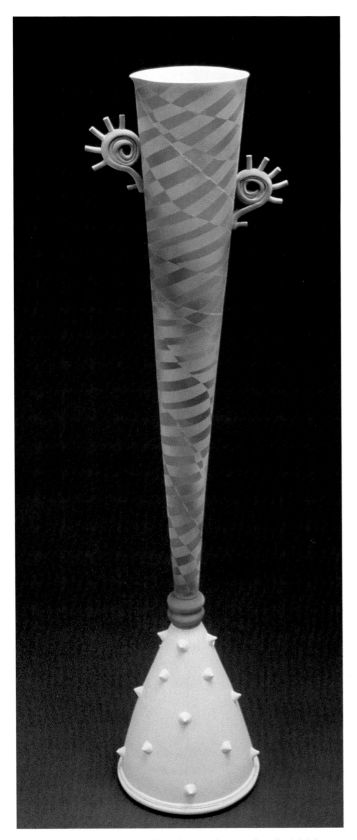

Conical Vessel with Handles, by Andrea Hylands 1993. Bone china, slip-cast and assembled, decorated with air-brushed colours, fired to 1240°C (2264°F) in an electric kiln.

in 1999. This is a beautifully considered and understated piece occupying space with its clean lines unimpeded by decoration.

In the first edition of *Contemporary Porcelain*, I described the work of **Andrea Hylands** (Australia) as some of the most unusual and exciting work being produced in porcelain and bone china with reference to vessel form. Those pieces displayed an obvious visual relationship to containers and were almost impossible to categorise. That work can be analysed, of course, in terms of geometric shapes assembled in various proportions and combinations while their surfaces can be appreciated for their colours, patterns and textures, but, beyond that, those works have more eloquence than can be expressed merely in words. They seem to be of an unreality given concrete form.

In her previous work, Hylands described the absolute whiteness of bone china as being 'ideal for the application of colour'. She combined both slip-casting and handbuilding in the construction of her pots but few clues remained to inform us of their origins or of the techniques used to arrive at the finished piece. Ceramic stains were mixed with frits or with porcelain and bone china slip and airbrushed to give a flat expanse of colour before bisque firing. Further colours were then applied over stencils in preparation for the final firing which was conducted in an electric kiln to around 1220°C (2228°F) with a half hour soak at the top temperature. Then the work was polished with silicon carbide paper (Wet 'n Dry) to achieve a surface sheen.

She explained how most of this early work was directly related to the vessel.

The vessel has an important physical function: that is one of containing. This function, owing to its familiarity, has a strong point of contact with an audience. The folded bowls were part of a series.

Lines and edges are prominent qualities in my work and I allude to feeling and touching. The starting point for basic shapes depends on previous work. I do not jump around from shape to shape arbitrarily, but simply evolve and modify ideas for forms. I enjoy making them look as if they have not been made from clay.

The later series was about reinterpreting the pot in an abstract way. These vessels were the products of an intricate process and they were complicated and enriched with decoration and embellishment. Using distortion and deception placed them between the ordinary and extraordinary, revealing some ambiguity of purpose. There was no overt symbolism in those pieces, but the familiar was turned into surprise, exaggerating the surreal aspect of a pot, as opposed to a pot as a commonplace object. In the later series of abstract vessels, I increased the scale of the work and some of my forms are a metre high.

Working to a particular theme concentrates the mind wonderfully. This may involve examining a certain form and trying to discover various options and nuances that give it fresh life and interest. Changing between techniques of making, decorating, glazing or firing may spark off new ideas or inspiration may be stimulated by the struggle to resolve problems of design or those judged to be inherent in the material itself.

Some works by **Tony Franks** (UK), especially his *Emerging Island*, appear to owe some allegiance to the vessel. Surprisingly, this robust object is made from bone china into which he has mixed unusual natural materials collected from fields and hillsides. Organic matter incorporated into the clay is burned away during the firing leaving traces of themselves that he refers to as 'fossil memories'.

Les Manning (Canada) works with a combination of three differently coloured and textured stoneware and porcelain bodies, starting with the darkest and most textured stoneware to suggest a foreground and middle distance, and

Emerging Island, by Tony Franks (UK), 2000. Bone china, 40 x 42 x 35 cm (15 ¾ x 16 ½ x 13 ¾ in.), fired twice to 1200°C (2192°F), then 1220°–1230°C (2228°–2246°F), sand-blasted, polished and coloured after bisque firing. *Photograph by Shannon Tofts.*

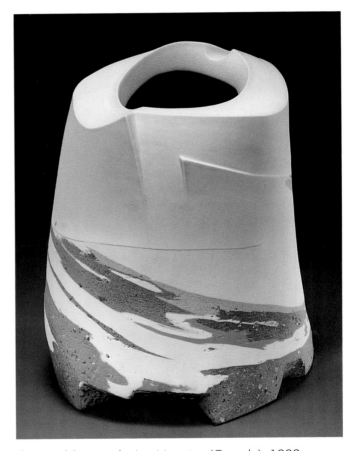

Corniced Summit, by Les Manning (Canada), 1999. Combinations of stoneware and porcelain bodies stacked together and wheel-thrown, altered, glazed and sandblasted, h. 29 cm (11 ¼ in.), w. 22 cm (8 ¾ in.). *Photograph by Howard Owen (Collection of The Canadian Clay & Glass Gallery).*

Boat, *Kamloops* series by Judi Dyelle (Canada), 2002. Porcelain, wheel-thrown and assembled, local earthenware slip glaze with oxides, reduction fired in propane gas kiln to cone 9 (1280°C/2336°F), 35 x 13.5 x 11.5 cm (13 ¾ x 9 ¼ x 4 ½ in.). *Photograph by Janet Dwyer.*

using porcelain as a background in his landscape sculptural forms. Each clay is wedged separately and stacked in an informal pattern. Porcelain is the dominate amount of material in the mix. Each body is carefully chosen to be within 1.5% shrinkage of each other in order to successfully survive the stresses of drying and firing without causing separation. The stacked form is thrown and altered, bisqued and glazed with a celadon glaze fired in reduction to Orton cone 9. After this the pieces are sandblasted to remove the shine and give the surface a smooth but matt quality. Any stress fractures that are not structural problems are then filled with silver amalgam to strengthen the surface and visually provide a silver accent.

Gotlind Weigel (Germany) also uses the wheel to throw the initial shapes for her sculptural vessels. She worked mainly in stoneware and only sporadically in porcelain for the past 20 years but, recently, porcelain has become her preferred material in the production of a series of 'boat' forms. Firing at high temperature required her to create a suitable porcelain body that was amenable to throw and would be stable enough to withstand the inevitable stresses incurred. She begins with a cylinder thrown without a bottom. This is then altered, cut and reassembled into

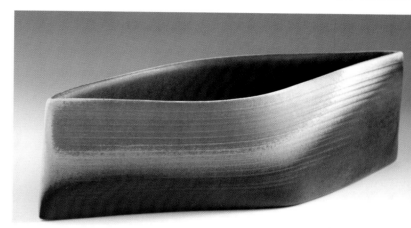

(Top) *Kahn (Ship)*, porcelain vessel, by Gotlind Weigel (Germany), 2002. Wheel-thrown and altered, 27 x 10 x 11 cm (10 ⅝ x 4 x 4 ⅜ in.), reduction fired to 1350°C (2462°F). (Bottom) *Blau-rosa (Cutter)*, porcelain vessel, by Gotlind Weigel, 2002. Wheel-thrown and altered, 32 x 10 x 10 cm (12 ½ x 4 x 4 in.). Reduction fired to 1350°C (2462°F). *Photographs by Baumann Fotostudio.*

asymmetric shapes with an appropriate new base fitted. She had to overcome a number of problems that arose during her initial exploration of these forms in porcelain. The high shrinkage rate ('up to 25%') is one disadvantage that all potters suffer, but this is generally much worse with porcelain. In addition, Weigel had to deal with cracks appearing between the joined sections.

I kept asking myself why it had to be porcelain after more disappointing setbacks than successes.

Perhaps it is the brightness of the material causing glazes to shine, or the weight in relation to the volume, or the translucency. I do know that working with porcelain has been a new challenge to my creativity, and striving after reliable answers is still exciting.

One porcelain potter who became well-known for her strongly thrown, classical shapes (and whose work was included in my previous books), but who felt an urgent need to pursue new directions in her vessel forms is **Catharine Hiersoux** (USA). She remains committed to the vessel as a point of

departure in her exploration of form but is prepared to adapt to any future changes that may develop. She built a wood-burning kiln to fire these new pieces because she wanted to use a process that just 'touched' the forms, enhancing, highlighting them. She felt that these pieces were 'still of the earth but not just natural. There are lots of problems with wood firing ... it's not very predictable ... but the chance for magic is much greater'.

My work in clay has been devoted almost exclusively to porcelain. Finding inspiration in classical forms, I prodded the traditional shapes into a dialogue with

Fish Bottle, by Catharine Hiersoux (USA), 2002. Porcelain, wheel-thrown and altered, h. 39.5 cm (15 ½ in.).
Photograph by the artist.

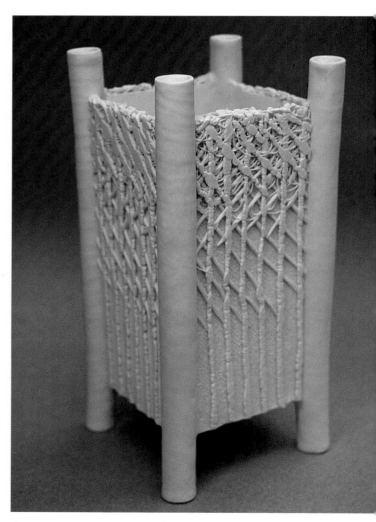

Japanese series, container by Gordon Cooke (UK), 2000. Porcelain slabs and coils, h. 20 cm (8 in.), l. 9.5 cm (3 ¾ in.), gas fired to cone 8. *Photograph by the artist.*

(Left) Handbuilt ceramic form, the result of collaboration in design and execution between two Belgian artists, Frank Steyaert and Chris Scholliers in 1993. It combines an earthenware base supporting a porcelain vessel decorated by nerikomi patterns, h. 60 cm (23 ½ in.). (Right) Vessel form, by Karl Scheid (Germany), 2002. Slab-built with coloured slip over tape resist, height: 29.8 cm (11¾ in.), reduction-fired to 1360°C (2480°F). *Photograph by the artist.*

new ways to be glazed, wood and soda firings provided an opportunity for an extended dialogue between maker and finished forms, where the kiln began to assume an ever more significant roll. The pieces were further enhanced by exposing them to the chance encounters of both the rigor and the magic of the fire. The fire is expansive, connecting us to forces much larger than the individuals. In this new relationship we experience both humility and a sense of awe.

personal and contemporary aesthetic problems. The metaphor of a cracked eggshell became the vehicle to explore the idea of vulnerability. Gradually, these vessels developed in or on rocks, sculpted from clay, expressing the ambiguity between shapes that represent new growth or those weathered through time. In pushing porcelain to its limits, so thin as to be translucent, even blistered, I am able to explore the polarities between inside and outside, fragility and strength.

As the emerging forms suggested

Textural interest in vessels by **Gordon Cooke** (UK) is created by adding thin coils, geometrically arranged, and rolled lightly onto the surface of thin porcelain slabs in a relief pattern. Whereas the vase by **Karl Scheid** (Germany) makes no use of texture as it rises up from a tapering base to flair outwards sharply angled at the top. Attention is drawn to this feature by precisely applied dark slip that continues downwards in narrow lines at each corner to end at the base.

Collaboration between **Frank Steyaert** and **Chris Scholliers** from Belgium began when Chris was one of Frank's students. They mounted Scholliers' small, tulip-shaped, neriage goblets on to Steyaert's sculptural stoneware sculptures when they discovered that the contrast proved to be a successful combination between the delicate porcelain and the coarser clay.

CHAPTER FOUR
SURFACE TREATMENTS

PAINTED DECORATION

The pure white porcelain body lends itself especially well to surface designs applied as stains, oxides, slips, glazes, lustres or enamels. Tools used may be paintbrushes of various sizes and shapes, sponges, rubber stamps, transfers, slip trailers, or spray guns and airbrushes. Colours can be overlaid and the piece fired and refired several times to different temperatures, and in all kinds of kiln atmospheres until the desired result is achieved. Resists and masks of paper, card, tapes, nets, latex and wax are often employed to widen the range of creative possibilities. Sources of both figurative and abstract imagery are infinite.

Bai Ming (China) demonstrates fluent brush work and supreme technique in his elegant porcelain vessels and imaginative ceramic sculptures. He is an artist with many talents not only in ceramics and painting but also as a prolific writer with numerous articles and several books to his name. His work evokes and restates many of the values we have come to

Structure, wheel-thrown porcelain by Bai Ming (China), 2000. Cobalt decoration, 47 x 18.8 cm (18 ½ x 7 ⅜ in.). *Photograph by the artist.*

(Left) Vessel form, thrown and altered, by Tony Laverick (UK), 2002. Decorated with gold and copper lustres, h. 25.5 cm (10 in.). *Photograph by Andrew Parr.*

Endless Life, by Bai Ming (China), 2000. Wheel-thrown porcelain with cobalt brushwork, 38 x 20 cm (15 x 8 in.). *Photograph by the artist.*

Porcelain vase, wheel-thrown, painted with cobalt pigments, by Alistair Whyte (Australia), 2002. *Photograph by Terence Bogue.*

recognise in traditional Chinese ceramics and develops them afresh. 'I like to develop two principles in my work, One is clearly that of the ceramic artist, a three-dimensional orientation toward real space, but there is also the conceptual sensitivity of a painter.' Although Bai Ming's blue and white porcelain are executed by conventional methods and techniques, his imagery exhibits a strong sense of the present without stylised decorative references to traditional ornamentation. His eloquent, abstract brush paintings bring to mind grasses and plants with the movement of wind and water. Each mark seems to be an essential part of the whole design. Thesse pieces are beautiful in their simplicity and refinement.

Alistair Whyte (Australia) spent several years studying porcelain ceramics in Japan and he acknowledges that Oriental influences remain strong in his work although he does not try to produce 'Japanese' pots. 'Apart from making use of learned techniques, I try to be true to my own feelings of design and decoration. I am strongly drawn to the use of blue and white on porcelain because I feel that it enhances the whiteness and purity of the material.' It was while he was in Japan that Whyte first began to use *gosu*, the natural cobalt blue colour to be found in *Kiyomizu sometsuke* (blue and white ware), which is a familiar aspect of much of his own work. At the present time, he is slowly exploring the use of a variety of glazes and more and more colour but he would probably regard himself as 'something of a purist'. He understands:

the meditative aspect of designing and carving the tools in the making process and of the patience that has to be learnt from the time of making and drying to the final firing of the kiln. The sense of satisfaction when, having created an object of beauty in porcelain, the light shines through between your fingers.

Large porcelain bowl by Mahmoud Baghaeian (Canada), 2000. Decorated with a blue wash over wax-resisted design, d. 40 cm (15 ¾ in.), fired to cone 9. *Photograph by Farinaz Agharabi.*

Mahmoud Baghaeian (Canada) creates vessel forms that he uses as canvasses upon which to design Persian-inspired motifs, but he defies the rules of symmetry typical of Persian tradition while respecting the essential harmony between form and surface. His brushwork swirls around and encompasses his generous vessel forms. For his wax-resist process, bisqued pieces are dipped in a black glaze containing up to 5% cobalt oxide. After this has dried, the piece is decorated with a brush using liquid wax emulsion and then dipped into a second, transparent glaze. The waxed area

on the surface of the piece repels the second glaze, much like the 'batik' patterns seen on textiles. This technique places two distinct glazes with different characteristics next to each other. Together, the result is quite different than when fired separately. Baghaeian states that a great deal of testing is necessary to avoid glaze problems. One of his best results came from a cobalt saturated black slip/glaze with a high-feldspar, transparent glaze on top. The cobalt from the first glaze actually leaches into the transparent second glaze on top and produces a

Blue covered jar, by Mahmoud Baghaeian (Canada), 2002. Porcelain, freely painted with wax resist brushwork, d. 28.5 cm (11 ¼ in.), fired to cone 9. *Photograph by John Carlano.*

pleasant, velvety blue glaze. A variation of this technique used by Baghaeian requires the bisqued piece to be dipped in a coloured glaze and allowed to dry. Then the piece brush decorated with liquid wax-emulsion resist before the entire surface is gently washed with a wet sponge to expose the bisqued surface. The pot is dipped again into another glaze after it has dried overnight for a similar fusion to take place in the kiln.

Painting with different coloured glazes that react and flow in different ways can produce some unusual colours and textures. Light colour applied over dark or dark on top of light, glossy over matt, matt over glossy provide obvious starting points for experiment. Results may range from subtle to spectacular depending on the respective glaze compositions. The del-icately coloured bowl by **Robin Hopper**

(Canada) displays textural variation within the freely painted glazes.

The beautiful, evocatively decorated vessels by **Soon Hyung Kwon** (Korea) demonstrate well his clear vision of form and surface. He explained that his work is focussed on a harmonious relationship between 'tradition and modern', and he emphasises 'the coexistence of abstract and non-abstraction' in trying to express his own experiences of life. He uses a title 'the natural phenomenon of the universe' in perfectly balanced, well finished, Korean white porcelain to describe his work. His pieces are clothed in a sumptuous white dolomite glaze with additions of colour from manganese, copper, cobalt and iron, fired to 1300°C (2372°F) in a gas kiln with an oxidising flame.

Freely painted brushwork in both lustres and underglaze stains is a strong feature of the work

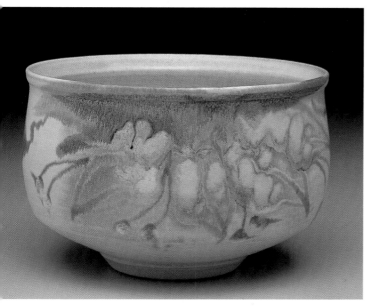

Squared deep bowl, *Clematis* series, by Robin Hopper (Can), 2002. Porcelain, multiple glaze application with brushwork, h. 12.5 cm (5 in.), w. 15 cm (6 in.). *Photograph by Janet Dwyer.*

Flying, by Soon Hyung, Kwon, (Korea), 2002. Wheel-thrown porcelain, painted with metallic pigments of copper, manganese, cobalt and iron oxides or carbonates, 27 x 26.5 cm (10 ⅝ x 10 ⅜ in.), fired to 1300°C (2372°F) in a gas kiln with an oxidising flame, dolomite glaze. *Photograph by the artist.*

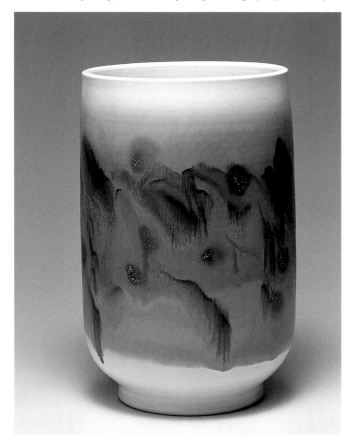

Red Mountain, wheel-thrown porcelain, painted with metallic pigments of copper, manganese, cobalt and iron oxides or carbonates, 37.5 x 22.5 cm (14 ¾ x 9 in.), fired to 1300°C (2372°F) in a gas kiln in oxidation, dolomite glaze, by Soon Hyung, Kwon, (Korea), 2002. *Photograph by the artist.*

by **Pippin Drysdale** from Western Australia. She lives in Perth which she describes as 'the most isolated city in the world – surrounded by desert and the Indian Ocean'. This feeling of isolation is reflected in her artistic endeavours giving it a regional identity. She states that all her life she has been surrounded by wide open land and seascapes and she has always been fascinated by contrasts of light, colour, space, texture and spirituality. Her work is directly inspired by her experience of that environment. She is noted particularly for her large, painterly platters which incorporate each of those elements expressed in terms of colour. All her pieces are individually made and decorated in wheel-thrown porcelain, bisqued to 1000°C (1832°F) and then painted with stains mixed in equal parts with frit 4712. Bentonite from the USA (3%) is added and the mixture is put first through a 150s and then a 200s mesh sieve to ensure even dispersal. The stains are applied in layers, hand-painted, sprayed and dipped on top of a white glaze using latex resist as a drawing agent. The base glaze has a wide firing range and contains tin oxide and

(Top) Porcelain bowl, *Russian* series, by Pippin Drysdale 1993. D. 20.5 cm (8 in.), h. 13 cm (5 ⅛ in.), wheel-thrown, with painted coloured stains on top of a white (tin/zirconium) glaze fired to 1200°C (2192°F) in an electric kiln, followed by lustre firings to 780°C (1436°F).

(Above) *Tanami Desert* series, large porcelain vessel, h. 37 cm (14 ½ in.), designed and decorated by Pippin Drysdale (Australia), wheel-thrown for her by Warrick Palmateer, 2002. *Photograph by Adrian Lambert (Acorn Photos).*

zirconium silicate with zinc oxide and barium carbonate. This is fired to Orton cone 4 or 5 (1180°–1200°C/2156°–2192°F) while lustres are

often applied for the third, fourth and, sometimes, fifth firings to Orton cone 016 (780°C/1436°F) on top of the painted and fired stains 'to add an extra skin which gives a rich dimension to the colours'.

Pippin Drysdale's painted designs are confident, bold and vigorously executed. Colours and shapes swirl over and around her pots as if in constant motion. She feels that the essence of her vessel forms is a 'solitary explanation of celebration' ... an embodiment of refreshed emotional response to my unique Western Australian environment, depicting subtle landforms and colours expressing light, skies, deserts, oceans and horizons'. She travelled extensively during the early 1990s to further widen her experience by working in a traditional Italian maiolica factory and teaching in Britain, Siberia and the United States. This provided her with the new influences, 'from Russian icon paintings to the flamboyance of Italian carnivals', which appeared in her work.

Drysdale's most recent work appears in a series of large vessel forms that were inspired by another intensely felt experience that started with a journey through the outback, over the Tanami Desert in northern Australia as a part of a recent Arts Council fellowship. She chose to produce this work in 'Southern Ice Porcelain' a body from Clayworks in Victoria. This is an expensive material but it has some wonderful properties that are discussed elsewhere in this book. All her large vessels are thrown for her by her assistant, Warrick Palmateer. He enjoys throwing with this plastic body although they encountered problems in drying and firing. Special cupboards were made so that the pots could dry very slowly and prevent distortion. Firing, also, required them to let the kiln become completely cold before opening because dunting (cracking) can occur when a considerable

(Right) *China Dolls*, handbuilt porcelain sculpture, 67 x 61 x 46 cm (26 ½ x 24 x 18 in.), by Rudy Autio (USA), 1984. *Photograph by the artist.*

thickness is left in the base. This causes a great deal of tension between top and bottom.

Rudy Autio (USA) enjoyed using some of the Arabia factory standard porcelain when he was in Helsinki, mainly because of its luminosity and hardness. After his return to the United States, he worked with it for a while, but (as in Finland) he found that it had a tendency to crack badly. Difficulties encountered in making large sculptures led him to believe that it was not the best material for handbuilding such pieces, some of which had a height of about 1.15 m (3.75 ft). Repairs with epoxy resin were less than satisfactory, since the filled cracks would yellow in time. He used nylon microfibres for strengthening the clay, plus porcelain grog, but this did not seem to solve the problem. This persuaded him to return to stoneware and intermediate temperature clay bodies that suited him better. He felt that the smooth, dry surface of porcelain was ideal for drawing, almost 'like parchment', and it provided an ideal surface for the application of colour.

Autio used nylon microfilament fibres (a small handful to 100 lb/45.4 kg) and a porcelain grog (Molochite) in his porcelain during the 1980s.

> As for the construction technique for all my clays, I used a combination of slabs and coils, but mainly slabs which are used much like a bricklayer lays bricks i.e., the edges are placed one on top of another in a circular course around the perimeter of the piece until the main body of the cylinder grows to the height I wish it to stand. Each edge upon edge is clawed together with the fingertips in a kind of gouging and joining process, then smoothed over with a hand tool like a pointing trowel or a steel edge of some kind. It's a fast handbuilding technique, a variation of pinching flattened coils together and it works quite well for me.

Painting with coloured slips enables the ceramicist to define precise areas with completely flat and opaque colour. They can be matt or shiny accord-

(Above) Porcelain bowl, by Ursula Scheid (Germany), 2002. Wheel-thrown, painted with vertical and diagonal stripes in black slip over tape resist, glazed, d. 16.6 cm (6 ½ in.). *Photograph by the artist.*

(Left) Vessel form, by Karl Scheid (Germany), 2002. Slab-built porcelain with coloured slip over tape resist, h. 30 cm (11 ¾ in.), reduction-fired to 1360°C (2480°F). *Photograph by the artist.*

ing to their composition. Normally, the same body provides the base material for making the slip but small additions of flux to this will encourage greater fusion and give the surface a sheen. Both **Karl** and **Ursula Scheid** (Germany) use slips on some of their porcelain vessels in conjunction with intricate, geometric designs made from arrangements of cut masking tape which articulates or

(Above) Porcelain bowl, by Johan Broekema (Holland), 2001. D. 12.5 cm (5 in.), with linear banding inlaid with black slip having 20% body stain added to the porcelain body and painted with coloured slips, sgraffito under a clear glaze composed of Potash Feldspar 24.5, Whiting 24, Magnesite 3, China Clay 19, Quartz 29.5, fired in a heavy reduction atmosphere to 1280°C (2336°F). *Photograph by the artist.*

(Right) Porcelain bottle, by Margaret Frith (UK), 2002. Ashed surface with blue celadon glaze and brushwork, h. 35 cm (13 ¾ in.). *Photograph by the artist.*

encircles and complements the forms with positive vertical and diagonal elements. The precise placement of the masking tapes is worked out directly on each unique piece before coloured slips are applied by painting. It is a fairly complex process. Finally, the slip decoration is covered by a transparent, matt glaze based on feldspar and barium, reduction fired to 1360°C (2480°F) in a gas kiln. The globular, swelling shapes of Ursula's bowls in particular seem as if they are stretching these patterns almost to bursting point, adding to their feeling of tension.

Coloured porcelain slips are used by **Johan Broekema** (Holland), painted on to contrast with the white body. Boldly cutting linear patterns through the coloured slip reveals the natural whiteness beneath. **Margaret Frith**

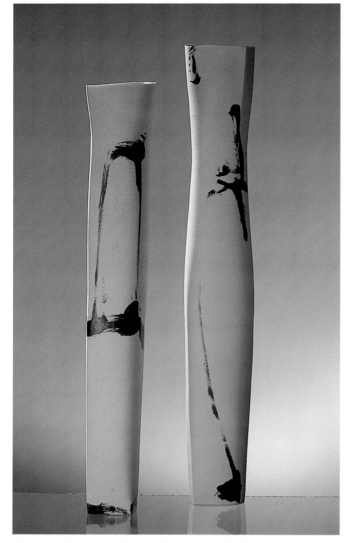

Two porcelain vessel forms, by Karin Bablok (Germany), 2002. Wheel-thrown and painted with basalt glaze, h. 58 cm (22 ¾ in.) and 62 cm (24 ½ in.), fired in reduction atmosphere 1280°–1300°C (2336°–2372°F). *Photograph by Joachim Riches.*

Claustrophobia, by Ilona Romule (Latvia), 1996. Limoges porcelain cup, gas-fired to 1400°C (2552°F) followed by china painting (790°C/1454°F), 9.5 x 12.5 x 8.5 cm (3 ¾ x 4 ⅞ x 3 ⅜ in.). *Photograph by Aigars Tukna.*

(UK) contrasts her traditional celadon glaze with a vertical area of wood ash glaze to support a dominant stripe of broad, black brushwork running from the neck to the base of her tall bottle, and the two tall, elegant vases by **Karin Bablok** (Germany) exhibit minimal but expressive linear marks in brush drawing with black basalt glaze on white porcelain. A much more precisely controlled, but equally eloquent, type of drawing can be seen in the onglaze, china painting by **Ilona Romule** (Poland) on the vessel form that she has entitled *Claustrophobia*.

Most of the artists in this book work completely independently. It is unusual to discover works jointly produced by two who come from very different backgrounds, but **Melissa Braden** (USA) and **Inguna Skuja** (Latvia) are two people who do cooperate fully in their enterprise. Melissa explained how they both visualise and produce their work as equal partners while enjoying the task of creating new shapes. They are attracted, particularly, to asymmetrical forms.

Our pieces are based on classical forms organically abstracted into new shapes. Then we want to push the shape further through the way in which we decorate the surface. As far as who does what: that is always the question and I think that most collaborative teams do indeed divide up the work according to individual talents. Usually in ceramics the husband and wife is the ultimate team with one person concentrating on the creation of the form and the other person concentrating on the surface

Lick, joint work by Melissa Braden (USA), and Inguna Skuja (Latvia). Slip-cast porcelain, inlaid with salts, high-fire and low-fire glazes, 30 x 30 x 5 cm (11 ¾.x 11 ¾ x 2 in.). *Photograph by Janis Banders.*

decoration. This is not how we work at all. Most other teams also tend to come from the same culture. We come from different countries, with different cultures, languages, historical and educational backgrounds. Inguna grew up in Communist Latvia and has a classical education rooted in traditionalism. On the other hand, I grew up in capitalist America, and have an education founded on Modernist or Post-Modernist ideologies. We work on everything together. We talk about our ideas and then we draw pictures for each other. We alter each other's drawings to see if we can not make the idea more perfect. Once we have both decided that the idea, the form and the design is a good concept we begin to build the forms. We make patterns from our drawings, and then coil build all of

our pieces. If we really like the form, we make a mould from it for slip-casting in porcelain. Usually, we make two pieces at a time and then continuously switch places to work on each other's forms. When people ask us who did what we cannot say because the boundaries of our individual marks have become blurred by the time each piece is actually completed. The ideas come out of conversations between Inguna and myself and are actually based on the breakdown between our collective understandings. In other words, we are fascinated by the difficulty in truly understanding one another's ideas and the point where we witness the vast distances created through miscommunication. Some of our most successful pieces are actually rooted in the space between understanding and misunderstanding.

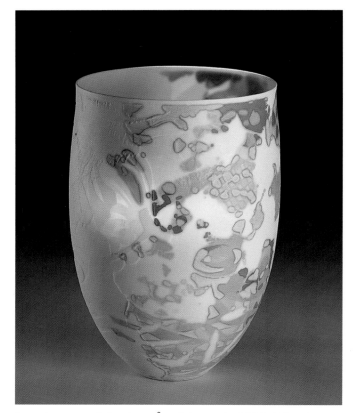

Porcelain vessel, by Arne Åse (Norway), 2000. Wheel-thrown and painted with metallic salts 'watercolour' technique, 22 x 15 cm (8 ⅝ x 5 ⅞ in.), unglazed, fired in reduction to 1250°C (2282°F). *Photograph by Glenn Hagebu.*

Two Lancet Forms, by Astrid Gerhartz (Germany), 1998. Porcelain, h. 19 cm (7 ½ in.) and 15 cm (6 in.).
Photograph by Helge Articus.

WATER-SOLUBLE COLOURANTS

One of the more unusual methods of applying colours to porcelain has been comprehensively explored by **Arne Åse** in Norway. His book, *Water Colour on Porcelain* (published in 1989 by the Norwegian University Press) deals with this in considerable detail. Rather than use the heavier pigments made from metallic oxides, Åse has conducted an enormous number of experiments with water-soluble colourants such as iron chloride, nickel chloride, ferrous sulphate, potassium dichromate and many others. He points out that most, if not all, of these materials are extremely poisonous and hazardous to health. They must be stored, handled and fired with great care. Åse compares the softer, gentler colours given by water-soluble metallic salts with effects achieved by using oxides and offers an

analogy with watercolour and oil paints. Certainly, the spectrum of colours developed by him is unusually delicate and distinctive. He expresses the view that 'ceramics is a pictorial art, artists relate to the world of visible phenomena from which they draw their inspiration and which governs their main modes of expression'. He refers to the changing role of contemporary ceramics and believes that the subject reveals evidence of 'a completely new branch of the fine arts on the verge of breaking through in all parts of the Western world'. He feels, as do I and many others, that ceramic art bears no direct relationship with traditional criteria of usefulness and function. Its more important purpose in a contemporary setting is the communication of thoughts, feelings and impressions through visual means.

Arne Åse has specialised in studying the effects of water-soluble colourants when used on unglazed porcelain fired to 1280°C (2336°F) in a reduction atmosphere. Concentrating his efforts in this way he has managed to produce a reliable palette of stable colours mixed in various solutions and combinations. Shellac is often used as a resist medium on his painted porcelain bowls. Sometimes, colourants are dissolved in glycerine or syrup to improve their workability. Occasionally, he combines phosphoric acid with the soluble salts or, possibly, a thickening agent may be added to the mixture to be painted under or over other colours. Solubles added to oxides extends the options even further so that the subtlety and range of colour effects appear to be infinite. This technique has been adopted by several ceramicists since publication of Åse's book, including two who are included in this book, Astrid Gerhartz and Les Blakebrough.

PRECIOUS METALS, LUSTRES AND ENAMELS

The most commonly used lustrous colours are those that are prepared and sold commercially. These metallic lustres are readily available in a wide range of iridescent colours made from bismuth, tin, silver, platinum, gold and copper all of which give brilliant, reflective surfaces on smooth shiny glazes. Matt glazes will also accept lustre painting but the effect is likely to be less dramatic. The precious metals must be dissolved in hydrochloric acid and the resulting chloride then mixed with sodium resinate suspended in oil. Since all the lustre colours appear brown and are difficult to distinguish until fired, some potters apply them separately using multiple firings for clearer control of colour relationships. They tend to thicken if kept for some time but they can be thinned with oil of lavender essence before painting. Soft-haired brushes are normally used to apply lustres and

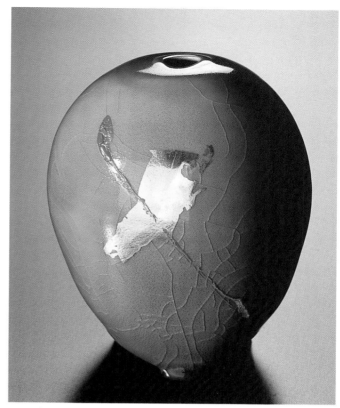

Tripod Vase, by Greg Daly (Australia), 2001. Wheel-thrown porcelain with gold and silver leaf and enamel over glaze, h. 23 cm (9 in.) fired to 1300°C (2372°F) followed by a lustre firing between 720°–800°C (1328°–1472°F) in electric kiln. *Photograph by the artist.*

they are best reserved solely for this purpose. Thorough cleaning is essential if they are to last for any length of time. Application is possible, also, by airbrush provided that it is carefully and frequently cleaned during and after use. The oil and resin components burn away in the electric kiln at around 750°C (1382°F) depositing a thin layer of metal on the glaze.

Greg Daly (Australia) is one potter who has developed an unusual and expressive technique using colour. Much of his work is an exploration of light and illusion with images which 'are abstractions of landscape and objects I have experienced in and around my environment'. Wheel-thrown plates, dishes, bowls and spherical forms with richly glowing glazes have long been a feature of his ceramics. Porcelain is a material perfectly suited to accept the high gloss glazes he favours. Clear and coloured

Tripod bowl, by Greg Daly (Australia), 2001. Wheel-thrown porcelain with enamel, gold and silver leaf over glaze, d. 28 cm (11 in.), fired in electric kiln to 1300°C (2372°F) followed by a lustre firing at 720°–800°C (1328°– 1472°F). *Photograph by the artist.*

glazes are used as the base or background for painted additions of lustres made from gold, cobalt, bismuth and zinc in different combinations. The addition of gold and silver leaf helps to enrich the surface imagery even further. Sometimes, linear patterns are etched into the coloured areas making a silky matt surface that acts as a foil for the lustres. Daly aims in this way to create illusions of colour and light that flow over the surface (drawing the viewer) into the depth of the glaze. The intensity of tones and colours changes when viewed from different angles and light sources.

Daly has had considerable experience of working with precious metals on ceramics and he says that he finds the application of gold and silver leaf is relatively simple to accomplish. The best results are usually produced when used on a glossy glaze but leaf can also be applied to ceramics for 'black firing' or on to a satin matt surface for different effects and with varying degrees of success. It is important to use the correct medium to attach the leaf because ordinary glues can leave surface scum on the glaze or a layer between the glaze and the leaf which prevents proper fusion taking place. The medium he uses is made from pine resin melted with a light oil such as lavender or eucalyptus with approximately 10 g (0.4 oz) of resin to 50–70 ml (1.8–2.5 fl.oz) of oil. This produces an oily, sticky medium that may also be used as a base for enamel painting. This medium is painted on to the surface to be decorated with the leaf which can then be manoeuvred into position quite easily to define a pattern. Daly recommends the use of high quality leaf and, in the case of gold, that it should be as pure as possible '22 ct at least'. When dry, a piece of paper is held over the leaf and light pressure applied to ensure consolidation with the ceramic surface.

Daly sometimes makes up his metallic lustres in a similar way to those used in conjunction with gold or silver leaf and these can be painted on together with enamels if required after applying the leaf and the whole is then fixed in the same firing. In some instances the leaf is placed on top of a previously fired lustre. Firing temperatures vary to allow for the different softening points of glazes used. Earthenware glazes soften at lower temperatures than stoneware or porcelain but generally the lustre and leaf firings are conducted between 720°–800°C (1328–1472°F).

Daly prepares his lustres by melting 10 g (0.4 oz) of pine resin and then adds metallic salts in the form of nitrates or acetates. For a 'mother of pearl' effect, he adds 3 g (0.1 oz) of bismuth nitrate and 2 g (0.07 oz) of zinc acetate by constantly stirring 'until the mixture takes on a glossy appearance, slowly adding lavender or eucalyptus oils (pure turpentine can also be used with the oils). Other lustre colours can be made in a similar way. Gold, in combination with other metals can give reds, pinks, blues and copper colours.' The lustrous coloured surface of these ceramics develops as the resin is burnt away *reducing* the constituent salts to a metallic state. This local reduction can take place in an electric kiln without causing damage to the elements but good ventilation should be ensured by leaving spy-holes open with the bungs out.

Another highly effective technique imaginatively used by Greg Daly is that of etching glazes with acid. An acid-etched surface provides an excellent foil for the lustre surface or a glossy glaze. In this case, more than one glaze may be used. If a solid lustre is applied over them, it will block out the underlying colour but etching through this reveals varying colours with a satin matt surface. Daly emphasises the attention he pays to safety when working with acids. Rubber gloves should always be worn and the process must be carried out in a well-ventilated area. 'The straight hydrofluoric acid is not very safe for this work but another form has bifluoride as an active ingredient. This may take a little longer to etch the surface but it is a little

safer to use.' The time needed for the acid to take effect depends upon the hardness of the glaze and the requirements of the design. Hot water is used to wash the piece and remove any wax resist followed by further washing with liquid soap to neutralise the acid and prevent any scumming from spoiling the surface.

Acid etching of ceramic glazes creates a surface which is very smooth to the touch and quite unlike anything achieved by sandblasting. Daly has discovered that 'the combination of different coloured glazes and finishes with lustres, gold and silver leaf, enamels and etched surfaces can lead to surface decoration which has great depth, illusion, colour, pattern and design. The exploration of these techniques releases the imagination through its countless subtle variations.'

Tony Laverick (UK) feels that every form he makes should be 'in equilibrium'. Between the rim, neck, shoulder, belly and foot of the pot there should be harmony and balance. He is

Round vase, by Tony Laverick (UK), 2001. Thrown and turned porcelain with metallic lustres, multiple firings, h. 25.5 cm (10 in.). *Photograph by Andrew Parr.*

not satisfied with a pot unless everything is in accord. The decoration of his pieces as well as the form has historical references, but the colours and textures are rendered in more muted tones giving a slightly more contemporary feel. There is a constant play between three-dimensional volume and a two-dimensional illusion of space. The overall effect of this surface pattern/form integration is one of visual stimulation and excitement. The eye is encouraged to explore the pot through shades of contrasting colours, squares, triangles, and lines, both straight and curved, richly coloured by metallic lustres and iridescence.

> There is playfulness in my work. Shapes jump out and recede, they intertwine, seemingly flat shapes become dimensional, straight lines become curved. I like to think that my pots are a melding of classical, cultural and contemporary influences. I have never thought of my work in Post-Modern terms but I suppose in many ways it fits the definition. My pots are based on traditional forms and engage in certain cultural appropriations in shape, design and decoration. My work is not Post-Modern in that I am not making any statements, conceptual, intellectual or social. There is no meaning or hidden metaphor in my work. I am committed to the idea of pure beauty. When it is finished the pot should be exquisitely beautiful.

Laverick's work is made from a porcelain body (Audrey Blackman from Valentine Clay) and fired, firstly, to between 1270°–1280°C (2318°–2336°F) with coloured glazes. Subsequent firings are carried out with lustres to 750°C (1382°F). Often, there are three or four lustre firings following the initial glaze fire in order to obtain subtle depths within the overlaid colours. Occasionally, also tin chloride and ferric chloride are used. Most of the colours achieved are the result of gold pigments and gold, thinned out with turpentine or special gold thinners, applied over other colours. Selected areas are masked with insulating tapes or latex

Porcelain dish, by Tony Laverick (UK), 2001. Thrown and decorated with metallic lustres, multiple firings, d. 41 cm (16 in.). *Photograph by Andrew Parr.*

masking fluid to protect underlying sections. Sometimes he makes and uses rubber stamps to apply patterns and textures. Different areas are quickly painted or stippled on with a brush or sponge. He never sprays the lustres as it is too hazardous.

I have discussed the painted lustres of **Geoffrey Swindell** (UK) at some length in my previous books and, although his many commitments in other areas have greatly reduced the amount of time he is able to devote to his own creative ceramics, the answers he gave in response to my questions precisely echo those of so many ceramists who choose to work in porcelain. Like Arne Åse, Swindell is not concerned with functional applications in the way that a teapot, for example, might be used for making and serving tea. 'But there are practical considerations like fired strength, stability and durability. However, the main function I aim for is that the 'presence' of the form should affect the

(Top) *Porcelain Object No. 3*, by Geoffrey Swindell (UK), 2002. H. 12 cm (4 ¾ in.), wheel-thrown and altered.
Photograph by the artist.
(Above) *Porcelain Object No. 4*, by Geoffrey Swindell (UK), 2002. H. 10 cm (4 in.), wheel-thrown and altered.
Photograph by the artist.

senses and give pleasure by its beauty as do many natural objects.' He admits that, for him, the nature of the materials used in his work have

a profound effect on the finished image. Combined with the techniques and the concept they are 'inseparable' elements in any good work of art or craft. Swindell says that the whiteness of porcelain gives him a perfect ground as it does not interfere with the purity of applied colours. He likes to make 'well-engineered, precise forms – almost mechanical – and then soften the appearance with a more "organic" quality of surface' with glazes that are textured with marbled lustres. It is through this image of 'precision and looseness that he attempts to communicate his interests in other objects that he collects, thus presenting a synthesis' of both man-made and natural qualities.

For much of his earlier work, Swindell evolved a technique whereby he painted commercially-prepared lustres on to glazed pots and then broke the surface tension of the medium with solvents such as paraffin or detergents brushed or sprayed selectively on to it. This action causes the lustres to retreat away from the solvent spot or line with a halo of concentrated colour around the edge. Further colours can be added and the piece might be fired several times with successive treatments until the visual texture and colour fully fits and complements the form. The technique was illustrated fully in *Studio Porcelain* (1980). This process is still used for some of his pieces but the effects have been developed further. He continues to work on a small scale but, more recently, these miniature objects sport visually variegated textures and, occasionally, extrusions bursting through or from the surface. Glazes applied in layers by spraying or brushing are adjusted by dropping spots of detergent into them while still wet in order to break the surface tension to create unusual textural effects. He describes his sources of inspiration and reasons for working with porcelain as follows:

I prefer to work on a very small scale developing groups of related vessels. I am inspired by a wide variety of visual sources including illustrations of marine creatures and science fiction hardware, fossils, tin plate toys and objects eroded by sea and time found on the beaches of South Wales. By extracting or abstracting essential visual and tactile qualities from these sources and investing them into my own work I try to create an intriguing vessel that reflects my fascination with this source material.

I use the egg or bud shape repeatedly because it suggests birth or growth. Sometimes these forms are not perfect, they can be scarred and eroded as if by natural forces, suggesting the vulnerability of all life forms which can be affected by environmental conditions and the power of nature to create, destroy and recreate. I hope to make ceramics that give pleasure to other people, paralleling my own delight in finding a strange object on the beach or a curious image in a book. The images and forms I work with require the fine texture and whiteness available with porcelain bodies. The body needs to be high-fired to give physical strength to the very lightweight, thinly walled structure of each piece. The lightness of the form creates a feeling of delicacy and preciousness similar to a seashell. Translucency is also produced, but this is irrelevant because most forms have openings too narrow to allow visual access to the interior. The whiteness of porcelain gives a good ground for the application of glazes without affecting the colours unlike a normal stoneware body. The porcelain body is smooth and characterless allowing me to control or impose my own texture upon it.

Gold, silver and platinum lustres are very expensive items in the potter's palette. Therefore, the traditional and more familiar use of precious metals in ceramics is to apply them sparingly as banding or outlining or to highlight details of the design. **Mary White** (Germany) makes good use of her training in calligraphy to paint gold lettering on some of her porcelain bowls and pots. Her calligraphic script is fluently executed encircling the forms as a full

Porcelain bowl, by Mary White (Germany). Wheel-thrown, decorated with brush-painted lettering, d. 28 cm (11 in.), fired to 1250°C (2282°F) in an electric kiln. *Photograph by the artist.*

Porcelain bowl decorated with enamels, by Marianne Cole (Australia), 2002. These small bowls, d. 14 cm (5 ½ in.), are thrown 'off the hump'. After bisque firing to 1000°C (1832°F), a shiny black glaze is applied and fired to 1240°C (2264°F) in an electric kiln. The design was drawn in gold lustre using a small 'batik' type pen. The powdered enamels were mixed with a grinding oil to a consistency of toothpaste before the painting process begins. This is followed by another firing to cone 017 which fuses the enamel into the glaze. *Photograph by Kulvanek.*

integrated part of the design.

Marianne Cole (Australia) makes vases, bowls and dishes, elaborately decorated with gold lustre and coloured enamels. Some of these are inspired by aboriginal painting and the Australian Outback. She describes her work as 'an ongoing experiment with ideas derived from many sources, in particular, the vast ceramic legacy left to us from ancient cultures'. Extensive foreign travel has enabled her to see such works in their environmental and cultural contexts. She feels that

their 'physical presence exudes an aura reflecting each culture's passion for form and decoration and these influences are in tune with her own 'unabashed zest for rich and complex surfaces'.

The painted decoration on top of a shiny, black glaze which has been fired to 1280°C (2336°F) in an electric kiln is undertaken in a dust-free room. It is a lengthy process, using commercial enamels and liquid bright gold. A special pen (a miniature version of a batik pen) is used to draw the network of fine gold lines. Gold

Porcelain bowl, by Mary Rich (UK), 2002. Gold lustre painted over coloured glaze. *Photograph by Simon Cook.*

'thinners' were added to allow the liquid gold to flow freely. 'It is a precise process requiring a steady hand, good light and good eyesight.' Although she has a *general* concept in mind when she begins decorating, the design actually develops on the bowl as she works.

Mary Rich (UK) prefers to cover her porcelain vessel forms with underglaze stains and coloured slips to provide a dark ground which is then fired with a clear, satin matt glaze prior to painting her intricate, decorative designs in gold lustre. Much of her work is small in scale from jewel-like, miniature bottles and bowls to cane-handled teapots, banded and cross-hatched with fine gold lines to make complicated, geometric patterns. Similarly involved patterning features in the work of **Russell Coates** (UK). Having won a scholarship to study ceramics in Japan, he spent a fruitful period during the 1980s learning about the art of underglaze blue painting and enamelling on porcelain (Kutani ware). His work remains strongly influenced by that experience and it still demands very careful planning and rigorous preparation.

Designs are worked out in detail on paper first and then transferred on to his dishes using tissue paper and charcoal. Colours are chosen as the work progresses.

Coates likes porcelain, especially for throwing. One of the bodies he uses is a natural porcelain from Japan similar to that first found at Arita where Imari ware is made. He says that the use of this clay 'tends to shift the emphasis away from translucency' (a quality which has been so important in Western porcelain), due to its iron content. He bisque fires between 800°C (1472°F) and 1000°C (1832°F) and then outlines his patterns in underglaze blue which is eventually covered with a clear, white glaze and fired again to Orton cone 9 (1270°C/2318°F) in a reducing atmosphere. (The plates and bowls are supported on setters in the gas kiln.) Further decoration is accomplished with five enamel colours, red, yellow, green, blue and purple, underpainted with black. Burnished gold may be included also and the final firing is taken to a temperature of 830°C (1526°F). Stylised birds, animals, fish, dolphins or plants encircle the rims in many of his decorative plates, surrounding an elaborate centrepiece reminiscent of Celtic designs. Describing his choice of subject matter for his painted designs, Coates says:

> Dolphins are liked by all and they introduce environmental and conservation themes. Creatures and plants look well painted in enamels which can be too hard and shiny for purely abstract or geometric patterns. In the last few years, I have been inspired by Cretan, Celtic, Anglo-Saxon and Mediaeval themes. Unfortunately, they take a long time to do.

He explains that the lengthiest part of the making process is the enamel painting on the fired glaze, at a point 'where the work of most potters has finished'. Coates admits that enamelled porcelain may have a limited appeal. 'It seems that although many people have heard of Imari ware, few potters even know much about "Kakiemon"

or "Dovetailed Colours" which are the roots of the tradition that I studied in Japan.' He feels it is unfortunate that 'the level of boredom bequeathed by Western transfer printed enamels is such that most potters lose interest at mention of the word'. Some of his detailed designs in painted enamels have been selected and adapted for a limited edition of porcelain vessels by the Spode factory in England. 'The Spode factory residency was part of the Year of the Artist 2000 project and I worked in "The Meadow" (the Spode design workshop) for five weeks. It is a truly astonishing factory in 18th century buildings. They have produced four limited edition pieces of my work and some derivative ones.'

Frederick Olsen (USA) worked with the Japanese masters Tomimoto Kenkichi and Kondo Yuzo in the 1960s where he was instructed in throwing and enamelling techniques. Tomimoto had advised him not to attempt porcelain for at least 15 years.

(Above) Porcelain dish, by Russell Coates (UK), 2000. Painted with enamels depicting deer, ibex, hare, fox and leopard, d. 44 cm (17 ¼ in.). *Photograph by Peter Lowry.*

Porcelain vessel, by Frederick Olsen (USA), 2002. Blue and green slip with inlaid blue lines, transparent glaze, cone 10 in reduction, followed by overglaze yellow (to cone 1) and red enamel (to cone 018). *Photograph by the artist.*

Porcelain lidded boxes, by Frederick Olsen (USA), 2002. Blue slip inlaid when leatherhard, cobalt oxide wash on the bisque, transparent glaze to cone 10 in reduction, overglaze enamels fired to cone 018. *Photograph by the artist.*

I took his advice and began working in porcelain again in 1983 (20 years later) and I was grateful for this because my own pattern and style emerged without being influenced from the years with them. I use Tomimoto's red enamel recipe for my yellow glaze fired to cone 01. This was a secret I learned about Hajime Kato yellow porcelain vases from remembering what Tomimoto had once said to me years ago when I overfired the red enamel. The enamel at cone 01 makes a beautiful non-grazing over-glaze on the non-graze porcelain glaze I use.

My scotch cups are porcelain fired in my anagama-style kiln. I use a shino style glaze that has been modified from a shino recipe by Fergus Stewart: (parts by weight) nepheline syenite 15, kaolin 5, salt 1, local clay (desert surface clay) 1, tin oxide 1. Thin is for flashing and thick is for white and, perhaps, crawling. My scotch cups are not tea bowls, because the Japanese would always find some fault with the way I do them, therefore as an expert in drinking scotch, I make scotch cups. A more versatile cup.

Olsen's patterns are all derived from his immediate environment in the high desert which abounds in animal and plant images. Rocks and surrounding mountains form the background with a touch of surrealism. The forms have developed from his interest in collecting pre-Columbian pottery.

There still is an appreciative audience for highly patterned wares at the time of writing but such detailed painting requires very thorough planning and great discipline in its execution. **Peter Minko** is an Australian potter who gained much of his inspiration from the wealth and variety of natural flora in the surrounding bush. Concentrating on fairly simple vessel forms, he has embellished them with an exotic range of richly coloured patterns. Each piece is wheel-thrown in a fine porcelain body and burnished at the leatherhard state to ensure the surface is smoothly compacted. Bisque fired to 920°C (1688°F) they are then individually painted with finely ground pigments (predominantly metallic oxides) and fired twice more to between 1280°–1300°C (2336°–2372°F) in oxidation to fuse the colours on the unglazed surface. Only the inside surfaces are glazed. Those pieces with gold lustre applied in parts are fired again to 760°C (1400°F). Minko says that he chose to work with this particular porcelain and technique because it was the only way in which he could

Goldfields 2, by Peter Minko (Australia), 1992. Porcelain plate, d. 30.6 cm (12 in.), wheel-thrown and burnished at the leatherhard stage. Bisque fired to 920°C (1688°F) and then individually hand-painted with finely ground pigments (mainly metallic oxides). Two firings up to 1280°–1300°C (2336°–2372°F) in oxidation conditions fuse the colours with the unglazed porcelain surface. Gold lustre is applied in a further firing to 760°C (1400°F).

obtain the kind of finish to display his detailed painting with complete clarity.

As with so many of the potters I have met, **Gordon Cooke** (UK) uses porcelain for its whiteness and close grain, and the opportunities offered by this property to work in very fine detail. One of his more unusual methods for manipulating surface texture was fully described in *Studio Porcelain* but his latest work is rather different in character and treatment. He aims to create a unity between form, surface and colour. He says that he is

motivated by many things ('not least the necessity to pay the mortgage!') but he thinks that it is the endless permutations that are possible in arrangements of texture, pattern and colours that appeals to him most of all. He especially likes the 'secretive nature of boxes and the element of surprise when the lid is lifted to reveal inner decoration'. His present work is influenced by African fabric patterns, natural form and the paintings of Gustav Klimt and Friedrich Hundertwasser. He is also fascinated by certain architectural details which he records

Porcelain form, by Gordon Cooke (UK), 1999. Carved and stamped slabs, with on-glaze lustres, h. 16 cm (6 ¼ in.), w. 95 cm (37 ¼ in.), gas fired to cone 8. *Photograph by the artist.*

Porcelain pot, by Gordon Cooke (UK), 2001. H. 8.5 cm (3 ¼ in.), d. 4.5 cm (1¾ in.), with on-glaze lustres, gas fired to cone 8. *Photograph by the artist.*

constantly in drawings and photographs. His pots are fired to a high bisque at cone 8. An earthenware glaze fired to 1100°C (2012°F) is applied to those areas which he wants to shine. Onglaze lustres are painted on to this as well as on some unglazed sections adding extra visual interest.

My ongoing work in porcelain is inspired by various observations. These are realised in forms which sit within the technical constraints of the medium. The main limitation is one of scale, although small objects in porcelain have a precious quality which can be enhanced by the use of onglaze lustres.

Some years ago, I went to Japan and a series of work was stimulated by the formality with which they treat natural materials. One specific example is their fence panels. These are woven meticulously into intricate patterns; very formal and regular, but offset by the random interruptions of the organic material.

Observations of things from outside are not always necessary. Sometimes, the process of making can start an idea for a piece of work or a series.

Recent work has been based on landscape views observed from flights over Bulgaria. I was interested in the effect which the physical elements in the landscape have had on the formal way the land has been divided up for agriculture. No photographs were taken of these views, but the seed of the idea has given an impetus to a whole range of work in porcelain and stoneware. The ability of porcelain to accept fine detail and to show the tiniest of marks has been exploited in these small works. Because of the flat, graphic nature of the idea, these works have been realised mainly in the form of panels, which are sometimes framed, either in metal, wood or ceramic, or left unframed. Some boxes have also been based on this idea.

Maps and plans have been a source of ideas for some time.

Again working within, or on the boundary of, the technical constraints of this beautiful but often frustrating medium, forms, and surfaces are sometimes based on an amalgam of collected and remembered imagery.

old Mine, by Philip Cornelius (USA), 1998. Porcelain with gold
stre, 25.5 x 25.5 x 7.5 cm (10 x 10 x 3 in.). *Photograph by the artist.*

Around You, by Ilona Romule (Latvia), 2002. English bone
china bowl, slip-cast, fired to 1235°C (2255°F) followed
by china painting and gold lustre to 790°C (1454°F), 18 x
35 x 28 cm (7 x 13 ¾ x 11 in.). *Photograph by the artist.*

Two Religious Birds, by Philip Cornelius (USA), 1999.
Porcelain form with painting in black and white, 25.5 x
25.5 x 25.5 cm (10 x 10 x 10 in.). *Photograph by the artist.*

PRINTED DECORATION

Ceramic transfers and printing methods have
long been used in decorating pots for mass
consumption but it is an aspect that has
received only scant attention from studio
potters. However, the techniques do present
opportunities for painting or printing extremely
detailed designs on to porcelain either in the
leatherhard and the bisque state or on top of
glaze. **Paul Scott** (UK) is one who has exploited
this method on both tile panels and vessel
forms. He uses a photocopier to make
transparencies of drawings which he intends to
reproduce as a ceramic print and then transfers
this image on to a silk screen coated with a light
sensitive film. The silk screen, with its light
sensitive face, is placed down on to the
transparency drawing and exposed to light from
a mercury vapour lamp for about five minutes,
making a contact print to fix the image. Then
the screen is washed out with warm water to
remove the areas not fixed by the exposure, i.e.

The Scott Collection, Cumbrian Blue(s): *Chapel Cross No: 3*, by Paul Scott (UK), 2001. In-glaze screen-print decal, collage on Royal Worcester bone china platter, platinum border, w. 38 cm (15 in.), l. 45 cm (17 ¾ in.) *Photograph by Andrew Morris.*

Scott's Cumbrian Blue(s) 2000, by Paul Scott (UK), 2000. Screen-printed decal collage and gold on Royal Worcester bone china plate, d. 25 cm (9 ⁷⁄₈ in.). *Photograph by Andrew Morris.*

the drawn images, and checked to ensure that the mesh is cleared of gel ready for printing. Screens made in this way can be used for printing directly on to tiles and slabs (Scott prefers to print on porcelain when the clay is becoming leatherhard) or for producing ceramic transfers for use on glazed pieces.

For printing underglazes on unfired clay, Scott mixes an 'ink' consisting of 10 parts of stain with 5 parts of powdered porcelain body (finely sieved) to 10 parts of a water-based print medium using a palette knife to blend the material thoroughly on a flat glass plate. The mixture is thinned slightly to increase its volume with the addition of between 5 and 10 parts of a textile printing medium. He points out that the consistency of the prepared 'ink' is critical to printing successfully but this can only be judged through a process of trial and error. Finally, the 'ink' is forced through the mesh of the silk screen and printed on to the leatherhard tiles. Powdered glaze replaces the clay for making transfers and this is mixed with an oil-based medium and

printed on to decal paper, a special paper coated with gum. When the printed images have dried, they are covered with a layer of transparent solvent-based resin applied through a blank silk screen. The transfers can be cut up when the 'covercoat' is dry. Soaking them in warm water allows the transfers to float off the paper ready for immediate application to glazed ware. Detailing his processes in an article written for *Ceramic Review* No. 140, Scott places great emphasis on safety when handling these materials. 'If you do make ceramic transfers, ensure that you get safety datasheets on the oil-based medium and the covercoat. Use good ventilation at all times, and store products safely.'

I use porcelain and bone china in two different ways. Firstly, for commissioned tiled work, I make panels where tile shape is integral to the overall design of the work. Here Harry Fraser Porcelain forms the backdrop upon which I collage, paint and print. Painting with underglaze colours takes place on bisque ware, printed elements (screen-printed decals or laser prints) are applied on top of the fired glaze tile, which is then refired to glaze maturation temperature ... the print then sinks into the glaze.

Secondly, I work increasingly on ready-mades, often porcelain and bone china ware bought from industrial ceramic manufacturers like Spode and Royal Copenhagen. Sometimes I use old plates. As with the tile work, I am primarily interested in the surface of the object, but I am also concerned with the historical and cultural connections created by the plate form. I use screen-printed decals to collage and compose, engaging with the commemorative traditions of printed ceramics. I am interested in the way composition, and time, have changed the meanings of landscape and narrative in the decorative surface of industrial produced ware. My engagement with printed blue and white provides me with a contemporary visual language. The historic roles of porcelain and bone china as prestigious ceramic materials are as important as the quality of printed image achieved on these surfaces.

Sylvia Hyman (USA) has been making sculptural arrangements of unpainted white porcelain 'documents, scrolls, diplomas', etc. for many years. These were displayed in stoneware boxes and baskets but it was only recently that she thought to try silk-screen printing. Initially, she intended only to use silk-screen printing on porcelain 'letters', 'envelopes' and 'cards' and following some instruction from Rimas VisGirda, she made a couple of small screens. But she discovered that the process of making the screens was too time-consuming, so she found a local company that could make her screens very cheaply. The first screens they made for her were taken from sheet music and then others were produced from some printed texts. The screens were very satisfactory but she realised that she was completely inexperienced in the process of actually printing on to porcelain.

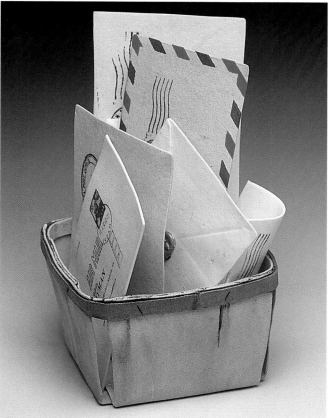

(Top) *Bark Ark with Scrolls*, by Sylvia Hyman (USA), 2002. Porcelain transfer-printed from *Genesis* and in four languages, in stoneware container, 33 x 37 x 28 cm (13 x 14½ x 11 in.).
(Above) *Berry Basket with Letters*, by Sylvia Hyman, 2002. Transfer-printed porcelain in stoneware basket, (8 x 15 x 15 cm (3 ¼ x 6 x 6 in.). *Photographs by John Cummins.*

It took quite a bit of experimentation to come up with a good printing 'ink'. After reading lots of information about engobes for printing and having difficulty with clogging screens as well as problems with faded looking print after firing, I developed a very simple 'ink' by just combining glaze stain with Speedball water-soluble Transparent Extender Base, which I believe can be purchased at any art supply store. I stir them together thoroughly to disperse the stain through the extender. I have never measured the proportion so I can't give you an exact amount. So far, I've only used black but I am thinking about trying other colours.

Several thin sheets of porcelain are rolled out and cut to the size she requires. Placing the silk screen on top of one of the clay sheets, the ink is forced through its fine mesh and onto the clay surface using a squeegee. Then, the sheet of plastic porcelain is quickly flipped over and rolled up around a coil of newspaper, taking great care not to smear the ink. She proceeds to print the other sheets of clay that have been cut to size and covered with plastic to keep them moist and, usually, manages to complete six similar scrolls during a printing session.

Maria Geszler-Garzuly (Hungary) is another artist who uses screen-printed imagery extensively in her work. She makes large porcelain objects that are fired in a wood-burning kiln taking between 14–20 hours to reach 1300–1320°C (2372°–2408°F) and three days to cool down. She had no instruction or, even, access to appropriate published information on firing big porcelain pieces without the protection of a saggar. Therefore, she was forced to experiment with several types of kiln until success, suffering many disappointments through breakages and much frustration in the process. She now has a 1200 litres kiln that can be sensitively controlled throughout the firing. Deeply

Volklinger Gesha, by Maria Geszler-Garzuly (Hungary), 2000. Porcelain plaque, screen-printed and salt-fired in a wood-burning kiln to 1300°C (2372°F), 72 x 29 x 3 cm (28 ¼ x 11 x 1 in.). *Photograph by the artist.*

affected by her environment, she observes and captures the most minute detail around her to both reflect and commentate upon many aspects of modern life. When Maria had graduated from the College of Applied Art in Budapest she started working as a designer in a run-down ceramics factory. 'I began to feel the smoke of the freezing towers, the lines of broken windows, the conveyor belts, women workers with their varicose legs, electricity pylons, the crane cemetery and the loneliness of the huge, badly lit production halls. Telegraph poles, aeroplanes in a sky coloured red with

Köningen der Industrie, by Maria Geszler-Garzuly, (Hungary). Porcelain wall plaque, screen-printed, wood-fired kiln, salt-glazed to cone 10 (1300°C/2372°F), 88 x 37 x 3 cm (34 ½ x 14 ½ x 1 ¼ in.). *Photograph by the artist.*

poisonous gases. I felt both wonder and dismay.' She began taking photographs and transferring the images to silk screens for printing on porcelain that she folded, crumpled and manipulated so that they moved with the form. Porcelain has an ideal surface for printing her astonishing line drawings. She refers to the multitude of linear patterns/writing) that surround us, 'the vee formation of flocking birds, tree branches against the sky, hands touching … footmarks in the earth, trains writing railway lines, factory chimneys breathing smoke. I write my life in clay.'

AIR-BRUSHING

The airbrush is a wonderfully versatile tool. There are many different types available from which to choose one best-suited to the work in hand. The most basic models provide a constant spray pattern but far greater control is obtained with those having a trigger action. The latter model can produce an infinitely variable spray from very thin lines to the coverage of broad areas and with textures anywhere between coarse and fine. Passing ceramic materials at quite high pressure through these instruments does have a more abrasive effect than when used with inks etc. and they require careful maintenance. It is necessary also to keep them meticulously clean while the work is in progress as well as after work is finished for they can easily clog up with compacted pigments, slips, lustres or glazes which stop them functioning correctly. Perhaps the most annoying and frustrating thing that can happen when pigment accumulates around the needle or when solid particles build up within the nozzle, is the sudden splattering of uncontrolled colour. This will most often occur, in my experience, when I have become so absorbed in the more expressive design aspects that I have neglected this elementary precaution and am approaching the final stage of the work! Since the main attraction of airbrushed colour is the smooth graduations that can be achieved, unintentional splatters or blobs will destroy the effect and illusion for which one aims.

I take the precaution of putting all my stains, whether commercially-prepared or mixed myself with an underglaze medium, through a 200s mesh cup sieve to ensure even dispersal with no lumps. The airbrush is dismantled and thoroughly cleaned after each session. While the work is in progress, also, clean water is frequently passed through the instrument so that no build up of hardened

(Left) *Mountain Sky: Evening*, by Peter Lane (UK), 2002. Wheel-thrown porcelain vessel with airbrushed ceramic stains over paper resist, fired to 1280°C (2336°F) in an electric kiln, h. 18 cm (7 in.). *Photograph by the artist.*
(Right) *Radial Light*, by Peter Lane (UK), 2000. Porcelain bowl, wheel-thrown and airbrushed with ceramic stains over tape resist, d. 30 cm 11 ¾ in.) fired to 1280°C (2336°F) in an electric kiln. *Photograph by the artist.*

material is allowed to impede the free flow of colour. The nozzle cap must be regularly removed and the aperture checked for the same reason. Great care is necessary during this procedure because the needle point is so fine that it can be easily damaged. A bent needle will affect the performance of the airbrush quite badly and delicate work will be ruined by uneven splattering of colour. It is advisable to always keep a spare needle handy as a replacement. A bent needle can sometimes be repaired by gently rotating the point against a smooth board in a stroking movement.

Underglaze stains are well-suited to airbrushing on to porcelain at any stage from dry to bisque or over unfired glaze. Bright coloured stains that will withstand high temperatures and remain close to their appearance when first applied have become readily available over recent years. Colours and patterns can be applied freehand but, more frequently, masks of one kind or another are used to control the exact placement of the medium. Hand-held shapes cut from paper or card are simple masks to use. They can be over-sprayed repeatedly as they are moved about the surface to build up multiple marks having a distinctive quality. Rich visual textures and tonal variations are thus possible with economy of means, provided that the mask does not become too wet so that the medium runs off and mars the design. Similarly, fixed masks made from paper tapes or other material must be dried out between successive applications if bleeding of one colour into another at the edges is to be avoided.

Masking tape of the kind used in the automobile industry and for protecting window glass when the frames are painted is ideal for use with an airbrush and I, and many other potters, have used it extensively. It can be purchased in different widths which can be cut and reshaped to suit most aims. Some brands are slightly less adhesive than others and this is an undoubted advantage when applying tape to areas previously sprayed with underglaze stains so that another colour can be added. Coloured stains are best prepared with a good binding medium which fixes the colour firmly to the pot and prevents smudging. A number of excellent underglazes mixed with a suitable medium are commercially available for this purpose. My own preference is to work directly on bisqued ware (previously sanded smooth) by airbrushing the lightest colours first and to proceed with progressively darker colours until finally, perhaps, black is reached. This may mean that the piece is almost completely covered with tape, obscuring the design, until peeled away. I use a hot air gun to dry the colours and stop the tape from becoming saturated to overflowing with liquid medium when building up complex patterns with tapes. (Tapes made from any kind of plastics must be used with discretion because they quickly become too wet. They have the added disadvantage that they will shrink under excessive heat and so cannot be force dried.) With care, the colour remains clear and unblemished when, eventually, the tape is removed. Working in this way from light to dark rather than the reverse process avoids the problems encountered when removing a tape that leaves a residue of adhesive on an area still to be over-sprayed.

Unless masks of one kind or another are

Porcelain bowl, by Peter Lane (UK), 2000. Wheel-thrown, with carved and pierced rim, green crackle glaze, d. 26 cm (10 ¼ in.), fired to 1280°C (2336°F) in an electric kiln. *Photograph by the artist.*

used with the airbrush, the spray pattern will always produce a soft edge even when the needle is set at the smallest aperture. This can be turned to advantage by combining soft and hard edges within the overall design. Colours can be merged gradually into one another so that the hues alter in the transition. Underglaze stains also offer the added convenience of remaining fairly true to their unfired colour when applied to pure white porcelain. It is easier, therefore, to assess the success or otherwise of the surface design before committing it to the kiln.

Slips and glazes are less amenable to airbrushing, although not impossible to use successfully, due to their nature and larger particle size. They tend to take longer to dry naturally. The hot air gun speeds this process but glazes usually remain friable to some extent and liable to disturbance while handling. Handheld masks are more appropriate in this case since tapes cannot be applied to unfired glaze. Resin-based lustres can also be used to good effect providing that the airbrush is thoroughly cleaned between each application of colour.

Clear glazes over stains make the colours appear brighter but many people find that a glossy, reflective surface lessens the visual impact while matt glazes tend to mute the colours. High-fired porcelain, therefore, is frequently left unglazed. Instead, pieces are polished smooth at several stages in the making process. Rubbing down any slight irregularities that appear after bisque firing can be done with a fine grade of sandpaper (I use a zinc-based type) and the surface is sponged clean of dust so that airbrushing can begin. (Sandra Black prefers to polish her porcelain bisque, after soaking it in water to avoid the usual build up of dust, by using firstly a 300 grade of wet and dry sandpaper and then the finer 600 grade.) Following the final firing to 1220°C (2228°F) or above, the work is thoroughly polished with a very fine grade of silicon carbide paper, 'Wet 'n Dry'. This action removes any hard particles which may have emerged as the clay contracted further in the kiln, spoiling the smooth surface.

Landscape and the ever changing colours and patterns of skies has provided me with much inspiration for my own work. Porcelain, with its fine texture, purity and whiteness, allows me to explore relationships between form and surface in a way that is more rewarding than with any other clay. For me, wheel-thrown vessel forms offer infinite opportunities for subtle variations, but my particular concern, while attempting to achieve harmony and balance in the work, is to express my feelings for the natural world through the positive radiation of light and colour. Skies, sea and landscapes, together with the multitude of flora, are a constant source of wonder, inspiration and delight to me.

I have always loved mountains since my wife first introduced me to the English Lake District when we were students at Bath Academy of Art in the mid-1950s. When we each decided to stop teaching in order to concentrate more fully on our own creative work (ceramics and textiles respectively) we went to live in Cumbria for four years. We were able to indulge ourselves in fell-walking, drawing, painting, photographing, enjoying the constantly changing effects of colours, light and shade in landscape and skies. Our house, high on a hillside overlooking Esthwaite Water and the village of Hawkshead, had expansive views of mountains. My airbrush painting on vessel forms is an attempt to capture some of that wonderful, atmospheric quality observed in successive layers of mountain ranges beneath skies at different seasons or times of day. I have experienced and photographed the Rocky Mountains in Canada and the USA also, as well as other magnificent mountain scenery in Europe and New Zealand.

Similarly, having lived all my life in the countryside, the structure and patterns of trees and plants were essential elements in much of my earlier carved and pierced porcelain vessels. Other source material comes from exotic flora I have seen in Queensland and other parts of Australia and New Zealand.

INCISING, CARVING AND PIERCING

Thrown and rolled or press-moulded porcelain offers an ideal surface for cutting into or incising. My earlier carved and/or pierced porcelain vessels evolved in response to nature observed in the form of plants, trees, the movement of water and other phenomena. The surface treatments involving carving, incising

(Above) *Blue and White Dyad*, by Marc Leuthold (USA), 2002. Unglazed coloured porcelain, deeply carved, 53 x 71 x 10 cm (21 x 28 x 4 in.). *Photograph by Eva Heyd.* (Opposite) Wood-fired porcelain vessel with carved surface, by Catharine Hiersoux (USA), 2002. H. 41 cm (16 in.). *Photograph by the artist.*

177

and piercing, in this work come from a mixture of physical expression and emotional experiences. It is not easy to distinguish between them. I still enjoy the tactile sensation of slicing through the surface of leatherhard porcelain and find the process quite seductive, but the marks so made come from the subconscious fusion of those previously mentioned sources rather than directly from prepared drawings or photographs.

Many others have found that porcelain is especially amenable to carving and piercing at various stages of making but, perhaps, it is at its most receptive when the clay has lost some of its moisture. Carving when the clay has dried out completely has its attractions for some potters but it does present a very real risk to health through inhalation of clay dust. For this reason I would not recommend carving unless a degree of moisture remains and that it is sufficient to bind the cut waste together as it is removed. *This waste clay should not be permitted to fall on the floor and be trodden to dust as it dries.* Another

Porcelain plate, by Thomais Kontou (Greece), 2002. Wheel-thrown, with sgraffito design through coloured slip (cobalt/copper/rutile), under Dolomite glaze, d. 43 cm (17 in.), fired in an electric kiln to 1250°C (2282°F). *Photograph by Sokrates Mavromatis.*

Porcelain bowl with inlay, by Marianne Cole (Australia), 2002. The wheel-thrown bowl, d. 38 cm (15 in.), is turned and then allowed to dry. When completely dry it is returned to the wheel and concentric lines are drawn into the surface using a sharp tool, following this a black slip is applied over the lines. Still on the wheel excess slip is removed with a steel kidney, exposing the clean black lines to reveal the white porcelain. After the bisque a satin finish cobalt blue glaze is sprayed onto the inside. After the final firing the outside surface is sanded with fine Wet 'n Dry paper. *Photograph by Kluvanek.*

important reason for working the clay while it is still damp is that it retains a certain flexibility and is thus less likely to crack or split under the pressure of carving tools.

Many different tools can be used and each will impart its own character to the work. Bent wire loop tools having a round section produce a slightly softer edge to cut channels than those made with a flatter section. Solid blades, whether metal or wooden, meet with greater resistance in the clay and can leave more obvious chatter marks. Both open and solid tools can be used to carve channels of varying width and depth in one movement in a rather calligraphic manner. Needle points give thinner linear marks which usually remain constant in width. Multiple, repetitive marks made in the surface of a pot with any tool produces a strong rhythmic texture. I have made some of my favourite tools from metal strips used in the building industry to bind parcels of bricks to a wooden pallet. These strips can often be found lying around on building sites or dumped in skips. Reduced into short lengths

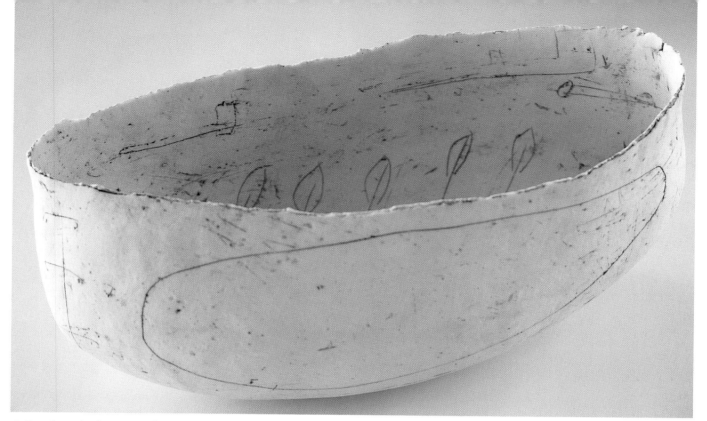

A Fine Line, by Raewyn Atkinson (New Zealand), 2001. handbuilt porcelain vessel with incised blue oxide wash, 28 x 14 x 11 cm (11 x 5 ½ x 4 ¼ in.), fired to 1250°C (2282°F). 'This work is from a series of pieces relating to early contact between Europeans and the Maori peoples.' *Photograph by the artist.*

(10–15 cm/4–6 in.) and cut across diagonally at one end, they can be sharpened on a grindstone to make ideal tools for incising porcelain. Vee-shaped linear incisions with one side of the vee longer than the other can produce surface effects rather like those to be seen on beautifully carved Chinese vessels with celadon glazes from the 10th and 11th centuries.

Greater care is necessary when piercing right through the clay wall not only in its execution but with proper regard to the fired strength of the finished piece. If piercing is done without sufficient understanding of the stresses which the form will suffer in the kiln, serious deformation can occur. The risk of slumping is reduced where the wall of the piece is vertical but special care is necessary where holes are cut through on sharply curved sections which have to support the weight of the clay above. Faults of this nature are more likely to be revealed in large forms. I well remember

problems I had to overcome with a series of porcelain bowls I used to make on the theme of 'trees'. This entailed cutting away a fairly extensive part around the circumference of a bowl. Each of those thinly-thrown bowls stood on quite narrow foot-rings from which they swelled up and outwards to the rim. The point at which the walls were pierced proved critical for their physical survival. If too much clay was removed below a certain level relative to any given profile, the walls would be weakened and unable to maintain their shape. It is always of the utmost importance to give sufficient support to the wall of a bowl with one hand while the other applies pressure in carving. This is especially so when working from the inside outwards because all the stress is centred over a very small area. Carving from the outside inwards is slightly less risky because, to some extent, the pressure is distributed more evenly around the circumference. I had to work fairly

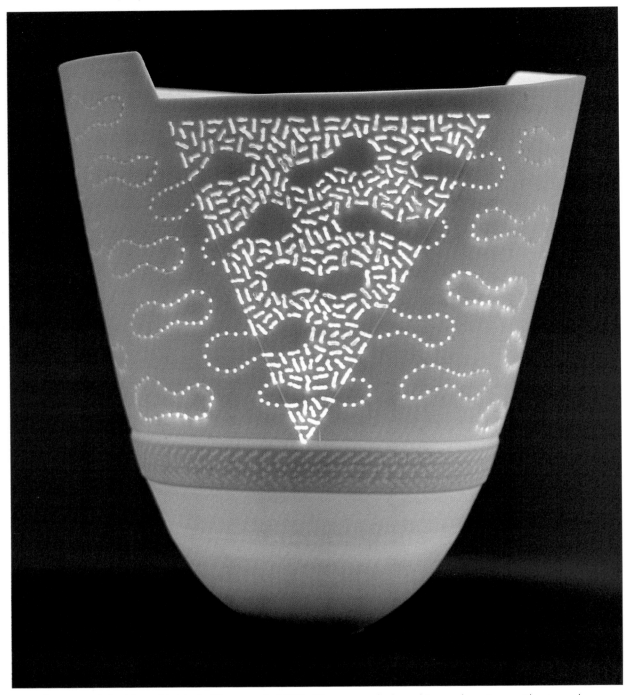

Porcelain vessel, by Horst Göbbels (Germany), 2001. Thrown and altered to oval section, with pierced design, h. 15 cm (6 in.). *Photograph by the artist.*

rapidly in order to counter the problem of the clay drying out as I worked. I have never liked to see carving which merely pierces through the wall leaving a crude cut edge as a sharp right angle within its thickness so I would always bevel the edges with the narrow-bladed scalpel immediately after completing the pierced

shapes. These would be softened further with a fine grade of steel wool when the piece was completely dry (see illustration on p.175).

Some of the finest filigree carving of porcelain in recent years has been done by the German potter, **Horst Göbbels**. When carving, he holds the pot carefully by one hand with its

Lidded box, by Horst Göbbels (Germany), 2001. Wheel-thrown, cut-glaze decoration, h. 16 cm (6 ¼ in.).
Photograph by the artist.

the mathematical precision of both the design and of the carving conveys a feeling of strength as much as fragility. There is little sense of fragmentation because that which has been removed is balanced by and of equal value to that which remains. The relationship of the inside and outside surfaces is accentuated. Colour and glaze are of secondary importance in such pieces and many are left unglazed. All his vessel forms are thrown using the KPCL porcelain from Limoges in France. Carved and perforated sections of the design are done with a broken saw blade when the piece has dried to the consistency of hard leather. The work is fired to 1280°C (2336°F) in a gas kiln with a reduction atmosphere.

Sandra Black from Western Australia has long been recognised for her carved and pierced porcelain and bone china vessels. Her designs are sometimes reminiscent of the angular patterns of the Art Deco period. Geometric carving in relief often has elements of the pattern cut away completely, giving emphasis to the rhythmic decoration and revealing the inner wall. Such pieces are frequently polished smooth but left unglazed. Her chosen motifs (e.g. 'fish and birds') are often interlinked or juxtaposed rather like an Escher drawing without the transmutation. She likes to make about 20 or more pots on the wheel and stores them in an old refrigerator to keep them damp. She stresses the importance of turning or trimming them to an even thickness of about 2 mm ($\frac{1}{16}$ in.) rather than leaving them too thick so that they lose translucency or making them so thin that they risk being cracked while carving or slump in the kiln. Black restricts herself to just four tools in the carving process, they are a surgical blade in a cane holder, a soft brush, a sponge and a water-sprayer. Piercing is done with a hand-held 'Dremmel drill' fitted with dental bits. Designs are first drawn on to the pot with the tip

base supported on his knee. This is at a critical stage in the process and it requires intense concentration. Göbbels' work has great delicacy and it usually displays much intricate, highly-ordered detail that is visually delightful. Many of his vessel forms have only minimal contact with the surface on which they stand. Bottoms are often rounded or raised on small foot-rings or elevated on integral pedestals. These devices contribute even more to the appearance of weightlessness and ethereality. At the same time,

of the blade and then cut into about half the wall thickness. The same blade is used on its side to remove excess clay and establish the relief. The soft brush is used to dislodge small particles without damaging the design and, finally, a damp sponge softens the edges and smoothes the surface. The work is bisque fired to 950°C (1742°F) and those that are to remain unglazed are soaked in water and sanded down, first with a 300 grade then a 600 grade of silicon carbide paper until they are completely smooth. Polishing the pieces while they are wet prevents dust flying around and from clogging the silicon carbide grit.

A more powerfully demonstrative kind of carving can be seen in the porcelain pieces by **Rolf Bartz** (Australia). His interest in carving was aroused initially by the work of prominent ceramicists using this technique and being heavily influenced by products of the Art Nouveau and Art Deco movements. The growth and shapes of plants provide him with ample subject matter to embellish a variety of vessel forms. He has always found much inspiration in his immediate surroundings, especially in the garden, and this source has been enhanced considerably since the installation of fishponds. His pieces have all been hand-carved, smoothed with steel-wool and then painted with underglaze pigments which, after firing to 1250°C (2282°F) develops a pleasant sheen that compliments the smooth porcelain surface. All the pieces have a white glaze inside. Sometimes, he allows the carving marks showing as a counterpart to the smoothness of the carved design surface.

(Opposite, top) Bowl, by Sandra Black (Australia), 2001. Slip-cast in Sealeys 'Ebony' porcelain, carved, pierced, fired to cone 7 and, finally, polished with silicon carbide papers. *Photograph by the artist.*

(Opposite, bottom) Three carved vases, by Rolf Bartz (Australia), 2002. Wheel-thrown porcelain deeply carved and painted with a black underglaze which, after firing to 1250°C (2282°F), develops a soft sheen contrasting the white glaze inside. *Photograph by Kluvanek.*

Porcelain bowl with green glaze over deeply carved 'Bird of Paradise' motif, by Rolf Bartz (Australia), 2002. The geometry of this flower and its leaves lends itself well to the carved design. The glaze is sprayed on with a heavy-duty air-brush to allow Bartz to manipulate the thickness of the glaze to emphasise the relief. *Photograph by Kluvanek.*

Bartz describes his carved, green bowl as:

one of my latest pieces: It harkens back to the very early stages of my career, when I was covering my carved design with this beautiful, rich copper green glaze (courtesy of Emmanuel Cooper). It also features one of my favourite flowers, the Strellitzia or 'Bird of Paradise.' The geometry of this flower and its leaves lends itself well to the carved design. The glaze is sprayed on with a heavy-duty airbrush to allow me to manipulate the thickness of the glaze in order to give even more dimension to the relief work. The manner in which the glaze breaks on the edges of the carved design further emphasises the carving.

Pieces are wheel-thrown with unusually thick walls because he likes to carve deeply into the porcelain to suggest different layers and overlapping shapes. No further clay is added to these pieces and the eventual form is decided

Porcelain platter, by Margaret Frith (UK), 2002. Carved under a blue celadon glaze, d. 28 cm (11 in.). *Photograph by the artist.*

purely by the amount of clay which is removed during the carving process. Having thrown a piece and allowed it to become firm and easy to handle, he trims it to perfect the shape, especially for his vase forms. Normally, he throws about six pieces in one session and this provides him with enough basic material for carving to keep him fully occupied for two weeks or more depending on the complexity of the design. Incising and excising is carried out when the clay has dried to a fairly hard state. Various tools are used for this work but his favourite for carving is a nib-shaped tool with a

curved head and shaft, sharpened on the edges and fitted into a handle. The abrasive action of the clay causes this to wear down very quickly. The flat wire type of modelling tools are particularly useful for smoothing and scraping between raised areas of the design. He has found that some dental tools are excellent for dealing with tight corners and narrow sections while flexible aluminium scrapers are ideal for smoothing away unwanted carving marks on larger areas. It can take anything between four and ten hours to complete a single carved form. 'Probably the hardest part of all is handling the pot while carving, especially in the latter stages as it becomes more fragile. On a number of occasions I have cracked a piece while carving the last part and seen several hours of work come to nothing.'

When the pieces have been thoroughly dried, Bartz uses a fine grade of steel-wool to finish smoothing the whole surface and then applies colours (commercially-prepared underglaze stains) painted with a brush or sprayed through an airbrush. The work is once-fired to 1260°C (2300°F) in an electric kiln before being given a final polish with 'Wet 'n Dry' emery paper. This gives the work a smooth, tactile finish which he feels is more sympathetic to the carved design than a glaze.

Margaret Frith (UK) likes to commence carving while the clay is at the softer end of leatherhard because she says that 'after handling for an hour or two it dries quickly and you have to be very careful not to break it as you near the end of the work'. She carves with metal tools made from old hacksaw blades set into wooden handles to make them more comfortable in use.

> I like to use them like drawing with a pencil so they must be nice to hold. The smoothness of the porcelain body makes it ideal for carving on open bowls and jars. These designs are mainly floral. I draw beforehand but I like to work directly on to the clay without copying so that I can achieve greater spontaneity and flow. Every imperfection shows on a pale blue, celadon, carved piece and losses can be frustratingly high. A piece of soft, malleable clay, nurtured through all its processes and carefully placed in the fire and coached to orange heat, never ceases to amaze me at the cooling of the kiln. A wonderful transformation takes place which can last for thousands of years. This is the force that drives me on!

Many contemporary potters continue to use

transparent coloured glazes, similar to those employed by Chinese craftsmen from the Sung period from the 10th century onwards. These glazes are designed to flow and pool in the depressions giving greater emphasis to incised or carved decoration. For example, the work of **Scott Malcolm** (USA) shows how his preference for delicate celadons can reveal the delicate drawings incised into the surface of his porcelain vessels.

Traditional celadon-type glazes have long been favoured by those who incise and carve porcelain. Every mark, even the smallest scratch in the clay surface is emphasised and revealed under these delicately coloured, transparent glazes when they liquefy during firing to pool

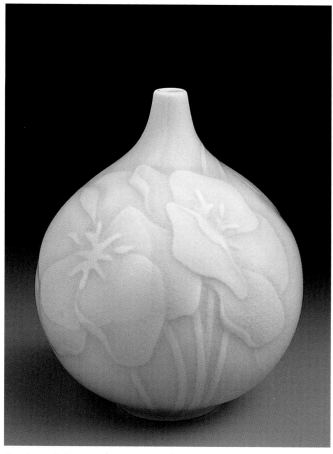

Bottle with Poppy, by Scott Malcolm, 2002. Porcelain, wheel-thrown and incised under celadon glaze, reduction fired to cone 12, h. 9 cm (3 ½ in.) *Photograph by Peter Lee.*

in, and emphasise, the slightest depressions. In the hands of a skilled carver today, pieces made in this way still possess the same seductive qualities that have charmed countless numbers over hundreds of years. Some of the most expressive incised work being produced in porcelain comes from the American potter, **Elaine Coleman**. The vessel forms on which she displays her imagery are thrown by her husband, Tom, whose work is also illustrated in this book. Coleman's fluent drawings that flow over and around to encompass the piece, are incised under a pale, green or turquoise blue celadon glazes. These vessels demonstrate the possibilities of the technique extremely well. It is essential to make positive movements with any tools used for

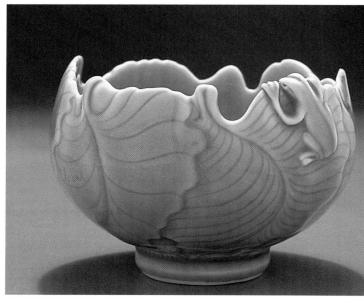

Incised and cut porcelain bowl, by Elaine Coleman (USA), 2002. Added clay frog, green celadon glaze, h. 10 cm (4 in.), w. 11.5cm (4 ½ in.). *Photograph by the artist.*

Incised porcelain bottle with clay lizards, by Elaine Coleman (USA), 2002. Iron blue glaze, h. 12 cm (5 in.), w. 7.5 cm (3 in.), fired to cone 10 in reduction. *Photograph by the artist.*

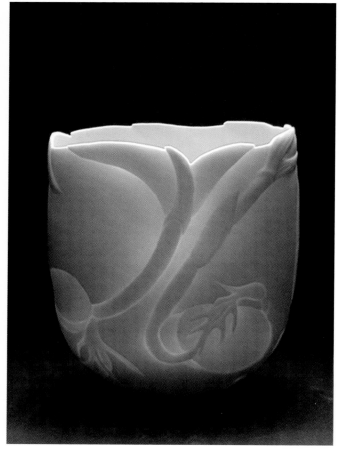

Porcelain bowl with carved walls and rim, by Hanneke Verhey (Holland), 2002. Dimensions: 9 x 7 cm (3 ½ x 2 ¾ in.). *Photograph by Frans Van Diepen.*

incising because a tentative or hesitant approach results in clumsy, awkward work that will be ruthlessly exposed under the glaze.

Harlan House (Canada) describes himself as a 'traditional potter' who admires much of the work by Chinese potters of the 10th to 13th centuries, and uses some of their techniques in the search for beauty, in form as well as in function. He uses rhythms and patterns taken from daily life in embellishing his pots. Occasionally, he will include a self-portrait emerging from the carved surface of a vessel.

For all intents and purposes my *only* source of inspiration is our garden, or our kitchen. When I was in Art School studying (painting), my teacher

impressed me with this opinion: 'Many artists think and look in the most awkward places for their subject matter.' He felt that they frequently overlooked the obvious. I agreed then, as I do now. Art and life are inseparable. If you are a potter, and have just made a fabulous sauce for some noodles but do not have the right bowl to put it in, you have all the right reasons to head to the studio and get to work. When cut flowers do not have proper homes a potter has a job to do. When beautiful events happen in your garden, it is time to share. Using forms reminiscent of the past; I try to answer some of today's reasons for bringing beauty into peoples lives. In doing so I place high value on the concepts surrounding elegance, beauty, grace and quietness as well as

Wave Delphinium Vase by Harlan House, 2002. Celadon and Imperial Snapdragon yellow glazes, h. 55 cm (21 ½ in.), w. 23 cm (9 in.). *Photograph by the artist*

Reed Section, by Harlan House, 2000. Carved, reed decoration with celadon glaze, h. 38.5 cm (15 ⅜ in.), w. 26 cm (10 ¼ in.) *Photograph by the artist*

Wheel-thrown, Southern Ice Porcelain bowl by Peter Lane, 2001. Acrylic medium resist painting to produce three levels of translucency, 14 x 19.5 cm (5 ½ x 7 ¾ in.), fired in reduction to 1280°C (2336°F). *Photograph by the artist.*

mystery/mastery. As a boy scout we were expected to leave a campsite in better condition than it was when we arrived. Almost 50 years later, I am unable to improve on that concept.

Most potters who choose to carve porcelain refer to the problems experienced in the latter stages when the pieces are drying rapidly and too much pressure applied while carving or piercing the thin walls can cause cracks which may not be evident until the work has been fired. I find that bowls, especially, can be thrown while leaving sufficient thickness in the base to provide a foot-ring which can be turned out from the inverted pot at the leatherhard stage. The pressure of the turning tools (I always use small, strap-wire tools for this purpose) helps to compress and align the clay particles sufficiently to avoid cracking occurring. Bowls are usually left to dry naturally, inverted on their rims. I check the state of dampness in each piece by holding its foot against a mirror which reveals a ring of condensation until completely dry.

RELIEF SURFACES IN ULTRA-THIN PORCELAIN

It is extremely difficult to incise into the surface of wafer thin porcelain at any stage. However, there are other ways to create relief patterns or imagery. Resist techniques painted on the bone-dry piece will permit a damp sponge to remove a layer from the unprotected clay. It may be possible to remove several layers this way. Care must be taken to allow the piece to dry out between each sponging in order to minimise the risk of loss caused by continual dampening. I use a hot air gun for the purpose. Some ceramicists wax while others, like **Arne Åse** (Norway), **Astrid Gerhartz** (Germany) and **Tim Gee** (UK), have all adopted a shellac solution to paint as a resist on bone dry pieces. For my own thinly thrown bowls, made in Southern Ice Porcelain, I prefer to use an *acrylic medium* that is water-soluble and much kinder to my

Porcelain cylinder, by Astrid Gerhartz (Germany), 1998. H. 26 cm (10 ¼ in.), d. 27 cm (10 ½ in.). *Photograph by Thomas Näthe.*

Porcelain vessel, by Arne Åse (Norway), 1996. Wheel-thrown, painted with shellac resist and sponged to produce varying levels of texture and translucency, 20 x 14 cm (8 x 5 ½ in.), unglazed, fired in reduction to 1250°C (2282°F). *Photograph by Glenn Hagebu.*

brushes. Either method will preserve even the finest and most delicate brush work while a damp sponge removes layers from the surface of dry porcelain. Several levels of translucency are revealed after the final firing. Gerhartz acknowledges the influence of Åse whom she met as a student at Hohr Grenzhausen although she pursues a very different direction. In some of her work, Gerhartz explores a theme of extremely elegant, thinly thrown cylinders treated by resist and sponging 'decoration' but she enlivens them further with precisely executed linear drawing over stained areas that have been subtly coloured by brushwork in metallic salts. These are clearly vessels but, in practice, their only function is to delight the eye and awake the tactile senses. The translucency and colour of the porcelain is enhanced by firing in a reduction atmosphere.

Marjan De Voogd (Holland) adds thin, wavy

fins, pinched into shape between fingers and thumb, or individually made, projecting spikes to some of her vessel forms. This technique enlarges the basic piece and creates extra interest.

NERIAGE, NERIKOMI AND INLAID TECHNIQUES

Porcelain can be easily coloured with commercially-prepared stains or combinations of metallic oxides to provide the potter with a reliable and scintillating palette. Marbling is the simplest way of using compound mixtures of coloured clays but the patterns produced are fairly random. Such mixtures are usually loosely wedged together before use and they inevitably develop linear patterns in a spiral formation around a wheel-thrown pot. Any 'muddy' slip created in the process of throwing is carefully removed from the surface with a sharp tool (flexible kidney-shaped steel tools are ideal for this purpose) towards the end of the throwing process. Subsequent turning will help to increase the clarity of the colours. Further visual interest can be given to pots thrown in this manner by rhythmic, vertical fluting with a wire tool when leatherhard. The Japanese term *neriage* describes this technique for wheel-thrown coloured clays.

When researching my first book *Studio Porcelain* in 1979, I found only a few potters specialising in the technique of nerikomi or marquetry which entails the use of multi-coloured porcelain sliced up and assembled so

(Top) Large bowl, *Forest Floor*, by Les Blakebrough (Australia), 2002. Southern Ice Porcelain, thrown, deep etched, unglazed, polished, d. 25 cm (9 ¾ in.), h. 20 cm (8 in.).
(Middle) *Goblet*, by Marjan DeVoogd (Holland), 2002. Porcelain vessel with applied and pinched fins, h. 17 cm (6 ¾ in.), d. 14 cm (5 ½). *Photograph by the artist.*
(Bottom) Pair of bowls, by Sasha Wardell (UK), 2001/2. Green interior, layered and sliced technique, h. 18 cm (7 in.) and 11 cm (4 ⅓ in.). *Photograph by the artist.*

Lidded jars, by Robin Hopper (Canada), 2002. Agate ware, white and two blue coloured porcelains, thrown and facetted, h. 20 cm (8 in.) and 16.5 cm (6.5 in.), fired in oxidation at cone 9. *Photograph by Janet Dwyer.*

that the pattern becomes an integral part of the form. Now there are so many more who have adapted this method because it allows the potter much greater control of the design than is possible in traditional marbling. It also requires far more care in the construction and a great deal of patience. Drying of forms made this way must be extremely gradual if cracking and separation of the constituent pieces is to be avoided. The slow building process has a certain advantage in that the maker can adjust the design as work proceeds. In addition, what you see is what you get, allowing for slight variations in the intensity of the colours in the final firing. Problems can arise, however, where stains or oxides cause uneven fluxing of the body so that some pieces shrink more than others pulling the joints apart. This can be overcome by (a) carefully testing the proportions of colour stain added to the base body to ensure compatibility and (b) firing very slowly to the optimum temperature. Some forms

Nautil, by Hans Munck Anderson (Denmark), 1999. Polychrome porcelain, handbuilt, d. 21 cm (8 ¼ in.) and 11 cm (4 ¼ in.). *Photograph by Ole Akhøj.*

may need to be supported in bisque moulds during firing to help them keep their shape without distortion due to the different fluxing effects of added stains.

Potters such as **Dorothy Feibleman** (UK), **Curtis Benzle** (USA) and **Thomas Hoadley** (USA), whose work has been featured in my previous books, have continued to refine the art of nerikomi while many others are now producing exciting and high quality work by the same method. In particular, the Dutch potter, **Judith de Vries**, and **Mieke Everaet** from Belgium have both chosen to use variations of this technique with considerable success.

Colour can be introduced into the white porcelain in several different ways. Selected ceramic stains or oxides can be intermixed and wedged thoroughly into the plastic body to supply a wide range of colours and tones. Another method requires the preparation of coloured porcelain in this way to be dried completely and ground into powder. A slab of plastic white porcelain is then covered with the coloured powder and rolled into the surface.

The powder absorbs moisture from the damp clay and ensures a perfect marriage between the two.

The method of joining strips and slabs of porcelain with slip is common to all handbuilding, but where coloured stains are likely to cause varying rates of shrinkage, and if this problem is further compounded by using slabs made up of many different elements, then drying becomes the most critical stage of the whole process. Anyone choosing to work with such combinations will require extreme patience. One artist told me that, occasionally, the necessary drying period can take as long as four months to a year according to the shape and thickness of the form and whether it is constructed as a single or double walled piece.

Nature provides much of the stimuli for the exotic vessels by **Curtis Benzle** (USA). His pieces are made up of multiple layers of coloured and patterned porcelain sheets laminated together and compressed while the clay is at the wet stage. In any one piece there may be up to six different layers.

The intended result is for the viewer to be confronted with a constantly changing imagery dependent on the available light. For me, this represents the reality of mentally processing the many elements of my environment simultaneously. For instance, when I gaze out of my studio window I see certain objects immediately brought into focus: trees, grass, flowers. As I continue to look, I bring into focus dew, mist, birds passing and a subtle shifting of light and shadow. To all this is added the remembered images relevant to the same scene: days of rain, snow, children playing, leaves changing and on and on. It is this 'layering' of imagery that encourages my layering of translucent porcelain surfaces.

During a residency in Seto, Japan in 2001, Benzle was able to set aside time to investigate

Porcelain vessel, by Curtis Benzle (USA). Handbuilt in Nerikomi technique, 20 x 20 x 7.5 cm (8 x 8 x 3 in.), fired in electric kiln to cone 8. *Photograph by the artist.*

and make some new forms that required the use of a castable refractory firing saggar. Due to the verticality of the walls of these vessels, a two-piece saggar was necessary. He needed to develop a 'locking device' to hold the saggar parts together. He constructed a third refractory component that encloses the two primary halves of the form. All this was an interesting challenge and beneficial also in that it opened up an array of new dimensional options for him.

> While in Seto and immersed in their wealth of ceramic history, culture and museums, another concern coalesced for me – that of firing cracks, damage and subsequent repair.
>
> Working as I do in a material prone to cracking and then extending the limits of that characteristic by narrowing the clay wall to a millimetre or less, I have always danced around the issue of naturally occurring fissures. In this realm, my interest has been encouraged historically – most notably by examples from the Momoyama period Igaware of Japan and

Porcelain vessel, by Curtis Benzle (USA). Handbuilt in Nerikomi technique, with gold leaf and epoxy resin, 25.5 x 15 cm (10 x 6 in.), fired in an electric kiln to cone 8. *Photograph by the artist.*

contemporaneously by artists sharing this fascination – most significantly, Bennett Bean. I have also been strongly influenced by the work of Rick Dillingham and his response to the reassembled results of archaeological discovery. As I said, I have danced around this issue for years by performing minor repairs and even applying modest gold leafing to highlight, instead of hide, my efforts.

All of this simmering fascination came to a head in Seto. Room after room of respectfully repaired ceramic icons merged with my unflinching determination to require no less of my indigenous Japanese porcelain than I would of my domestic home brew back in the US. As my pieces emerged from the Seto kilns bearing ample evidence of the structural strain on sub millimetre clay walls, I realised clearly that these stress fractures and fissures were no less a natural indication of my process than flashing in a wood firing. And, surrounded by the masters of history represented so well in the museum collections of Japan, I was encouraged to respond to this natural reaction to firing by accentuating the visual evidence of response to structural challenge.

His research helped Benzle to understand that, traditionally, cracks or fissures were filled with adhesive and then enhanced with a metallic overlay. This is the technique he uses himself now. While he continues to produce the occasional, unblemished piece, they now seem somehow less to him for their apparent perfection. Those pieces that are embellished with what he describes as 'beauty marks' resulting from the fire and his 'stubborn desire to see the warm glow of light through resistant fired porcelain walls' do seem to be rather special. These scarred and blemished pieces, 'like creases in octogenarian skin, speak volumes about our fascination with the natural effects of fire'.

The extremely complex decorative patterns seen in the work of **Judith de Vries** (Holland)

Ocean Bowl, by Judith De Vries (Holland), 2001. Porcelain in white and coloured Limoges body, 18 x 24 cm (7 x 9 ½ in.), fired to 1220°C (2228°F) in oxidation. The bottom is wheel-thrown and nerikomi elements built up and adjusted. *Photograph by Ron Zijlstra.*

were made piece by piece with multiple strips of coloured clays. The bottoms were thrown on the wheel and slabs were added later. These were rhythmically arranged in overlapping layers which, to some extent, dictate the evolution of the forms and produce a strong sensation of movement. The coloured stains and oxides were mixed with water before kneading and wedging into the white porcelain. The colours go right through the wall of the piece or, when fixed onto a backing slab, the white from the background is revealed as very thin lines between the applied patterns. Occasionally, she uses moulds to support the bottom, or bottles or cans as props inside vertical vessels while she is working on them. Some of the forms also require supporting in moulds while in the kiln if they are not to suffer deformation. The finished work has undergone several stages of scraping, refining and sanding before it was fired in an electric kiln, first to 1000°C (1832°F). The insides were then glazed and pieces fired again to 1220°C (1868°F). Finally, the vessels were polished until satin smooth with Wet n' Dry silicon carbide paper. She has found that this

Blue Winged Bowl, by Judith De Vries (Holland). Porcelain in white and coloured Limoges body, 24 x 17 cm (9 ½ x 6 ¾ in.), fired to 1220°C (2228°F) in oxidation. The bottom is wheel-thrown and nerikomi elements built up. *Photograph by Ron Zijlstra.*

technique requires great patience and perseverance because, occasionally, slight cracks can appear between the different layers to spoil the work.

Dorothy Feibleman refers to her particular technique of assembling sections of poly-coloured porcelain as millefiore. In one of her methods she rolls out, separately, several thin, even slabs of clay of different colours on finely textured cloth. The slabs are coated with thin layers of slip between them and then bonded together using a rolling pin. A sharp knife is used to cut a slice vertically through the layered slab and each strip is then turned on its side to reveal the striped surface. These are rejoined with slip (often of a contrasting colour) and pushed tightly together to make into a new slab which can itself be recut in a variety of

Floating in Moonlight, by Dorothy Feibleman (UK), 1999. Nerikomi porcelain form, 26 x 14 cm (10 ¼ x 5 ½ in.). *Photograph by Mark Johnston.*

directions and reassembled until a particular design is achieved. Eventually, the new slab with its pattern appearing on both sides can be cut to fit a plaster mould into which it is gently coaxed. The whole is then wrapped in polythene to allow gradual drying to take place. Any smudging of the colours occurring during assembly are scraped carefully away when dried to a leatherhard state and, finally, smoothed when the pot is bone dry.

It was in 1969 that, first inspired by millefiore and ancient mosaic glass, she began to work with coloured porcelain. Every change in colour, texture, or translucency is structural. The forms are also dependent on the movement of the above elements in the construction, drying and especially the firing, where the movement can be dramatic. All these elements, and their relation to the atmosphere and

temperature in the kiln, can be altered for very different images using the same materials. She keeps and sometimes uses patterns she made 20 years ago and says that it is 'like saving some nice pieces of wood and thinking how you would like to use them for the next project'.

Feibleman spent the summer of 1995 at the International Ceramic Studio in Kecskemet, Hungary and discovered another porcelain clay that proved suitable for use with her own porcelain (which she had formulated and used and later, sold commercially). This enabled her to make white nerikomi.

The high-fire Hungarian clay served as a structure for my own, low-fire porcelain to melt within and, depending on the atmosphere in the kiln, I had the options of texture in oxidation or no texture in reduction. I have experimented and worked mainly

Suspense, by Dorothy Feibleman (UK), 2001. White/white textured with gradations of blue on black/black porcelain/ stoneware 'grown in the kiln'. Due to the additions to the black clays, they expand in the kiln and are restricted by moulds so that they 'grow' but change shape in the kiln due to the structures of the different clays and the moulds that restrict them. 'I call them Kiln Bonsai. Grown, controlled, restricted but allowing for the structures they are made of. Working with the structures and melting process in the kiln.' 56 x 50 cm (22 x 19 ¾ in.) black piece, 2.2 x 1.7cm (¾ x ⅝ in.), white/white with blue gradations and textures due to different melting temperatures of the white clays. *Photograph by Osaki Studio.*

with whites since 1995 although I tried to alter my clay before that to change the texture and translucency. Rather than trying to lower the temperature of my clay, I found that working with many different porcelains and using their intrinsic differences in translucency, whiteness and melting temperatures, was a better solution for me rather than trying to use and alter only one clay. I have used textures in my coloured work since 1979. On a small scale, I liked changing the shape of the pieces (through structure and chemical alteration) and the textures by firing. They go in the kiln with smooth texture and come out with patterned textures. By building forms to restrict the growth and, depending on the nerikomi patterns which are structural and determine the movement, I can predetermine the fired shape and movements of the surface. It can be consistent.

In Japan during 2002, Feibleman worked out a new method for inlaying images in tiles. This technique can achieve any type of pattern, and the tiles can be polished. She describes it as a sort of nerikomi process with industrial possibilities. She explains that this way of working is not traditional. She made fake rock – with fossils in it as a prototype. But, any image can be used. During her time at Inax this year, she made a new, translucent, strong white clay with a softly smooth surface that can be fired in one hour in tunnel kilns. 'It is also nice for hand-building and takes colour very cleanly. It is very reliable in long firings also. It is like having found a good dance partner. It is similar in use to my previous clay, but it has a different personality and holds its shape very reliably. I can use it with my old clay as well, as the structures are similar.'

Glazes are rarely used by potters using neriage or inlaid techniques because the clarity of the patterned surface could be obscured or become too reflective. The crisp designs and bright colours to be seen in the work of **Mieke Everaet,** for example, would be, in a sense, cheapened by a covering of shiny, transparent glaze. She has developed a uniquely personal style that brought her international recognition soon after completing her studies in Antwerp. Despite some unexpected results and failures caused by technical difficulties with uneven shrinkage of porcelain mixed in different colours, she has produced many exquisitely beautiful designs. Her pieces are well-conceived and executed with a remarkable liveliness considering their graphic complexity, while colours are carefully coordinated to unify pattern and form.

Everaet speaks of the forms, composition and colours of her pieces as evoking 'exotic influences, emotions inspired by nature or the memories of recent styles transcribed into artistic language'. The bowl is a favoured shape with its open character offering both inner and

(Top) *Composition of Three Porcelain Bowls*, by Mieke Everaet (Belgium), 2002. Inlaid coloured body, fired in an electric kiln to 1280°C (2336°F), d. 14 cm (5 ½ in.), 16 cm (6 ¼ in.) and 20 cm (8 in.). *Photograph by Fabien De Cugnac.*
(Bottom) *Porcelain Object*, by Mieke Everaet (Belgium), 2002. Double form, d. 30 cm (11 ¾ in.), inlaid coloured body, fired in an electric kiln to 1260°C (2300°F). *Photograph by Michèlle Franken.*

outer surfaces to view and, since the design is echoed precisely within and without, there is little room for confusion. The simplicity of these basic forms can support complex graphical imagery to a degree that would overwhelm a more consciously articulated shape. Light, especially when strategically placed, is gathered and diffused through extremely thin walls, and adds a certain magical quality. Black slip used to join the fragments of coloured porcelain appears as black boundary lines of varying thickness. The density of the black contrasts delightfully with the variable translucency of the

coloured areas. Many of her bowls have thin strips of colour alternating with thinner black lines rising up vertically and radially from a small base to form a broad encircling band. This often constitutes a large part of the bowl which supports another band with contrasting colours and tones around the rim which defines the personality of the piece.

Whereas my earlier bowl-shaped objects have a more lyrical, emotional composition (with rolls of coloured porcelain, clearly influenced by agate motifs), my later bowl-shaped objects are more

Double Form, by Mieke Everaet (Belgium), 2002. Porcelain with inlaid mosaic pattern and platinum lustre, d. 14.5 cm (5 ¾ in.). *Photograph by Michèlle Franken.*

subtle compositions of geometric motifs and intense colours. I drew my inspiration from African baskets. These baskets are finely woven with painted types of grass, a technique which also results into a very tactile structure. Another source of inspiration was the inventive use of geometric decorations in the Maya temples of Uxmal in Mexico. The forms of nature provide standards for proportion and harmony, regarding the growing process and the coherence of the form, the colour and the decoration. For example, if one looks closely at a cross-section of plants or roots, one can discover the geometry of nature, which brings order and rhythm into being. The art of the islands of Polynesia is also dominated by a natural ornamentation. I am also attracted to exotic fabrics and batik patterns.

Everaet explains how the decoration itself forms the actual structure of her pieces creating clear rhythms over the whole surface. She says that, in her recent work, endless repetition of coloured porcelain strips seems to have evolved into a kind of 'modern minimal dance'. She continues to explore variations in both shape and volume. All her work is fired in an electric kiln to 1280°C (2336°F).

The inlaid work by **Elisabeth Schaffer** (Germany) is constructed from porcelain slabs made from slip poured on to plaster with coloured porcelain elements inlaid. She builds her cube forms from carefully cut, square slabs painted with different coloured slips (coloured with oxides and body stains). She cuts into the surface of these so that they can move and open a little more during the firing process.

Of course, another way to make precise placements of colour is to inlay slips and stained plastic clay made from the same body to ensure compatibility. I use some of the dried trimmings from my wheel-thrown work as the base material. This is thoroughly dried and reduced to fine powder ready to be weighed for the additions of carefully measured percentages of stains or colouring oxides. After mixing with water this is then sieved several times through an 80s and 100s mesh to obtain even dispersal

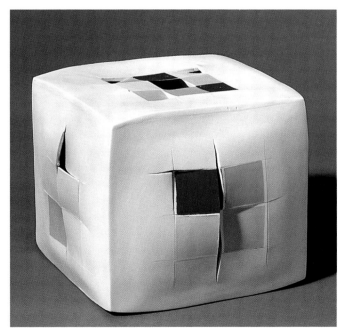

Kubus, by Elisabeth Schaffer (Germany), 2001. Cube, slab-built porcelain painted with coloured slips, 23 x 24 x 24 cm (9 x 9 ½ x 9 ½ in.), bisque fired to 950°C (1742°F) and second firing to 1300°C (2372°F) in a neutral atmosphere. Cuts made in the wall of this piece are intended to open further during the firing. *Photograph by Antje Anders.*

of colour throughout the mix. Unless the mixture is required to be used as a slip for painting, spraying or inlaying, I pour the slip mixture into a plaster mould previously lined with a fine muslin cloth and leave it to stiffen to a plastic state. The cloth enables the clay to be easily removed from the mould without sticking. It can then be kneaded to a workable consistency as a coloured body for inlaying or assembling into neriage-type patterns or for making one-piece forms.

Coloured porcelain can be placed directly on top of slabs of the same body and in the same condition, whether white or coloured, and then pressed into the parent slab by rolling. This method causes the applied pieces to spread under pressure of the roller and allowances must be made for that in the design. The inlaid slabs may be used in various ways to build any kind of form but one of the most suitable is to lay the rolled slab face down over a plaster or bisque hump mould to create a dish or bowl with its decorated surface uppermost. Inlaid slabs made by the rolling method offer other possibilities when they are stretched in the opposite direction. Instead of bending the decorated surface inwards as described above, the slab can be bent round into a cylindrical shape with the pattern outside. This movement causes the inlaid elements to separate slightly from the parent slab so that a narrow crevice appears around the outline. This fissure can itself be inlaid with slip, oxides or stains. Rolling white into white porcelain and painting a dark colour in the cracks is particularly effective. Any excess colour is removed with a metal scraper or steel wool when the work is dry.

For even greater control of the placement of colour, the completed object can be incised (up to half the thickness of the wall) or areas removed from the surface and then inlaid with slips or with plastic clay only slightly damper than the underlying form. Slow drying is usually necessary to prevent separation or cracking. Again, excess clay is cleaned up when the piece is dry. Slips must be applied until the inlay stands proud of the surface to allow for shrinkage as it dries out. Compressing the slip into the incisions when it has stiffened helps to ensure a good bond.

Thomas Hoadley (USA) cites the countless varieties of patterns to be found in nature as providing his primary source of inspiration but other influences 'range from fabric designs to styles of contemporary music, to painting and graphic design'. His earlier distinctive bowl forms were begun by draping a disc of soft clay, whether patterned or a solid colour, over a bisqued hump mould. When it has stiffened enough to hold its shape, it is removed from the mould and turned upright on to a batt with the outer edge supported by wads of clay. The rim is then moistened and scored so that slices taken from variously patterned, laminated blocks can be attached and built up into the main walls of the pot. The sides are then paddled on the outside while a cloth-covered wad is used for support on the inside. More recently, pieces are made from softer clay that he stretches from the inside with a rubber rib until the required shape is formed. This forming process is followed by slow drying, scraping with a metal rib at the leatherhard stage, and several sandings both before and after the bisque and high firings.

Inlaid coloured porcelains which are polished with silicon carbide grits rather than glazed have a special visual and tactile appeal. Without a 'skin' of glaze distancing the observer from direct contact with the piece, the colours remain clean and clear. Matt glazes tend to obscure the patterns while transparent glossy ones produce reflections, which disturb the form. Some pieces have the addition of gold leaf which is applied after the last firing but, since the leaf is not fired, it remains somewhat fragile.

(Left) Nerikomi vessel, by Thomas Hoadley (USA), 2002. Handbuilt with coloured porcelain and gold leaf, h. 24.5 cm (9 ⅝ in.). (Right) Nerikomi bowl, by Thomas Hoadley, 2002. Handbuilt with coloured porcelain, h. 15 cm (6 in.). 'I like to create fluid or undulating forms because to me they reflect the sensuous and flowing qualities of the soft clay. Some of the patterns that I create reflect these qualities as well and are accentuated by being juxtaposed with more geometric designs.' *Photographs by the artist.*

My current ceramic work reflects an investigation into several areas of interest and an attempt to unify solutions to various visual problems. One interest is in the vessel as an abstract sculptural form and its many associations, both literal and metaphoric. Another is pattern and colour and how a collection of abstract elements can create various feelings or impressions. A third is an interest in the integration of surface pattern and three-dimensional form. The technique that I use, which results in a penetration of the pattern through the thickness of the wall so as to be visible on both the outside and the inside, is a partial solution to the problem; but from a strictly two-dimensional standpoint I am also concerned with how the pattern relates to the form as seen in profile.

A certain degree of illusion of depth is created by some colour/pattern combinations and I enjoy the play of this implied visual depth versus the 'flat' modulating surface of the pot versus the real depth that is present in the interior space. My aim is not, however, to create strong illusions nor representational or abstracted pictures on the pots.

My initial attraction to the nerikomi technique came from its organic union of pattern and structure. Rather than the former being applied to the latter, as in most decorative pottery traditions, the two are one and the same. The natural world abounds with this sort of union and as a result, offers endless inspiration for pattern making. The other aspect that was particularly attractive to me was the translation of the physical properties of clay into a visual format. By this I mean that the very plasticity of the clay is made visible in the way that an imposed pattern is altered. Straight parallel lines are created by stacking up slices of variously coloured clays but in the manipulation of the resulting soft block of clay, the lines become undulating or are perhaps made to taper down to a hair's breadth. Porcelain of course shows off this quality to its greatest extent but the principle is the same with any clay. I think of my patterns as being a collaboration between my imposed structure and the clay's wise alteration of that structure.

In addition to the natural sources, I have found inspiration for patterns in a number of other areas. Fabric design has recently been of great interest to me as well as a variety of non-ceramic craft traditions. Graphic design of all sorts serves as visual stimulation and colour ideas can come as easily from a magazine advertisement as from a rock, shell, or flower.

The techniques of Japanese neriage, English agate ware, and marquetry also inspired **Kalliope Tsoutsoura** (Greece) who has worked with this technique since 1980. She continues exploring ways of using stained porcelain to integrate colour and ornamentation into her vessel forms. She uses simple press moulds to build up the walls and patterns together as the

work takes shape. The addition of Molochite strengthens the larger pieces. After drying slowly to a leatherhard condition, the surface is scraped back to reveal the pattern. Finally, the whole piece is burnished to seal the surface without the need for glaze. Each vessel is dried slowly and fired once to between 1250°–1280°C (2282°–2336°F). Some of her designs give the impression of woven fabrics. Recently, she has inlaid coloured elements into rolled slabs of plastic porcelain before press-moulding them, 'experimenting with spinning tops, egg forms, wall panels' in this way.

Sony Manning (Australia) works rather differently with inlaid coloured porcelain to depict certain aspects of landscape. Many of these images refer to childhood experiences of land formations, rock strata and animals. To do so successfully, she learnt to understand and control what she calls 'the mechanics of inlay'. The broader shapes are carved out and inlaid first before other figurative elements are added. She uses metallic oxides added to a white or creamy porcelain body to obtain the effects she

Vessel form, by Kalliope Tsoutsoura (Greece). Handbuilt with coloured porcelain. *Photograph by Socratis Mavrommatis.*

(Left) *Millefiore Cup*, by Sony Manning (Australia). Coloured porcelain clays were laminated together in various ways so that slices taken through a cross-section provides a predetermined profile. These slices were press-moulded to form the cup, h. 9 cm (3 ½ in.), burnished and fired in reduction to 1300°C (2372°F). *Photograph by Terence Bogue.*

(Above) Two beakers, by Sony Manning (Australia). Coloured slips first laid out in thin layers on a plaster batt to form pieces of landscape imagery. When firm enough to lift it is placed carefully into a plaster mould before casting. Fired in reduction with a glazed interior to 1300°C (2372°F). *Photograph by Terence Bogue.*

requires, 'a unique quality which can define the depth of field and moody light of the inner landscape'. Rates of expansion and contraction will often differ according to the proportions and natures of the oxides used to stain the porcelain. She finds it necessary to thicken the walls of her pieces in order to compensate for any tensions set up between different colours inlaid side by side.

(Right) *Isaphahan*, by Hans Munck Anderson (Denmark), 1999. Polychrome porcelain, handbuilt, d. 27 cm (10 ½ in.) and 11 cm (4 ¼ in.). *Photograph by Ole Akhøj.*

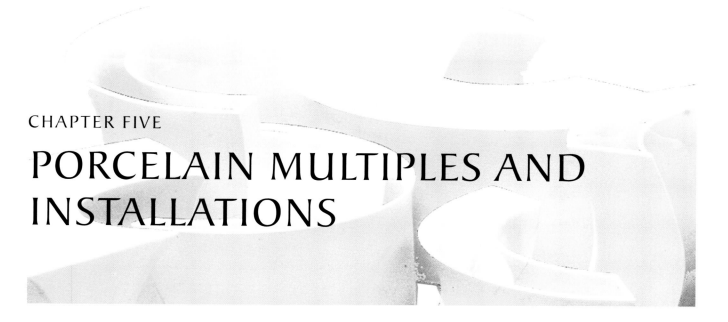

CHAPTER FIVE

PORCELAIN MULTIPLES AND INSTALLATIONS

Bottles, bowls and vases are common vessels that are normally considered in isolation or as individual pieces displayed in a gallery but they acquire extra interest when grouped together. Of course, this is taken for granted when pots are seen in a domestic setting but a group of pieces purposely designed to relate together and be viewed as a composed still life or installation assumes a totally different character. **Gwyn Hansen Pigott** (Australia) produced a number of 'still life' groups consisting of

beakers, bottles and bowls without decoration under simple transparent glazes. **Elsa Rady** (USA) explores similar themes with a series of 'still life' compositions featuring elegantly classical vessel forms in single, double, triple, or more combinations of both similar and dissimilar forms. Her work is highly disciplined and precise with sharply defined profiles. The individual elements interrelate with each other and the immediate space in perfect harmony.

Phillipe Barde (Switzerland) and **Ulli**

(Left) *No: 1 Lily Still Life V,* by Elsa Rady (USA), 1996, (Collection of Isitah Museum, Tokyo). Porcelain on painted, aluminium shelf, 42 x 51 x 35.5 cm (16 ½ x 20 x 14 in.). *Photograph by Paul Sanders.*
(Above) *Summer Parade,* by Gwyn Pigott (Australia), 2001, (Philip Bacon Galleries). Limoges porcelain, 9 pieces, w. 66 cm (26in.), h. 16.5 cm (6 ½ in.), d. 18 cm (7 in.).

(Above) *Stone reduction*, by Philip Barde (Switzerland), 1995. Porcelain, fired at 1250°C (2282°F), h. 300 cm (118 in.). (Opposite) *100 Bluten – 100 Blossoms*, by Ulli Bömelmann (Germany), 1999/2000. 100 suspended flowers, porcelain, each is 21 cm (8 ¼ in.). *Photograph by the artist.*

Bömelmann (Germany) are two artists who have employed multiple elements made in porcelain to create installation pieces in which the relationship of the individual parts combine with each other and space for particular effect. Barde does not utilise the translucent property of porcelain as in the traditional sense. Above all he is interested in the process of casting and in the many possibilities offered by this technique. Whiteness and precision of slip-cast porcelain is fundamental to him. In one aspect of his work, he takes plaster casts from chunks of rock. Slip is poured into the casting to make the same form in porcelain. Using further moulds taken from each of ten successive castings he is able to produce identical forms that become increasingly smaller as the operation proceeds. These pieces are then

installed together creating a group of related forms. Similar cast elements are left with one open side allowing the interior to be seen, revealing different aspects and adding considerable visual interest in relation to other elements making up the installation. Sometimes he has picked up stones from a particular location during his travels for this purpose because their use allows him to make a geological chronicle of his journey.

Ulli Bömelmann works in a completely different way with porcelain. Her floating objects and installations are focussed on the essentials of fragility, transparency, weightlessness, and what she describes as 'spaces of time and spaces in space'. Porcelain, paper and silicone are the materials which give substance to these subjects. The work confuses the spectator because the

porcelain elements appear to be made of paper because they are so thin and delicate.

Firstly, for some of her installations, Bömelmann makes paper patterns in the shape of a flower. These fragile pieces are supported in plaster moulds so that a thin film of porcelain slip can be lightly brushed over the paper 'flower'. As it dries she pierces three holes through the 'petals' so that the flower can be suspended on silicone threads. The dried flowers are put in the kiln, each held in its own pre-formed bed of fire-clay-sand and fired by electricity to 1320°C (2408°F) in a normal kiln atmosphere. The paper disappears completely

(Above) *Pears*, by Andrea Hylands (Australia), 2002. Bone china, slip cast and handbuilt in wooden container, 22 x 29 x 12.5 cm (8 ¾ x 11 ¼ x 5 in.).

(Opposite) *Still Life* series, by Andrea Hylands, 2000. Bone china, platters from soft slab, hand constructed, 'fruit' is slip-cast, each set of fruit fired to reduce size, and individual moulds made to create increasingly diminishing fruit, so that each piece of fruit is identical to its larger companion (x 5 times), l.100 cm (39 ½ in.), largest platter: w. 48 cm (19 in.), smallest platter: w. 20 cm (8 in.).

Photograph by Andrew Barchem. (Collection, Taipei County Yingo Ceramic Museum. Taiwan, 2000–2001).

Jeroen Bechtold (Holland) displays some of his slip-cast *Towers* in linear groups for greater effect while **Andrea Hylands** (Australia), also, makes multiple castings of a particular form and assembles them in groups, sometimes within a rectangular frame. She works in a range of media often combining ceramics with painting and what she describes as 'transformational media'.

I no longer use colour as a form of expression in my recent ceramic work but, instead, I rely on the whiteness of the material to define a sculptural form. This work is related to the physical environment and to the relationship between peoples and nature, investigating the fragility of landscape and my concern for the living world. The egg, as a symbol, has been important in my work, also.

Bone china is the whitest of ceramic materials and is therefore compatible with the way I make my sculptural pieces. I use combinations of slip-casting, press-moulding, soft slabs and other handbuilding techniques. The casting slip is made from the plastic bone china body to which I mix quantities of water and Dispex only.

I have made numerous large plaster batts with an assortment of surface textures that I am able to transfer onto the clay body to use in various ways. This process is either by manipulating plastic (soft slab) clay, or by pressing or pouring the clay onto a plaster batt. These textures enable me to provide information and expression about the physical aspects of landscape.

The work is fired in an electric kiln to around 1250°C (2282°F). Towards the end of the firing cycle the kiln is soaked (held at the top temperature) for about 30 minutes. I do not normally use a glaze on these pieces. Finally, the bone china or porcelain is polished with a fine grade of wet and dry sandpaper.

Wall panels and assemblages by **Elisabeth Schaffer** (Germany) rely on duplication and

during the firing. As the flowers have a thickness less than 0.1 cm (⅛₂ in.) the wastage rate can be as high as 50–70%. The most difficult part of the process is in removing the dried paper and slip 'flowers' from the mould without breaking them. She describes this as 'very exhausting work, but I think of them floating in the air and keep on doing it!'

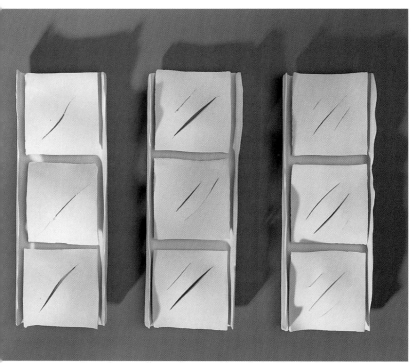

Porcelain wall installation, (detail), by Elisabeth Schaffer (Germany), 2000. Dimensions: 38 x 27 cm (15 x 10 ½ in.). *Photograph by Antje Anders.*

repetition with subtle variations. Incisions slashed through the surface of thin porcelain sheets, built into shallow boxes, move, open and change shape in the heat of the kiln. Groups of these similar but different objects are mounted together in sequence.

Malgorzata Dyrda-Kujawska (Poland) enjoys working in a factory environment with its busy atmosphere with large spaces, machinery and production kilns. Her imagination is strongly stimulated in this situation. She prefers to explore sculptural works following a specific idea. Sometimes a particular cycle can occupy a lengthy period over several years, subject to continuous modifications, until a new theme is begun. All her works consist of many elements, usually prepared separately and later fixed, mounted or assembled together.

I remember the strong impression made upon me when I saw a column of bisque-fired plates, damaged by a factory worker, that were piled one on top of another. It was a sharp image that had

Vertical objects in motion, by Malgorzata Dyrda-Kujawska (Poland), 2000 (at the exhibition in Keramion, Frechen Germany). Unglazed porcelain, metal base (detail), up to h. 300 cm (118 in.). *Photograph by Lukasz Kujawski.*

connections with circular movement, like a spiral stretched in time. I started to cut plates into squares and stacking them on top of each other to create 'Vertical objects'. Piled up and narrowing upwards – they were like chimneys. Different thickness of the edges of these flat elements made graphic lines of shadows between them (twined around an axis) – these factors were most important for me. Sometimes I used colour – but the whiteness of porcelain is the most beautiful feature for me.

A higher level of discipline was demanded by my 'Sphere' cycle, which began in 1992. Spheres were made by sticking individually-cast elements together. The forms ultimately produced were fired on a supporting bed of quartz sand to ensure they remained complete. Diameters of these pieces were up to 50 cm (18 in.) although this was really difficult to achieve in porcelain. Sometimes I organised them into a constellation of spheres – like planets.

Dyrda-Kujawska continues to explore the interrelation of harmony and dissonance in resolving her ideas, because, for her, a work of beauty can be associated with a shiver of delight as well as with emotions of suffering, destruction and emptiness.

Vertical Objects in Motion have their origins in circular movement. I worked as a ceramic designer in a small factory in the 1990s, using the wheel much of the time. It was a kind of meditation for me, comparable to taking a walk on an empty sand beach. Then I began to look at mathematical structures and the geometry of seeds and plant life. This led me to prepare moulds based on a cone construction of a green cauliflower. I assembled these cast objects in different ways, to achieve specific vibrations of the structure, resembling circular movement. Later I arranged multi-element compositions, with shapes associated to working on a wheel – objects with increasing or decreasing diameters, up to 3 m (10 ft) high. Whiteness was still essential, helping light to play on particular parts of the forms.

Hideo Matsumoto (Japan) has given the title 'Kakomitotte Mederu' for his large-scale,

(Left) *Vertical Object*, by Malgorzata Dyrda-Kujawska (Poland), 2000. Unglazed porcelain, metal base, h. 293 cm (115 ¼ in.).
Photograph by Lukasz Kujawski.
(Above) *Kakomitotte Mederu XIV, Subterranean-Moonlight-Episode 01*, by Hideo Matsumoto (Japan), 2001. Porcelain, bone ash glaze, ceramic pigment, 340 x 340 x 30 cm (133 ¼ x 133 ¼ x 133 ¼ in.), fired at 1240°C (2254°F). *Photograph by Takashi Hatakeyama.*

multi-layered works since 1990. Roughly translated, he says that the title means 'enjoying the space surrounded by a fence'. In other words, enclosing 'nature' or natural space so that it becomes a garden in the Japanese fashion as opposed to the artificial, man-made landscaping creations commonly found in Europe. He explained that his term describes the way of creating a Japanese garden in the Middle Ages. He is interested in such historical references and says that the title also relates to the methods he uses to build his sculptural pieces. He expressed his continuing interest in working into the wet surface of plastic clay as he did when a child.

(Opposite, top) Group of porcelain sculptures, by Sueharu Fukami (Japan), 2001 (exhibited at Mie Prefectural Art Museum). Slip-cast under pressure, pale blue celadon glaze, reduction fired in a liquid petroleum gas kiln. *Photograph by Takashi Hatakeyama.*

(Opposite, bottom) *The Endless Possibilities of Form...*, by Janet DeBoos (Australia), 2001. Cedar and three porcelains (Limoges, Southern Ice (Australia), Walkers Superior white (Australia)), wheel-thrown porcelain vessels, h. 95 cm (37 ¼ in.), w. 110 cm (43 in.), d. 15 cm (6 in.), clear glazed, oxidation fired to 1260°–1300°C (2300°–2372°F). 'The same action, different shapes – endless possibilities in the results from essentially the same performance. I used different porcelains, fired in oxidation in different kilns (gas, electric) to make the differences more noticeable – but still in a very reduced palette.' *Photograph by Greg Daly.*

(Top) *Kakomitotte Mederu XV, Subterranean-Moonlight-Episode' 02*, by Hideo Matsumoto (Japan), 2002. Porcelain, bone ash glaze, ceramic pigment, 480 x 100 x 70 cm (189 x 39 ½ x 27 ½ in.), fired at 1240°C (2264°F). *Photograph by Yo Nagata.*
(Bottom) *The Container – Process and Forms*, by Bai Ming (China), 2002. Porcelain (detail from a linear installation of 23 similar cylindrical forms, each treated differently, 600 cm/ 236 in. long). Individual elements: 61 x 11 cm (24 x 4 ¼ in.). *Photograph by the artist.*

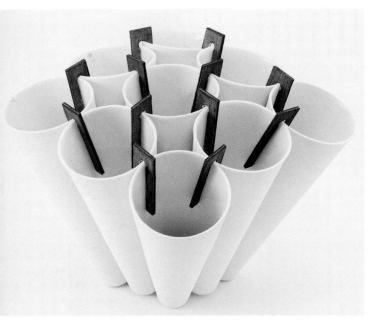

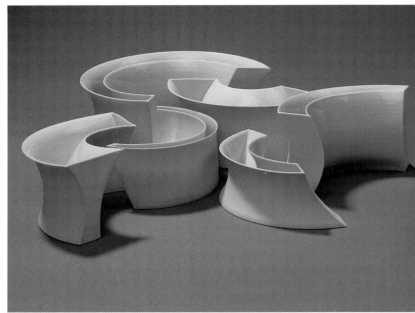

(Top Left) *Vase Object*, by Johanna Hitzler (Germany), 2001. Porcelain, wood, nine porcelain cones, 11 x 28.5 cm (4 ¼ x 11 ¼ in.), flexible fixed with twelve wooden clamps, fired in reduction to 1410°C (2570°F). *Photograph by Gunter Binsack, Leipzig.*
(Top Right) Group of *Segments*, by Astrid Gerhartz (Germany), 2001. Porcelain, h. 10–18 cm (4–7 in.). *Photograph by Peter Oszwald.*
(Bottom) *Auf Hohem Sockel*, by Volkmar Kuhn (Germany), 1996. Slip-cast porcelain, 212 cm x 300 cm (83 ½ x 118 in.)

Hydrogen, by Piet Stockmans (Belgium), 1998. Installation in slip-cast porcelain, exhibited at the former headquarters of the Eisden-Maasmechelen Mine. *Photograph by B. Cielen.*

216

CHAPTER SIX

GLAZES FOR PORCELAIN

The chemistry of glazes is a vast subject and open to limitless possibilities far beyond the scope of this book to deal with in any detail but a suggested reading list will be found at the end of the book. It is a subject that is of only passing interest to those ceramicists who either use no glaze at all or who prefer to rely on commercially-prepared glazes that they know will perform reliably for their purposes. However, it is an area of ceramics which, despite many publications covering every aspect of the technology involved, continues to fascinate or mystify many.

The colour response of white porcelain has been previously mentioned with regard to stains, oxides and slips but even the most simple of glazes on porcelain can have unequalled luminosity. A classic example is a glaze composed of just two natural materials:

Cornish stone	85
Whiting	15

Deep Sea, by Soon Hyung Kwon, (Korea), 2002. Wheel-thrown porcelain, painted with metallic pigments of copper, manganese, cobalt and iron oxides or carbonates, 27 x 28 cm (10 ½ x 11 in.), fired to 1300°C (2372°F) in a gas kiln with oxidising flame, dolomite glaze. *Photograph by the artist.*

Cornish stone is a feldspathoid containing feldspar, quartz, kaolinite, mica and a small amount of fluorspar so it consists of enough of the right constituents to melt into a glassy state on its own but to produce a reliable glaze other materials are normally added. A number of alkalis such as potash, soda, calcia and magnesia are introduced into a glaze composition by Cornish stone but in the above recipe further calcia is added in the form of whiting (calcium carbonate) to act as a flux. This well-known glaze is one which I have used extensively for its ability to craze evenly over porcelain. The resulting fine network of lines can be stained in various ways to emphasise the crackle pattern. Experience has taught me that the thickness of the glaze coating dictates the nature of the crackle. The more thickly glaze is applied, the wider apart the (initial) crackle lines will be. The converse is also true but if the glaze is too thin no noticeable crazing will occur. However, if the combined thicknesses of glaze on inner and outer surfaces exceeds that of the body wall it can cause cracks and splits around the rim of a bowl. Crazing is likely to continue for a while and so the resulting crackles can be stained with one or more colours. Ink is normally used for this purpose but finely ground

Round vase, by John Tilton (USA). Crystalline glaze with cobalt, 14 x 14 cm (5.5 x 5.5 in.). *Photograph by the artist.*

Lidded vessel, by Johan Broekema (Holland), 2001. Porcelain with celadon crackle glaze, 14 x 12 cm (5 ½ x 4 ¼ in.). The crackle has been stained and emphasised with Indian ink after firing. *Photograph by the artist.*

oxides of iron, copper, cobalt or manganese can be mixed with a medium and rubbed into the lines and the piece refired to produce further visual texture. New crackle patterns occur on cooling and these can then be stained with inks for extra interest. This glaze has a fairly wide firing range and I have used it successfully at temperatures between 1220°C (2228°F) and 1300°C (2372°F). Without additions of colouring elements and in the relatively clean atmosphere of an electric kiln, the glaze becomes a glossy, slightly warm white, but under reduction conditions in a live flame kiln, it is affected by minute traces of iron present in the materials making up body and glaze which produces a cooler, bluish tint. This simple glaze offers many possibilities for use under or over other coloured glazes, over

coloured slips or when stains are added to it. One can take it as a starting point for further development and experiment. Adjustments can be made by progressively substituting small amounts of china clay for some of the Cornish stone, for example, to produce a satin rather than a glossy surface. Natural oils in human skin can impede the application of water-based inks into the crackled glaze so pots destined to be stained should be handled carefully and protected with cloth until the process of inking has been completed.

Glaze chemistry is something of a mystery to many amateur potters and there is also a surprising number of professionals who admit to having little knowledge or interest in the

Porcelain platter, by Tom Coleman (USA), 2002. Thrown and altered, Crystal Matt and Barium Matt glazes sprayed on the surface with dry mesquite ash sprinkled on top, d. 58.5 cm (23 in.), fired to cone 10 in reduction. *Photograph by the artist.*

subject. The search for an ideal, reliable glaze that will transform pots with its magical qualities certainly occupies a large proportion of pottery students around the world. Glaze tests are often fitted into odd spaces in the kiln as part of this quest. Ultimately, most sensible potters rely on very few glazes which they get to know and understand intimately.

CRYSTALLINE GLAZE EXPERIMENTS

A great deal of effort is sometimes put into trying to grow crystal patterns in glazes. The oxides which act as crystallisers and opacifiers in a glaze are provided by baria (BaO), calcia (CaO), magnesia (MgO), tin (SnO_2), titania (TiO_2), zinc (ZnO) and zirconia (ZrO_2). Porcelain bodies are particularly well-suited to crystalline glazes, which can have a kind of mystical quality, but they are not universally popular. Large, flamboyant crystals spreading over the surface of a pot can tend to dominate and distract from the form. The maker's satisfaction is often in achieving these random effects irrespective of whether they properly complement the form. The nature of the glaze composition and the degree of control exercised during the firing cycle will, to some extent, condition the results but a good deal must be left, inevitably to chance. **Hein Severijns** (Holland) has had extensive experience of crystalline glazes over many years and he warns ceramicists who do not fully comprehend glaze technology against adventuring into the crystalline field. It is not his intention to discourage experiments with such glazes but he feels that it is too easy to be seduced by them and that too often excellent crystalline effects are used in the 'embellishment of imperfect inappropriate pots'.

Severijns started his career as a laboratory assistant in the ceramic industry and was trained as a ceramic engineer, chemist and technologist. He worked for the ceramic industry, developing bodies, glazes and products in factories for sanitary ware, tableware, refractory wall and floor tiles for seven different companies in several countries. At the same time he always had his own private ceramic studio. He chose to work in industry for three main reasons that he explained as follows:

Firstly, I could collect a lot of ceramic knowledge

Porcelain bottle vase, by Hein Severijns (Holland), 2002. Satin-matt, crystalline glazes, h. 46 cm (18 in.), d. 14 cm (5 ½ in.). *Photograph by John Hermans.*

and technical information, which I could apply to my studio work. Secondly, I was not dependent on financial income from my studio and I could work more freely, without needing to consider the demands of public taste. Finally, but not least, my studio kept me mentally alive and protected me

220

Oval vase, by Hein Severijns (Holland), 2001. Porcelain with satin-matt, crystalline glazes, h. 30 cm (11 ¾ in.), d. 15 cm (6 in.). *Photograph by John Hermans.*

from the pressures of my industrial work. It helped to keep me sane.

Working in industry, Severijns soon learned to be very critical and disciplined about the quality of his own work. He was able to call upon the

technical expertise and developments in modern ceramic technology that are rarely accessible to the studio potter and he always had well-equipped laboratories available for glaze research and for solving difficult problems. The modern fast-firing technology developed for industrial processes, with its uniformity and streamlined production lines, inevitably provoked a counter-reaction to his aim for perfect craftsmanship. He had the desire to use porcelain, 'the most challenging material', to make unique pieces in his personal work. It seems logical, also, that he chose to utilise the extremely slow firing and cooling cycles necessary for crystalline glazes and, in addition, to create those more difficult and unpredictable, matt surfaces.

Severijns studied many articles dealing with the subject and was surprised to find similar glaze recipes appearing in which the main component is an American Ferro frit, difficult to obtain in Europe, without suggesting alternatives. He rarely uses the brighter, shiny crystalline glazes because he prefers the silky touch of satin matt surfaces even though they provide more of a challenge to produce. They are more unreliable and, he says, their success depends on many more factors than those that influence the glossy types. They are more aesthetically appealing to him with their smaller, rounder crystals embedded within the surface 'like a starry sky'. He aims for perfection through simplicity with vessel forms that have no practical function, other than to display an aesthetic presence. He believes that shiny crystalline glazes often destroy forms with their exploding colours and spectacular crystal shapes. Satin matt glazes with more subtle surfaces and smaller crystals appeal to the tactile senses, achieving harmony between form, colour and surface quality. He tries to 'see' the finished pot with his fingers with his eyes closed.

Severijns' work is all thrown, trimmed and

refined on the wheel before bisque firing between 1100°C (2012°F) and 1120°C (2048°F) and then glazing. The glazes are composed with combinations of zinc, barium and titanium together with various metal oxides for colour. Application is by spraying and brushing in three to seven different glaze layers. They are fired to 1270°–1300°C (2318°–2372°F), mostly over repeated firings in a kiln cycle taking up to 20 hours.

The development of crystals within a glaze is dependent upon (a) the chemical composition and its physical properties and (b) the temperature and duration of the firing and cooling cycles. In his excellent book on *Ceramic Glazes* (see bibliography), Parmelee stresses the important role played by the nature of the glaze.

> Chiefly because it must serve as a solvent for the silicates which are later separated during cooling and because its physical properties, notably the viscosity during that period, must be favourable to the growth of the crystals. This is shown by the widely different types of glazes in which zinc silicate, for example, may be induced to crystallise. The reaction of the glaze and the body, in so far as the solution from the latter is concerned, may be important in some instances since a fundamental relationship is thereby disturbed.

Severijns' glazes are based on 'the crystallisation of zinc-barium-silicates with quite complex crystal structures whereas the shinier glaze crystals are mainly composed of willemite Zn_2SiO_4 with colouring oxides taken into the crystal matrix'. The basic formula for his glazes varies within the following limits based on the molecular or unity method devised by Seger:

KNaO	0.15–0.20		
ZnO	0.35–0.50		
BaO	0.20–0.40	Al_2O_3 0.15–0.20	SiO_2 1.5–2.2
CaO	0.05–0.15		
MgO	0.05–0.10		

For the first layer of glaze, Severijns adds 5% of SnO_2 and 5% of TiO_2 plus some quartz to make it somewhat stiffer and reduce the risk of running. His pieces are placed on a thin disc of soft refractory brick to absorb any glaze runs during kiln firing. This can be ground away and polished later if necessary. This initial layer is applied quite thickly. Subsequently, glaze is put on with a brush or by spraying very thin layers of the base glaze coloured with natural oxides from cobalt, copper, iron, manganese and titanium. Up to seven layers may be used. It is interesting to note that base glazes with less than 0.35 ZnO and more than 0.35 BaO give rose-red colours with 2% nickel oxide, while the same percentage of nickel oxide in a glaze containing less than 0.20 BaO and more than 0.45 ZnO produces blue crystals against a light brown background. Thin layers of glaze rich in zinc silicates are applied in between and the final layer contains compounds of molybdenum, tungsten or vanadium to influence and improve the crystallisation.

Limoges porcelain bodies (mixtures of TM10, TM18 and 45937) are mainly used for Severijns' wheel-thrown vessels. Bisque firing is taken to the slightly higher than usual temperature of 1100°C (2012°F) to reduce the eventual reaction between body and glaze. The final glaze firing is first taken up to 1270°–1300°C (2318°–2372°F) and then the kiln is rapidly cooled to 1080°C (1976°F) to assist the formation of nuclei before raising the temperature again to be held at 1150°C (2102°F) for three hours. This is followed by a gradual firing down process which involves dropping the temperature in a series of cooling steps to 1120°C (2048°F), 1100°C (2012°F), 1050°C (1922°F), then back up to 1100°C (2012°F), 1070°C (1958°F), 1040°C (1904°F) and 1000°C (1832°F) for periods each varying between half an hour and three-quarters of an hour. He has found that the firing cycle contributes as much as the glaze composition to the ultimate success of crystalline glaze development but he insists that it is for every potter to discover his own personal 'signature' through the many variables involved.

Personally, I prefer to work empirically with dry batches of glaze materials measured by weight rather than to work out formulae by molecular equivalents. As long as careful and thorough records are kept, not only of the materials used but also concerning the placement of pots in the kiln, the kiln atmosphere, the pattern of firing and cooling and the temperature reached, this method can suffice for most potters. A crystalline glaze recipe, which resulted from such practical experiments I conducted several years ago, has a silky smooth surface similar to those favoured by Hein Severijns. This glaze proved well-suited to porcelain, providing that it was applied to the right thickness, without such a lengthy cooling programme. Doubtless it would have produced more consistent crystalline results had I not lacked sufficient patience to watch over the kiln and had attempted a longer period of cooling to allow time for the crystals to grow! The recipe for my glaze could be used as a starting point for further exploration so I give the details as follows:

Nepheline syenite	50
Barium carbonate	15
Zinc oxide	20
Flint	15

Up to 4% light rutile should be added to the above (or titanium dioxide which gives slightly different results) to 'seed' the crystals. Colouring carbonates of copper (0.5–2%) or cobalt (0.25–1%), or oxides of iron (2–4%), manganese (up to 4%) or nickel (up to 2%) can be added also singly or in combination (to a suggested total maximum of 4% colourant) for a variety of coloured crystal formations when fired in an electric kiln to 1260°C (2300°F). Bungs and spy-holes should be left closed and the kiln unopened until completely cold. Crystalline glazes are under a great deal of compression and if the above glaze is applied too thickly, it can cause thinly thrown porcelain to fracture, but if too thin few crystals will appear. This is very much a matter for trial and error experiments as with all the recipes printed in this book.

Another potter who conducted extensive tests and experiments with crystalline glazes, **Derek Clarkson** (UK), differs in his approach to the subject from that of Severijns although they share much common ground. Clarkson wrote an article published in *Ceramic Review* (No. 137 in 1992) describing his methods in some detail and he has generously supplied further information for the purposes of this book. He declared that he can offer no rational explanation for the attraction crystalline glazes holds for him. 'It can be a passionate, obsessive affair overriding one's good sense!' His practical work, after several years, is still experimental with each glaze having a different firing cycle. The use of a fairly small (0.06m³/2 cu.ft.) electric kiln with a programme controller and containing no more than six to eight pots per firing makes this a practical, economical proposition. His 0.3m³ (12 cu.ft.) gas kiln is 'much more inhibiting' for these experiments.

Clarkson uses a chemical balance to accurately measure and make up just sufficient glaze for each pot. Colouring oxides are sieved through a 120s mesh cup sieve before adding to the glaze, and the complete mixture is twice passed through an 80s mesh sieve to ensure even dispersal. The glaze, mixed to a creamy consistency, is brushed on to the pot with a one-inch brush, applying the bulk of it on to the top third (most of his crystalline glazes are used on narrow necked 'bottle' forms and approximately 100 g (3.5 oz) dry weight is used to coat a bottle form 26 cm (10 in.) high with the inside left unglazed). Wider necked forms are glazed inside with a non-crystalline glaze in order to avoid cracking the piece by the pooling of glaze in the bottom were a crystalline type to be used. A further layer of crystalline glaze is applied by brush over the first for 5–6 cm (2–2 ¼ in.) down the neck of the piece. 'This glaze flows down over the first giving a linking crystalline effect.'

For the development of large crystals on a plain background, the glaze has to be quite fluid. This can create problems with glaze running off the pot and on to the kiln shelf. In order to deal with this occurrence, Clarkson uses a flat-bottomed saucer (bisque fired from the same porcelain body to equalise the shrinkage) to contain any excess glaze, and a pedestal about 3 cm (1 in.) high is also made from the same body to lift the pot above that pooled glaze in the saucer. The pedestal is made to fit exactly to the diameter of the foot-ring in the base of the pot. After bisque firing, a mixture of $\frac{2}{3}$ flint and $\frac{1}{3}$ china clay is generously applied between the pot and its pedestal to assist separation after the glaze firing. Separation is then achieved by first scratching through the glaze surface all the way around the junction with a glass or tile cutter and then tapping gently with a chisel around this line. The foot-ring is then smoothed with a flint tungsten carbide disc mounted in an electric drill and finished off with carborundum paper or block.

The colouring oxides mainly used by Clarkson are cobalt carbonate, copper carbonate, manganese dioxide and red iron oxide in different combinations using all four or just one in amounts from 0.05% to 6%. A limitless range of colours, varying in subtlety, are possible and which can be repeated accurately. He finds that there need be no end to experimenting in the search for more matt glazes, more muted

Porcelain bottle, by Derek Clarkson (UK), 2000. Green crystalline glaze, h. 14.5 cm (5 ¾ in.). *Photograph by Peter Lane (author's collection).*

colours, the introduction of a wider range of materials into the glazes, and in 'seeding' to obtain the crystal formations. 'The number of crystals forming in the glaze and their location on the pot cannot be controlled precisely. However, with careful attention to every detail of the making process, some repetition of fairly similar characteristics can be achieved. The

Round vase, by John Tilton (USA). Crystalline glaze with uranium, 15 x 18 x 18 cm (6 x 7 x 7 in.). *Photograph by the artist.*

clay, the glaze composition, its application and the firing cycle all play a vital part!'

Clarkson conducts the usual bisque firing but takes his glaze kiln up to 900°C (1652°F) as for a normal glost and proceeds from that point to fire up to around 1260°–1290°C (2300–2354°F) as quickly as possible before switching off the kiln. The temperature is then encouraged to drop rapidly by opening vents and spy-holes (to prevent glaze running too much) until 'somewhere between 1150°C (2102°F) and 1020°C (1868°F) at which temperature crystals develop'. All openings in the kiln are then closed and the electricity switched on again to hold the temperature steady within this range for up to five hours. The kiln is then switched off and allowed to cool naturally. 'Periods of moving to higher and/or lower temperatures will produce concentric bands within the crystals.'

Titanium dioxide is an important ingredient for aiding crystal formations in glazes. Amounts about 5% tend to make the glaze less shiny and the background becomes a darker, opaque tan colour and above 10% larger crystals begin to break up into the more familiar mottled surface obtained in many glazes with titanium/rutile compositions.

Zinc oxide also encourages crystal growth and it often contributes about 25% of the glaze recipe. Clarkson found that the high shrinkage problems associated with zinc oxide can be reduced by calcining it in a bisque-fired bowl to about 1000°C (1832°F). Its volume will decrease but its weight will be reduced only slightly by calcining.

John Tilton (USA) uses crystalline glazes extensively so he devised a useful tool for holding his pots while applying glaze and avoiding finger marks. He discovered a product called 'Fern-Co bushings' in a plumbing store, and realised he could adapt them for his work. These are rubber bushes fitted to the outsides of different sizes of plastic sewer pipe that are held together by a stainless steel band tightened with a screwdriver. They are used to join different diameter pipes together by slipping the bushes over the end of the pipe and tightening the band. He had only to cut them in half (each bushing yields two different sizes of holders), had an insert made to fit, and attached them to a vacuum pump via a hose. His system is quick to assemble and disconnect so that the right diameter of pipe can be selected to apply suction and hold the pot securely while dipping in glaze. As soon as it has dried sufficiently the pot handled without disturbing the glaze surface. He described his glazing techniques as follows.

At a very early point I realised that my glazes were incredibly sensitive to thickness of application and wanted to somehow measure the way that they were applied. I decided to construct a glaze micrometer and measure the glaze after it was applied to the bisque, rather than try to figure out how to standardise the glaze slip. Searching catalogues revealed the Starrett 643JZ Dial Depth Gauge – it was this tool that I took to a machine shop and had them modify the shoe so that it fits nicely onto the surface of a pot and gives a thickness measurement that is correct to a half thousandth of an inch. I have found it to be the most useful tool in my workshop – I never glaze pots without it. I do not measure the glaze on every pot, but have a good idea of the variation from piece to piece. It is a somewhat tedious process but it does remove a lot of the mystery in application.

I observed that the matte crystalline glaze was very unforgiving with respect to drips and runs – if they were there, they would show in the finished piece every time. The zinc crystalline glaze is more forgiving in this way, but it is still quite sensitive to variations in thickness – at least in the way that I use it. For both the matte crystal and the zinc crystal, I apply them to a thickness of .0012 inches – at least that is my target – they will be OK but different between .0010 and .0014 inches.

I have found it easiest to apply the zinc crystals by spraying and really enjoy the process of spraying them. It also allows me to mix much less glaze and to vary the ingredients more often. But the matte crystals are best applied by dipping and for this I devised a vacuum system to hold the bottoms of the pots while they are dipped in glaze.

CRYSTALLINE GLAZE RECIPES

John Tilton provided the following basic recipes:

Matt Crystalline Glaze: Cone 10 Reduction (usually needs to be re-fired several times).

Nepheline syenite	85
Barium carbonate	65
Whiting	20
EPK kaolin	15

Titanium dioxide	15
Plus colourants	

Zinc Crystalline Glaze: Cone 10 Oxidation

Frit 3110	134
Zinc oxide	88
Silica	64
EPK kaolin	6

Titanium dioxide (varies according to how many small secondary crystals wanted in the glaze)
Plus colourants

His experience suggests that different brands of zinc oxide have different strengths, so it would be best to line blend the zinc oxide into this formula in order to maximise results.

The glaze recipe and firing cycle used by Derek Clarkson is as follows:

Ferro Frit 3110	42.0
Calcined zinc oxide	31.5
Flint	20.0
Titanium dioxide	5.5
Alumina hydrate	0.4
China clay	0.6
+ 6% Copper carbonate	

This glaze was fired in 2 hrs. 5 mins from 900°C (1652°F) to 1260°C (2300°F), then cooled to 1095°C (2003°F) and held there for 1 hr. 25 mins, then cooled to 1065°C (1949°F) and held there for 1 hr. 30 mins, then cooled to 1055°C (1931°F) and held there for 15 mins, then cooled to 1045°C (1913°F) and held there for 15 mins, and then allowed to cool completely.

Another recipe and firing cycle from D. Clarkson:

Ferro Frit 3110	43.0
Calcined zinc oxide	29.0
Flint	19.0
Titanium dioxide	8.0
Alumina hydrate	0.5
China clay	0.5
+ 0.4% Copper carbonate	
1.2% Manganese dioxide	

This glaze was fired in 1 hr. 50 mins from 900°C (1652°F) to 1260°C (2300°F). Then cooled to 1093°C (1999°F) and held there for 1 hr. 25 mins, then cooled to 1069°C (1956°F) and held there for 1 hr. 45 mins, then cooled to 1053°C (1927°F) and then held there for 1 hr 30 mins. Then it was cooled to 1041°C (1906°F) and held there for 25 mins, and allowed to cool completely.

The variables are infinite but the meticulous record-keeping shown in these two examples by Derek Clarkson indicate the importance he attaches to noting every detail of the process involved in the successful creation of crystalline glazes.

FURTHER GLAZE RECIPES FOR PORCELAIN

Sandra Black uses the following glaze for 1260°–1280°C (2300°–2336°F) which has a 'dry' surface:

Whiting	50
China clay	50
Feldspar	50

Colours are produced by adding different glaze stains up to a maximum of 10% to obtain the intensity of colour required. Glazes are sieved through at least an 80s mesh. For carved pieces where greater emphasis to the design is wanted, a clear glaze is used 'originally developed for hotel china' with a firing range of 1220°–1300°C (2228°–2372°F) but which performs best between 1260°–1280°C (2300°–2336°F). This glaze has proved to be very reliable and has a low rate of thermal expansion. Its quality can be improved further by ball milling and it can be coloured in the usual way or made opaque by the addition of 5% tin oxide:

Nepheline syenite	29.3 parts by weight
Whiting	9.7
Barium carbonate	6.4
Zinc oxide	7.9
Talc	3.9
China clay	10.1
Ball clay	5.0
Silica	27.7

Large porcelain pot, by Paul Davis (Australia), 1993. Wheel-thrown, with a black crystalline glaze composed of feldspar, the local Albury slip (similar in nature to the well-known Albany slip from the USA), and a high proportion of manganese dioxide, d. 75 cm (29 ½ in.). Fired to between cones 10 and 11 in a reducing atmosphere. (The full recipe for this glaze is: potash feldspar 67.3; whiting 2.79; talc 1.35, kaolin 4.45; silica 3.6, red iron oxide 76; manganese dioxide 20.5, all parts by weight.)

Paul Davis supplied the following recipes for reduction firings to 1300°–1320°C (2372°–2408°F):

Celadon Glaze (for cone 10)

Potash feldspar	61.26
Talc	0.04
Whiting	10.22
China clay	2.57
Silica	26.41
Iron silicate	4.00
Red iron oxide	0.02

Apricot Lustre Shino Glaze (for cone 10)

Nepheline syenite	50.9	
Potash feldspar	39.2	Spray over top of glaze
Terracotta clay	6.1	with pine ash for rich
China clay	9.2	lustrous orange.
Salt	3.6	

Chun Glaze (for cone 10)

Potash feldspar	61.25
Soda feldspar	1.70
Talc	1.24
Whiting	18.29
Bone ash	0.57
Silica	16.90
Red iron oxide	0.28
Yellow ochre	1.60

Johan Broekema uses the following glazes in reduction firing to 1280°C (2336°F):

(a) Matt black glaze

Feldspar	25	
Whiting	11	
Magnesite	15	add 8% black body stain
China clay	14	
Quartz	25	

(b) Clear porcelain glazes

Feldspar	24.5	Potash feldspar	42
Whiting	24.0	Soda feldspar	9
Magnesite	3.0	Whiting	12
China clay	19.0	Magnesite	4
Quartz	29.5	Barium carbonate	8
		Zinc oxide	6.5
		China clay	9.5
		Quartz	33

(c) Copper red glazes

Soda feldspar	42	Potash feldspar	42
China clay	8	China clay	8
Whiting	15	Whiting	15
Quartz	33	Quartz	33
Calcium borate	5	Magnesite	2

+ zinc oxide 2%, tin oxide 2%, copper carbonate 1%

(d) Celadon crackle glaze

Nepheline Syenite	42
Whiting	19
China clay	14
Quartz	25
+ Yellow ochre	2.5%

Porcelain vase, by Johan Broekema (Holland), 2002. Painted with an ilmenite-bearing slip, copper red glaze sprayed over a transparent glaze, 15 x 11 cm (6 x 4 ¼ in.), fired in reduction. *Photograph by the artist.*

(e) Semi matt glaze

Soda Feldspar	75
Wollastonite	12
Magnesite	3
China clay	10

'This produces a beautiful Chun glaze sprayed over tenmoku.'

Hein Severijns offers two crystalline glaze recipes with the amounts given as percentages for quick reference. Both are for 1260°–1280°C (2300°–2336°F).

Matt/semi-matt base glaze

Potash feldspar FFF or B411	33
Soda feldspar F7 Ventilato	12
Zinc oxide	15
Barium carbonate	18
Lead bisilicate frit	5
China clay	3
Talc	5
Quartz	5
Whiting	4

'Add colouring oxides and apply many layers. In between these, very thin layers of glaze having 80% $2ZnO.SiO_2$ (zinc silicate), quartz, whiting and talc, eventually with 5% iron oxide.'

Shiny-brilliant base glaze

Frit (Reimbold & Strick A2120)	34
Frit (Reimbold & Strick A3389)	16
Zinc oxide	25
China clay	2
Titanium dioxide	5
Quartz	18

'Add colouring oxides and apply thickly!'

Derek Clarkson provided the following recipe for his favourite celadon glaze:

Cornwall stone	80
Ball clay AT	5
Molochite	5
Wollastonite	10
Talc	6
Bentonite	1
Red iron oxide	1

Clarkson applies his crystalline glazes by brushing but dips pots into his ash glaze. This glaze needs a generous thickness but requires careful application because any unevenness in the glaze will remain after firing. He holds his bottles at the rim/neck and dips them, base first, into the glaze up to the narrowest part of the shoulder. As soon as the glaze is dry enough to touch (almost immediately) the top of the bottle is then glazed down to meet up with the previously glazed area. The inside is left unglazed. Brush decoration is carried out whilst the applied glaze is still damp because dry glaze on the porous porcelain body sucks the water-mixed oxide pigment too quickly from the brush, thus making long thin brush strokes difficult. 'Inadequate brush strokes cannot be "touched up" but it is possible to scrape off a little pigment (shortening a too long brush stroke or slimming one too fat). However, this should be kept to a minimum.'

I prefer to spray all my glazes because I want to have an even layer with no 'runs' or finger marks to mar the surface. It is essential to do this in a properly vented spray booth. Porcelain bisque is notoriously difficult to dip glaze because it can become easily saturated and take a very long time to dry. Some potters try to overcome this problem by dampening the bisque slightly to lessen the absorption, but it is better either to adjust the glaze suspension with the right amount of water or to fire the bisque to a higher temperature to reduce its porosity. Double dipping of glazes is much easier to accomplish on stoneware bisque. Overlaying one or more glazes offers interesting possibilities. This is especially true when, for example, a 'dry' or matt glaze is applied on top of a more fluid one. The first glaze melts and begins to flow dragging and breaking the surface of the drier glaze. When one glaze is dark in colour and the other light, even greater visual interest can develop. One method which I have found very rewarding to explore is a kind of glaze sgraffito. This entails spraying one glaze which can be drawn into, as soon as it is dry, with a sharp tool (not necessarily pointed, almost any shape will do) right through to the underlying body. Traces of glaze will be left and, even with a white glaze, there will be a marked difference between the sgraffito and the glaze when fired. The first layer of glaze and sgraffito can itself be over-sprayed (preferably before it is *completely* dry in order to lessen the risk of lifting off the first layer which can cause 'crawling'), with another glaze different in character, colour or tone and the two will interact but the design will remain clear to see. This is a very direct way of working that can be extremely satisfying. I have achieved some of my best results when using this glazing method with a clear, transparent glaze under a matt, or even dry, glaze stained with various oxides. Rich blues, greens and reds (from cobalt and copper in combination or with other oxides) can appear where the two glazes merge together and the more linear sgraffito design is picked out with contrasting, darker colour.

I rarely do more than make simple, experimental 'line blends' when working out new glaze compositions. Since I use a spray booth to apply all my glazes, the 'waste' glaze which gathers on the inner walls is added to that which is fettled from the bases of pots to mix together into new glazes. These are usually fairly predictable in colour and texture but I make regular tests, nevertheless, and am occasionally surprised by the results. More often, adjustments are made to each batch of any size until I am satisfied with its appearance and performance. It is a simple matter to increase the flux content of any glaze which is too dry, or to add china clay to those which would benefit from a more matt surface. This seemingly haphazard procedure reduces the waste that would otherwise occur when sprayed glazes of different kinds are in constant use in a small workshop.

One of my favourite glazes works equally well for porcelain in both oxidation and reduction firings and the recipe and also for others better-suited to oxidation are as follows:

1260°C–1280°C (2300°–2336°F)

Potash feldspar	65
China clay	5
Barium carbonate	20
Dolomite	10

Add (a) 0.75% copper carbonate and 0.25% cobalt carbonate or (b) 0.25% cobalt carbonate and 2% red iron oxide or (c) 0.75% copper carbonate and 2.5% rutile or other combinations for colour.

Smooth matt 1250°C (2282°F) *(Oxidation)*

Nepheline syenite	45
Barium carbonate	13
Zinc oxide	20
Flint	20
Lithium carbonate	3

Smooth matt surface with crystal inclusions. Interesting variegated colour from additions of 3–4% rutile together with up to 2% copper carbonate or up to 1% cobalt carbonate. Titanium dioxide may be used in place of rutile with slightly different results. Slow cooling will aid the growth of crystals. Too thick an application of glaze can cause runs and risks cracking thinly made porcelain.

Shiny porcelain glaze 1260°C (2282°F) *(Oxidation)*

Nepheline syenite	70
Whiting	9
Zinc oxide	9
Flint	10
Lithium carbonate	2

Shiny glaze studded with tiny crystals. Inclined to run above 1260°C (2300°F) if applied too thickly. The addition of 2–4% rutile or titanium dioxide in combination with up to 2% copper carbonate gives good results but it is worth experimenting with small amounts of cobalt, iron, manganese also.

Bryan Trueman (UK) uses a variety of overlaid glazes with wax resists to produce rich visual textures. He has always tried to apply glazes in a very personal way, calling upon his previous experience in painting and printmaking, with masking techniques that allow him to convey sensory responses to things around him:

Porcelain platter with abstract landscape, by Bryan Trueman (UK). Wheel-thrown and decorated with multiple glazes over wax resist, d. 49 cm (19 ¼ in.), fired in reduction to 1300°C (2372°F). *Photograph by the artist.*

By orchestrating an exotic collection of high temperature glazes and anticipating their movement, distortion and interaction with each other and experimenting with different temperatures and kiln atmospheres have been the most significant aspects of my work. The challenge has always been the 'freeze frame' effect of shutting down the kiln at the precise moment when all the melting and colour maturation has taken place and you think that you have achieved what you had set out to do. These refined critical judgements are the results of numerous firings in which failures as well as successes combine to establish parameters that enable me to develop greater understanding of the process.

Trueman's images were produced by using opalescent and opaque glazes overlapping and interlapping (edge to edge) over a black glaze. The base glaze is a dark tenmoku formulated to remain stable at cone 10. This stability prevents subsequent glaze layers from running and distorting too much. A wax resist is brushed over parts of the tenmoku prior to pouring more fluid glazes. Interlapping parts of the design are controlled by painting wax to mask areas of one glaze where it is due to meet another edge to edge. The unwanted section of glaze can then be sponged off and left to dry before pouring another glaze in its place. This method ensures a clearly defined boundary between the two glazes.

The two main opalescent glazes used by Trueman are a pale blue Chun and a copper red.

The Chun glaze is responsive to various oxides applied over images painted in wax resist, particularly chrome and cobalt. Rutile over the tenmoku provides an opaque effect which can be controlled by the thickness of the rutile painted on. I use several methods of applying glaze over the wax images but pouring, brushing, sponging and slip trailing are the most common. Each provides different linear and textural qualities to the finished piece.

Bryan Trueman offered the following glaze recipes for cone 10 reduction firing:

Chun glaze 1

Potash feldspar	52.40
China clay	0.75
Magnesium carbonate	2.55
Whiting	3.55
Silica	24.00
Zinc oxide	5.50
Bone ash	0.90
Red iron oxide	0.75

Chun glaze 2

Potash feldspar	50
Silica	23
Whiting	14
Zinc oxide	11

Tenmoku glaze

Potash feldspar	46.50
Whiting	14.25
China clay	8.75
Silica	19.50
Red iron oxide	8.50

Copper red glaze

Potash feldspar	36
Silica	36
Borax frit	10
Whiting	15
Tin oxide	2
Bentonite	1
Black copper oxide	0.5

Caroline Whyman (UK), wanting to change her glaze palette from soft toned subdued colours to bright sunny colours, used one of Emmanuel Cooper's recipes, from his book of glazes. This was a useful starting point. Her first tests produced a very dry, rough, textured surface with strong colour response from the alkaline nature of the barium-based glaze. She then tried a combination of fluxes in a series of line blends to try to create a more silky surface. Eventually, she found a glaze that had the vibrant colour response required together with a suitably silken surface. Having worked with this base glaze over many years she discovered that it performs best for spraying when it has bentonite added, as this greatly improves the suspension in water and dramatically increases the durability of the raw glaze while handling the pieces and loading the kiln. However these glazes did not yield good colour with added commercial stains such as yellow or red.

Satin Matt Turquoise glaze

Cornish stone	25
Nepheline syenite	25
Barium carbonate	50
China clay	12
Lithium carbonate	3
Bentonite	2
Copper carbonate	1

(substitute copper carbonate with 0.5 Cobalt carbonate for deep blue glaze)

Tom Turner (USA) has experimented with crystalline inclusions in his copper red 'oxblood' and 'flambé' glazes. He tries to encourage the growth of crystals in the glaze in his normal reduction firing schedule without a special cooling programme. Another glaze which has proved to be of considerable interest is made from a natural clay found beneath his house in Delaware, Ohio. The clay is ball-milled and 1% iron oxide is added to it. 'It's a gorgeous,

Male & Female Couple, by Caroline Whyman (UK), 2001. Wheel-thrown porcelain inlaid with black porcelain slip, under satin matt turquoise glaze, h. 29 cm (11 ¼ in.) and 23 cm (9 in.). Photograph by the artist.

natural *hare's fur* glaze with crystals where thick.' He has named this slip glaze 'Peachblow' after the road in which he lives. All his pots are wheel-thrown porcelain and reduction fired to cone 10 in ten hours. 'The reduction period starts at 1010°C (1850°F) with an ACI oxy-probe reading of 0.70 and no changes or adjustments are made until the kiln is turned off and the damper closed. We use no clean up period nor do we quick cool. The kiln is cooled in about 40 hours and unloaded without gloves.'

Tom Turner suggests the following glaze recipes as *starting points* for experiment ('never before published because chemicals and kilns vary so much. I doubt whether they will work for anyone else. When I lived in Florida, I did not protect the copper red pots during firing but when I moved to Ohio and put my kiln inside tall barns, the taller chimneys required that we semi-saggar them. By this I mean that soft bricks are set alongside the pots on the fire side *(to act as baffles to divert the direct action of the flames)*. Other formulae don't require this adjustment either, b*ut mine does!* My copper red is a product of years of experiment with the Chun base glaze given in Carlton Ball's books.'):

Cover jar, by Tom Turner (USA), 2002. Oxblood, Flambé, with iron oxide, 23 x 23 cm (9 x 9 in.). *Photograph by the artist.*

Satin celadon glaze

Cornish stone	25
Silica	25
EPK china clay	34
Whiting	25
Alumina hydrate	1
VeeGurn T	1
Iron oxide	1.7

'This is a variation of the David Leach recipe with additional clay and some alumina hydrate to promote a satin surface that appears frosted. VeeGum T is the whitest and most plastic material I've ever found. It's a plasticiser and lubricant that does not burn out!'

Tom Turner oxblood glaze		*Tom Turner flambé glaze*	
Kingman feldspar	72	Kona A3 feldspar	150
Silica (325 mesh)	45	Silica	90
Whiting (low Mg)	25	Whiting	30
Kaolin	4	Kaolin	6
Gerstley borate	8	Gerstley borate	40
Magnesium carbonate	7	Dolomite	20
Barium carbonate	7	Barium carbonate	14
Zink oxide	3	Zinc oxide	6
Tin oxide	1.5	Tin oxide	3
Copper carbonate	0.75	Copper carbonate	1.5
Frit 3134	1.25		

Gail Russell (USA) works in porcelain, also, because its fine particle size retains and displays the amount of intricate detail that she requires for making the sprigs and stamps applied to the surface of her bowls. This feature is enhanced under a fluid coloured glaze.

(Top) Porcelain bowl, by Gail Russell (USA), 2002. Sprigging applied under a copper red glaze. *Photograph by the artist.*

(Above) Porcelain platter by Margaret Frith (UK), 2002. Reduction fired glazes, including copper red, d. 22 cm (8 ¾ in.). *Photograph by the artist.*

FIRING METHODS

Reducing atmospheres can be introduced into live flame kilns extremely easily by altering the ratio of fuel and air. Cutting back on the air supply alone encourages the excess carbon from unburnt fuel to search out oxygen from the metallic elements contained in bodies, slips and glazes and thus altering the colour and appearance of the pots. The drama and additional involvement experienced by potters working with reduction glazes in live flame kilns is quite different from the more detached, almost clinical, practice of firing with electricity. It is possible to introduce similar conditions in electric kilns for short periods but with some risk to the life of the wire elements and this is not normally advisable. However, one method used by Derek Clarkson to achieve respectable copper reds in some of his crystalline glazes, without the same degree of risk to the elements, is worthy of mention. He discovered that he could obtain fine copper red glazes (containing between 0.25% and 2% copper carbonate) just by pouring old or used vegetable cooking oil from a tablespoon through the top central vent of his kiln. The vent was restricted to a hole no more than 11 in. (10 cm) wide (closed with a bung) and a bisque saucer was placed on the floor of the kiln directly under the hole with pots arranged around it. A spoonful of oil in every few minutes, and the bung replaced, over a period of an hour and a half while the temperature was dropping from 850°C (1562°F) to 650°C (1202°F). At this stage the kiln is no longer switched on but is cooling naturally. Approximately half a litre of cooking oil was used in the process. The main disadvantages to this method appear to be, firstly the constant attention required during the period of reduction and, secondly, the unpleasant smell that clings to the workshop for several days afterwards!

Correct firing of the kiln is essential when

Porcelain bowl, by Peter Lane (UK), 1998. Wheel-thrown, with copper red glaze, h. 14 cm (5 ½ in.), fired in gas kiln to 1280°C (2336°F). *Photograph by the artist.*

the aim is to produce reliable copper red glazes. **Chris Hogg** (UK), who has made a serious study of copper red glazes, sent me some excellent notes with detailed information about his experiments. He also emphasises that the key to success with copper reds lies in the firing process.

The firing cycle is much more important than the glaze recipe in achieving good reds. It is no use putting a few copper reds into a normal reduction firing and expecting to get good results. To get the best colours you have to use a firing schedule specifically designed for these glazes.

The temperature for the onset of reduction is critical in avoiding bleached glazes. But it is also vital that copper reds in their final form are not over-reduced, as this gives opaque reds that are muddy and dull. Because the atmosphere in studio kilns cannot be controlled so precisely as to give only cuprous copper in the glaze, another way has to be found to produce it. This is by re-oxidation of the glaze at top temperature, a technique already used by some studio potters to brighten their copper reds. The advantage of re-oxidation of a melted glaze is that it is a relatively slow process and can be controlled to give exactly the required results. But even with a period of oxidation at top temperature, my glazes still lacked brilliance. After years of experimenting, I found the best way to get brilliant colours was to complete the firing in an electric kiln, and now I no longer fire copper reds to maturity in a gas kiln. My current schedule is to fire in my gas kiln to 1100°C (2030°F) with moderately strong reduction above about 800°C (1472°F). Both these temperatures should be increased if there is no boric oxide in the glaze, depending on its melting temperature. At about 1100°C (2030°F), when the glaze has melted, the kiln is turned off and allowed to cool. At this stage the glazes are matt or semi-gloss, dirty purple and often covered in large blisters; they look pretty awful!

Reduction firing at low temperatures can deposit a lot of soot. This in turn can cause problems with bloating if it becomes sealed into the body of the pot. To keep the burner flame from being too sooty, have the primary air to the burners wide open, and control the reduction using the flue damper. The pots are then refired in an electric kiln to a pyrometer reading of about 1270°C (2318°F) with a 30 to 60 minute soak, approximately equivalent to Orton cone 11. When cool, the glazes are the rich dark transparent blood red that I most admire. Although 1270°C (2318°F) is rather higher than the normal maturing temperature for many of these glazes, it seems necessary to get the best colour. At lower temperatures, re-oxidation can be very slow.

Chris Hogg provided the following recipe for his favourite copper red glaze:

GK487 (Gas Kiln)

China clay	5.1	SiO_2	62.9
Dolomite	2.0	Al_2O_3	11.7
Quartz	23.0	B_2O_3	5.5
Talc	3.5	CaO	11.7
Whiting	12.8	MgO	1.7
Calcium borate	10.2	K_2O	3.7
FF feldspar	11.8	Na_2O	2.4
Potash feldspar	11.7		
Soda feldspar	13.2		
Nepheline syenite	6.7	(from Norway)	

Add:

Tin oxide	1
Copper carbonate	0.3
Iron oxide	0.15

GK487 is my best glaze. It came about because after every glaze experiment, I would put the leftovers into a bucket. Every so often, I would test the mixture to see how it performed. At one point, the results were superb, but of course I had no idea of the composition. I stopped adding more residues, and had the glaze chemically analysed. The recipe above is a close match to that analysis, using a greater number of materials than is probably necessary, to simulate the range of materials that went into the original mix.

In summing up his glaze research, Hogg makes the point that colour in copper red glazes is due to a mixture of colloidal metallic copper and cuprous oxide, but in the glazes with the richest colours, colloidal cuprous oxide dominates. This is most easily made by first reducing the copper to its metallic state before the glaze melts, followed by slow and controlled re-oxidation at higher temperatures to produce the cuprous oxide. Tin oxide in the recipe buffers the reduction-oxidation balance in the glaze during re-oxidation at just the right level for cuprous oxide formation.

Hogg believes that most copper red failures happen either because reduction is started too soon before the glaze has melted, allowing all the copper to volatilise, or because reduction is started too late, after the glaze has sealed, when no reduction of the glaze occurs.

Nothing can quite match the excitement of firing with living flames. When we moved to our present address in Hampshire in 1990, it proved impossible to take my excellent gas kiln with me and the glazes which I had perfected for reduction firing lacked the attraction and element of surprise when transferred to the

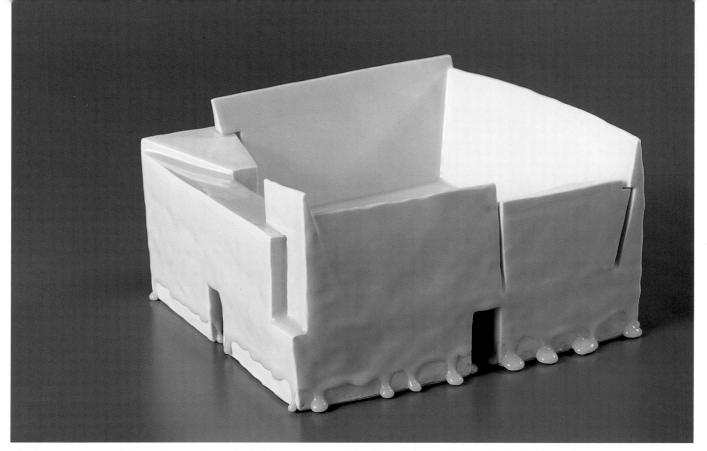

Kayho, by Masamichi Yoshikawa (Japan), 2002. Porcelain, 34 x 35 x 21 cm (13 ¼ x 13 ¾ x 8 ¼ in.). 'I am concerned about how much life I can give to the inorganic nature of geometric shapes with the fresh and soft texture of bluish-white ceramics, in other words, about the fitness of organic and inorganic, as I enjoy the process of taking out from a mass of clay the rise of shape and the quality, power and the flesh of material.' *Photograph by Sigeru Murai.*

more detached and predictable firing by electricity. There seems little point in trying to imitate those uniquely attractive effects of reduction firing in an electric kiln, although many potters attempt to do so. Eventually, I bought a new kiln fired by liquid petroleum gas (LPG) to renew some of the well proven reduction glazes that I had formulated previously. This required considerable experimentation and much patience before I could adapt those glazes to work well enough in the new kiln with its different internal layout and burners. Each live flame kiln has its own firing characteristics and its performance can be affected by its immediate environment as well as the way in which it is packed.

Both oxidation and reduction offer ample opportunities to experiment and to achieve very satisfactory results with or without glazes. In

either case, it requires a supreme act of faith on the part of the potter to commit the result of his or her labours perhaps the work of several months, to be transformed by such intense heat. The most radical changes, of course, are wrought by the glazes which will be no more than dull, powdery coverings to the underlying ceramic objects. Hence the excited anticipation which accompanies many glaze firings, especially when experimental work is involved.

The most simple of familiar, traditional, oriental porcelain glazes can acquire a fresh and exciting appearance when applied to contemporary ceramic forms. Copper reds of different shades have long been a challenging and popular choice for many potters. Likewise, celadons ranging from the palest blues through greys to pale and deeper olive greens are frequently chosen to enhance incised work and

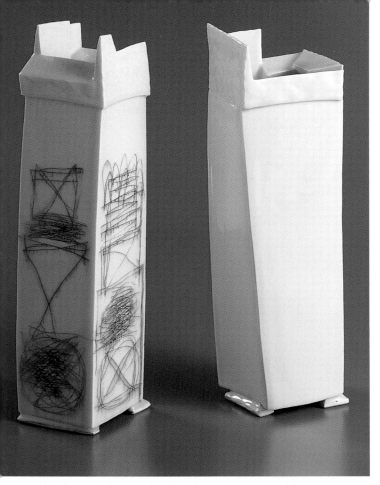

Kayho, by Masamichi Yoshikawa (Japan), 2002. Porcelain, h. 58 cm (22 ¾ in.) *Photograph by Sigeru Murai.*

surface carving. The grey-green version of this glaze, so revered by the Chinese from the T'ang period onward for its jade-like appearance, is generally accepted as the original and, therefore, proper colour for 'celadon', although there is some confusion over the origin of the name. The delicate colour variations and soft luminous quality of Chinese celadons comes from differing amounts of iron present in the glaze and/or body together with countless undissolved particles and tiny bubbles held in suspension within the glaze. Fired in a reducing atmosphere, even small amounts of iron are sufficient to contribute colour to the glaze.

The Japanese potter, **Masamichi Yoshikawa**, clothes his monumental pieces with a particularly sumptuous, pale blue celadon glaze. Made from very thick slabs of porcelain, his work is sometimes decorated with incised,

linear drawing picked out with cobalt. The visual power of these forms is in complete harmony with the glaze that seems to flow with great depth over them.

Reduction firing, however, is not always possible for those who live in an urban conurbation. However, the greater predictability of electric kiln firing has proven perfectly satisfactory for the needs of a considerable number of potters whose work is illustrated in this book. Porcelain bodies are relatively inert compared to those more commonly associated with stoneware and which rely for effect on their positive contribution to the final results achieved through the reaction between body and glaze. Iron spots burning out from stoneware bodies to enliven even the dullest reduction glaze would, in most cases, be inappropriate blemishes on porcelain.

Without the need to make ceramics that must conform to fit functional, domestic requirements, potters are no longer bound to make vessels watertight. In this book are illustrations of the work of potters who have chosen to dispense with firing porcelain to the high temperatures necessary to mature the body. This liberty has allowed them to produce objects of beauty and interest serving purely decorative purposes. Others may fire their pieces many times with multiple glazes at both high and low temperatures. The options are infinite and the directions chosen for exploration are the decision of each individual. That which appeals to one will be anathema to another.

The freedom from any of those traditional constraints has encouraged fresh, adventurous approaches to working with clay. There can be little doubt that the enormous variety of forms, surfaces and expressions which we see today in porcelain and ceramics generally, will continue growing, enriching our environment and adding to our cultural heritage with each succeeding generation.

CHAPTER SEVEN

CONCLUSION

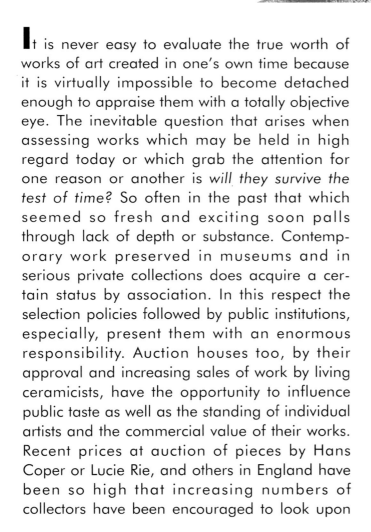

It is never easy to evaluate the true worth of works of art created in one's own time because it is virtually impossible to become detached enough to appraise them with a totally objective eye. The inevitable question that arises when assessing works which may be held in high regard today or which grab the attention for one reason or another is *will they survive the test of time?* So often in the past that which seemed so fresh and exciting soon palls through lack of depth or substance. Contemporary work preserved in museums and in serious private collections does acquire a certain status by association. In this respect the selection policies followed by public institutions, especially, present them with an enormous responsibility. Auction houses too, by their approval and increasing sales of work by living ceramicists, have the opportunity to influence public taste as well as the standing of individual artists and the commercial value of their works. Recent prices at auction of pieces by Hans Coper or Lucie Rie, and others in England have been so high that increasing numbers of collectors have been encouraged to look upon

Candle Transformation, by Sarka Radova (Czech Republic). Porcelain sculpture, h. 85 cm (33 ½ in.). *Photograph by M. Polák.*

contemporary ceramics as worthy of serious investment. Nevertheless, in comparison with other branches of the art market, ceramics still offers a relatively inexpensive purchase for anyone wanting to possess original works.

For many people the term 'pottery' implies the making of functional vessels intended primarily for domestic use but we have seen that the majority of those individuals whose work is represented in this book are more concerned with expressing personal feelings in response to the various stimuli that impinge upon their lives. In some cases 'function', in the recognised sense, remains an important element. In others, vessel forms provide a springboard for fresh explorations and invention. The reworking of traditional forms in porcelain such as bowls, vases or teapots etc., need never be a dull exercise, especially when translucency, delicacy and purity contribute their cherished qualities to the final appearance. Expressions possessing subtlety and sensitivity can create long-lasting impressions while demonstrations of extrovert flamboyance may be soon forgotten. Anyone who takes an interest in ceramics learns to recognise even the simplest objects as being from the hand of a particular craftsman or woman. Their identity

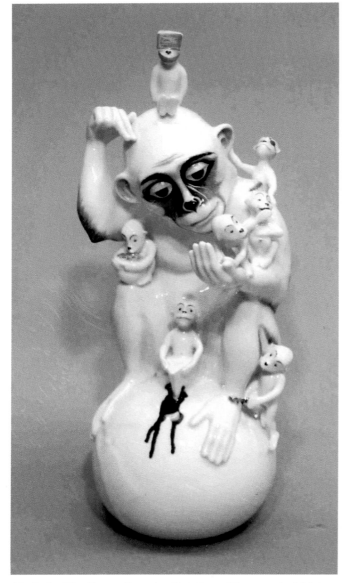

Afe Dek –The Seven Sins, by Kati Zorn (Germany), 2001. Modelled and slip-cast porcelain. *Photograph by Ulrich Fischer.*

Untitled, by Aline Favre (France), 2002. Porcelain sculpture, 60 x 40 x 30 cm (23 ½ x 15 ¾ x 11 ¾ in.). *Photograph by Jean-François Claustre.*

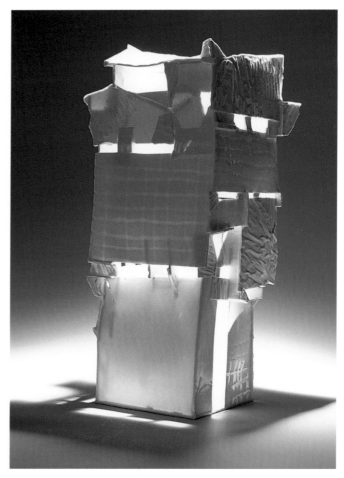

Tower, by Peteris Martinsons (Latvia), 2002. Porcelain sculpture, slip-cast and handbuilt, partly glazed, 39 x 19 x 18 cm (15 ¼ x 7 ½ x 7 in.). *Martinsons' work exploits complexity, translucency and fragility. Photograph by Maris Kundzins.*

may be revealed through extremely subtle visual clues. Slight nuances in the profile, the way in which the form rises up from its base, perhaps the style of decoration or maybe just the choice and arrangement of colours and glazes will provide enough information for instant recognition. No more than a quiet, restrained elegance may suffice. Recognising the indefinable quality that gives a ceramic object a kind of 'presence', irrespective of any label or category assigned to it, is an ability which

ROW, by Jeroen Bechtold (Holland), 2001. Slip-cast porcelain inlay and onlay, 13 x 13 x 47 cm (5 x 5 x 18 ½ in.).

Porcelain vessel, *Boot (Boat)*, by Gotlind Weigel (Germany), 2002. Wheel-thrown and altered, 30 x 25 x 22 cm (11 ¾ x 9 ¾ x 8 ¾ in.), reduction fired to 1350°C (2462°F). *Photograph by Baumann Fotostudio.*

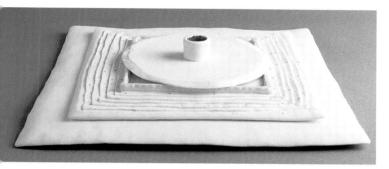

The Blood Well, by Marta Nagy (Hungary), 2000. Handbuilt porcelain sculpture with glaze and lustre, 4 x 34 x 34 cm (1½ x 13½ x 13½ in.), fired to 1380°C (2516°F). *Photograph by István Füzi.*

Coral to Yellow Asymmetrical, by Dorothy Feibleman (UK), 1996. Nerikomi porcelain form, d. 23 cm (9 in.), h. 12 cm (4 ¾ in.). *Photograph by John Ward.*

becomes more refined as experience in the field grows. In *Studio Porcelain* (1980) I wrote that, 'a simple bowl may possess a quiet, unassuming "presence", no less impressive than the most complex sculpture, whether designed for use or otherwise'. The best solutions to aesthetic problems are often remarkable for their simplicity! But, whatever form the work may take, it can express the very essence of considered ideas as well as revealing something of the emotional involvement of the individual who made it.

Unusual images or surprising uses of a traditional material may capture the imagination but without substance or, perhaps, further development, they are rarely likely to offer much more than a passing fancy. As mentioned previously, sculptural objects created from clay by modern ceramicists have often been underrated or even dismissed as being of little significance. In part this may be because they are difficult to categorise. Should they be labelled as 'fine art' or *merely* pottery? Indeed, does it really matter? Undoubtedly, it is often easier to accept and absorb that which conforms to traditional concepts. Anything which appears to violate normal boundaries may need more time to become familiar and understood, and therefore, acceptable. The new can excite but it may also offend sensibilities. Therein lies a dilemma, for entrenched attitudes impede the progress of thought, ideas and expression. One can cultivate an 'open' mind without necessarily conceding personal principles or granting *carte blanche* approval to a work merely on the basis of its 'originality'. At the very least, we can appreciate that each object, whether in the form of a 'simple' vessel or as figurative or abstract ceramic sculpture, is the concrete realisation of multiple and complex strands of human feeling.

The resolution and production of each ceramic piece requires the artist to work with ingenuity and sensitivity, to have a thorough understanding of materials and processes, and a sincerity of purpose if it is to successfully appeal to a wide audience. We may choose to deny *any* worth in works which do not happen to coincide with our own personal tastes or does not conform to some established or perceived ideal but, if we try to value any genuine human endeavour with open minds, we can learn to judge each piece on its individual merit and will be enriched by the experience.

Japanese Bathers, by Melissa Braden (USA), and Inguna Skuja (Latvia). Slip-cast porcelain with inscribed design, salts, high-fire glazes, and glass from a wine bottle, 36 x 23 x 5 cm (14 x 9 x 2 in.). *Photograph by Janis Banders.*

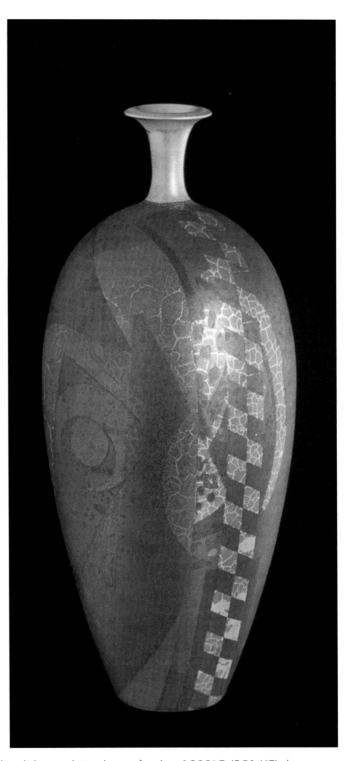

(Top) *Terra Blanca*, by Annika Teder (Estonia), 1998. Handbuilt solid porcelain objects fired to 1380°C (2516°F), h. 10–15 cm (4–6 in.), w. 7 cm (2 ¾ in.). 'Porcelain is expected to be small and fragile but this material has its hidden strength and monumentality. I compare porcelain with piece of earth covered with white vanishing snow or eternal ice. In my childhood I played with snow, cutting and breaking it into parts. This, what I did with porcelain – cut solid blocks of porcelain – building of them 'terra blanca', like with snow in childhood'. *Photograph by Annika Teder.*

(Bottom) *All Equal, All Different*, by Phillipe Barde (Switzerland), 1997. Takeo stone, porcelain, 25 cm (9 ¾ in.).

(Right) Bottle form, by Tony Laverick (UK), 2001. Thrown and turned porcelain with metallic lustres, multiple firings, h. 25.5 cm (10 in.). *Photograph by Andrew Parr.*

(Right) Porcelain sculpture, by Sueharu Fukami (Japan), 2000. Slip-cast under pressure, glazed, pale blue celadon glaze, reduction fired in a liquid petroleum gas kiln, 181 x 45 x 42 cm (71 ¼ x 17 ¾ x 16 ½ in.).
Photograph by Takashi Hatakeyama.

OPPOSITE PAGE
(Top left) *Glacial Bowl*, by Les Manning (Canada), 1997. Combinations of stoneware and porcelain bodies stacked together and wheel-thrown, altered, glazed and sand-blasted, w. 24 cm (9 ½ in.), h. 14 cm (5 ½ in.), l. 32 cm (12 ½ in.).
Photograph by Howard Owen (Collection of The Whyte Museum of the Canadian Rockies).
(Top right) Porcelain, multi-lipped bowl, by Victor Greenaway, (Australia), 2002. Celadon, w. 23 cm (9 in.), h. 14 cm (5 ½ in.).
Photograph by Terence Bogue.
(Bottom) *Dyad with Vertical Form,* by Marc Leuthold (USA), 2002. Carved and handbuilt porcelain, unglazed, 23 x 25.5 x 2.5 cm (9 x 10 x 1 in.). *Photograph by Eva Heyd.*

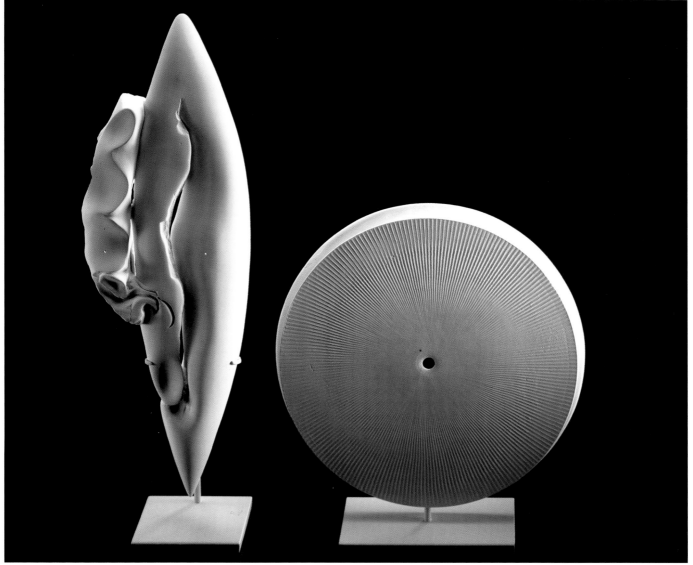

GLOSSARY

Agateware
Ceramics assembled from layers of different coloured clays (usually prepared with body stains or metallic oxides), laminated and sliced through.

Airbrush
An instrument which operates with compressed air to propel a fine, adjustable spray of coloured material (stains, slips, glazes, lustres) onto the ceramic.

Albany clay
An American clay from Albany, New York, containing a high proportion of fluxes and a fine grain size, which is used as a brown/black slip glaze at temperatures above 1240°C (2264°F).

Albury clay
An Australian clay having similar characteristics as Albany clay.

Alkali
Opposite to acid. Potash, soda and lithia are strong fluxes. Potters also use alkaline earths such as calcium, barium, magnesium and strontium as fluxes.

Alumina
Aluminium oxide. An important ingredient in clays and glazes. It provides the plasticity in clay and acts as an opacifier, stiffener and matting agent in glazes. Usually added in the form of china clay.

Applied decoration
Often describes additions of pieces of clay to the main form. Can also be decoration with slips, oxides, stains and glazes used in various ways.

Ash glaze
A glaze containing a proportion of ash from burnt organic material, mainly trees, straw, grasses, etc.

Ball clay
An extremely fine-grained, light-coloured, sedimentary clay, sometimes used as a plasticiser in porcelain bodies.

Ball mill
A porcelain jar filled with pebbles and used to grind minerals and glazes to a fine particle size.

Banding
The application of horizontal stripes of oxide, stain, slip, glaze or lustre to pots on a rotating wheel.

Barium
An alkaline earth. Barium carbonate (poisonous) is used in glaze recipes for particular surface and colour effects (notably with copper and nickel).

Batt
This can be a kiln shelf, a removable wooden disk attached to the wheelhead for throwing making it easier to remove freshly thrown pots, or a slab of plaster or low-fired bisque used to dry wet clay.

Bentonite
A clay with a very fine grain, used to plasticise porcelain and added to glazes in small amounts around 2% to aid suspension in the slop state.

Bisque
Unglazed ware, usually porous.

Bisque firing
The first firing of clay into ceramic. Usually conducted prior to glazing or other treatment because it is easier to handle than in the raw state.

Blunging
Mixing clay with water in a blunger to produce a smooth slip.

Bodies
Any clay or mixture of clays. Few clays are used by potters 'as dug'. Normally they use mixed clay bodies with different qualities for specific purposes.

Body stains
Colours prepared from metallic oxides to mix into slips and clay bodies.

Bone ash
Calcium phosphate made from calcining cattle bones. It is used in certain glazes to give a milky quality and is a major constituent of bone china.

Bone china
A very translucent white ware with a high proportion of bone ash.

Bung
A ceramic stopper to fit in the spy-hole of a kiln.

Calcine
To heat materials to a sufficiently high temperature to drive off chemically-combined water.

Calcium
The carbonate form is extensively used as a flux in glazes.

Carborundum
The trade name for silicon carbide, a hard grit used for polishing ceramic and, occasionally, added to glazes to cause local reduction in electric kilns.

Carving
Cutting into and removing clay from the surface of (usually) leatherhard clay.

Casting slip
Deflocculated mixture of clay and water in suspension for pouring into moulds.

Celadon glaze
A high-fired, grey-green glaze often used over incised or carved decoration. Blue and grey glazes having similar characteristics are sometimes described as 'celadon' types.

China clay
Kaolin, a pure form of primary clay, high in alumina and extremely refractory.

Chun glaze
A thick, opalescent glaze and bluish tint caused by scattered blue light waves.

Cobalt
Small amounts of the oxide and carbonate forms of this mineral give strong blue slips, bodies and glazes.

Coiling
Coils are made by rolling clay between the fingers or by extruding through a machine. Forms can be built up with coils joined together.

Cones
Elongated, three-sided pyramids composed of ceramic materials graded to measure the actual 'heat work' in a kiln and designed to collapse at specific temperatures. Cones can be observed through the spy-hole during the firing.

Copper
The oxide and carbonate forms are used to give greens, blues and reds in slips and glazes according to their composition and the kiln atmosphere.

Copper red glazes
In reduction firing small amounts of copper produces red in reduction.

Crackle glaze
A glaze designed to craze by shrinking more than the body. The pattern of crackle lines is often stained after firing to give them greater emphasis.

Crazing
This occurs when the glaze does not fit the body due to uneven expansion and contraction. Either can be adjusted by the addition of silica.

Crystalline glaze
Glaze with crystals visible in and on the surface. Usually 'seeded' with titania, zinc or zirconium to encourage the growth of crystals. Slow cooling also helps.

Cup lawn
A small, cup-shaped sieve with a fine mesh.

De-airing
The removal of all air bubbles in a plastic clay prior to working.

Deflocculation
The dispersal of fine clay particles suspended in a slip prepared for casting. Soluble alkalis are added so that the slip can contain a high proportion of clay to a small amount of water without loss of fluidity.

Dolomite
A natural mineral, containing calcium and magnesium, used as a flux and crystalliser in high temperature glazes.

Dunting
Cracking of the body during firing or cooling.

Earthenware
Porous pottery usually fired to temperatures under 1100°C (2012°F).

Engobe
Slip applied to pots at either the unfired or the bisque stage.

Engraving
Shallow incisions made into the surface of a ceramic at any stage.

Extruded
Plastic clay can be shaped into various sections by forcing it through a metal dye.

Feldspar
One of the most useful material in ceramics. Used as a flux in bodies and as a natural frit in glazes.

Feldspathoid
Mineral with similar properties to feldspar e.g. Cornish stone and nepheline syenite.

Fettling
Trimming away excess clay, slip or glaze before firing.

Flambé
A bright, glossy glaze streaked with reds produced by the use of copper in reduction.

Flint
Silica for bodies and glazes.

Fluting
Cutting vertical or diagonal grooves in the surface of a pot.

Flux
An oxide which lowers the melting point of a glaze mixture and aids vitrification in bodies.

Foot-ring
The thrown or turned ring of clay supporting a bowl.

Frit
Glass or glaze which has been ground to be added to a glaze or body recipe. Frits are often prepared to make soluble materials insoluble for use in glaze mixtures.

Fusion
The melting of ceramic materials.

Glaze stain
Pigments made from oxides and added to give colour to glazes.

Grog
Fired clay body ground and graded to pass through various mesh sizes. It is added to bodies to provide extra wet strength and reduce shrinkage.

Inlay
Clays and slips, usually of different colours, inlaid into the porcelain body.

Iron
An important source of colour in ceramics. Rust reds, browns, tans, blues, greens and blacks can all be produced from different forms of iron oxide in various compositions and kiln atmospheres.

Kaolin
China clay.

Kidney steel
A small piece of flexible steel shaped like a kidney and used for shaping and scraping clay.

Kneading
Mixing plastic clay to an even consistency by hand.

Latex resist
A liquid rubber solution which can be painted or trailed on to a pot. When dry it resists water-based mixtures of colour, slip or glaze.

Lawn
A fine mesh of wire or fibre for sieving wet materials like slip or glaze etc.

Leatherhard
Clay in a stiffened condition but with sufficient moisture content to accept carving, piercing, inlaying and slipping.

Lithium carbonate
A strong alkaline flux used in glazes.

Lustre
Metallic salts of copper, gold, silver, platinum, bismuth and tin are mixed with resin and oils to deposit pure metal on the surface of pots in a localised reduction firing at a relatively low temperature around 750°C (1382°F).

Magnesia
Used in bodies and glazes. Contributes opacity and mattness when percentages between 20%–30% are used in high temperature glazes. Often added in the form of dolomite.

Manganese (carbonate or dioxide)
Used as a colourant in bodies and glazes giving browns, blacks and purples.

Molochite
A refractory grog made by English China Clays (now Imerys Minerals) in Cornwall.

Neriage
A form of decoration where slabs of contrasting coloured clays are laminated together, cut into strips and reassembled into patterns pressed into moulds.

Onglaze enamels
Soft, coloured glass with a low melting point for painting on top of fired glaze.

Opacifier
Materials in a glaze composition which remain suspended in the fired glaze. Tin, oxide, titanium dioxide, zinc oxide and zirconium dioxide are the principal agents.

Oxidation
This occurs when there is an ample air supply in the kiln during firing.

Oxide
A chemical compound formed between oxygen and another element.

Oxidising atmosphere
A clean kiln atmosphere where plenty of oxygen is present.

Paper porcelain
Porcelain slip mixed together with paper pulp and cast and rolled into sheets.

Plasticity
The essential property that allows clay to be shaped and reformed, but excess plasticity can make a clay unworkable or increase the amount of shrinkage when fired.

Polishing
This term is used to described the method of smoothing fired porcelain with silicon carbide 'sandpaper'.

Potash (potassium oxide or carbonate)
A strong alkaline flux and an important constituent of porcelain bodies and glazes.

Press mould
A hollow mould, made from plaster or from fired clay, used to form clay pressed into it.

Pyrometer
An instrument to measure temperature in the kiln.

Quartz
Silica. Used in body and glaze composition.

Raku
A Japanese word used to describe a particular type of low-fired ware made from a refractory clay able to withstand the shock of removal from a red hot kiln with tongs and rapidly cooled in water, or covered with combustible materials to create reducing conditions for special effects.

Reducing atmosphere
An excess of carbon is introduced into the kiln, usually about 900°C (1652°F), so that oxygen atoms are extracted from the oxides present in the ceramics to produce often radical colour changes in glazes, notably from copper and iron.

Reduction firing
See **Reducing atmosphere**

Refractory
Resistant to high temperatures.

Rib
A tool usually made of wood or metal and used in throwing or for shaping.

Rutile
A natural titanium dioxide used to modify other colouring oxides. Alone, it has small traces of iron which produce tan colours. It is also used to give mottled colour effects in glazes. It is often used in crystalline glazes.

Salt glaze
Common salt thrown into the kiln fire at high temperatures decomposes and volatilises to combine with the alumina and silica in the clay body to produce an uneven glaze surface resembling orange peel in texture.

Satin glaze
A semi-matt glaze.

Sgraffito
Decoration scratched through the surface of slips or glazes or painted oxides.

Silica
All ceramics contain silica. It occurs as flint or quartz or sand. It is the essential ingredient of glass and glazes. Clay is a combination of silica, alumina and water.

Silicon carbide
A compound of silica and coke used for its refractory properties and in grit form, as a powerful abrasive.

Slip
A creamy mixture of clay and water. The potter's glue. Can be coloured and used to completely cover a pot, or used for inlay and other decorative purposes.

Slip glaze
A fusible clay which melts to form a glaze at high temperatures.

Soak
A period during which the kiln temperature is kept constant to allow glazes and body to mature.

Soluble salts
Chlorides, nitrates and sulphates of metals commonly used as colourants in ceramics.

Sprigging
Adding pieces of clay as relief decoration.

Stannic oxide
White tin oxide, used as an opacifier in glazes.

Stoneware
A vitrified ware, usually fired to temperatures in excess of 1200°C (2192°F) with low porosity (no more than 5%).

Talc
Magnesium silicate. Used as an insoluble form of magnesia in bodies and glazes.

Tape resist
Paper masking tape used to protect areas of a design when painting, spraying and dipping slips, glazes and coloured stains.

Tenmoku
A high-fired glaze containing a large amount of iron oxide. It is usually brown to black in colour with streaks of rust, especially where thin on rims and carved edges.

Throwing
Making hollow pottery forms by hand on a rotating wheel.

Tin glaze
An opaque, white glaze containing tin oxide. This glaze forms the base for painting coloured pigments as seen in maiolica and delftwares.

Titanium
A creamy coloured opacifying agent which also produces crystals in a glaze.

Trimming
Turning or trimming waste clay away from a pot rotating on the wheel. This is usually done at the leatherhard stage.

Turning
See **Trimming**

Underglaze stains
Prepared ceramic pigments applied to the raw clay or bisque and normally covered with a transparent glaze. Colours which are capable of withstanding high temperatures are often used on porcelain without a glaze coat.

Vanadium oxide
A rare metallic oxide used to produce yellow pigments with tin oxide or zirconia, and blue pigments when combined with zirconium silicate.

Viscosity
Without the property of viscosity, glaze runs off a pot as molten glass. Viscous glazes hold their position due to internal friction between the particles of their composition. The alumina content in a glaze is one of the factors affecting viscosity.

Vitrification
The point at which the glassy materials within a body melt and flow into and fill the spaces between the clay particles and interact with them fusing them together. The vitrified state is the furthest point at which the body will hold its shape prior to deformation.

Wax resist
Molten wax or a wax emulsion design painted or trailed onto unfired clay, bisque, or glaze, resists water-based colours, slips and glazes with great clarity.

Wedging
The preparation, or restoration, of plastic clay by kneading into a smooth, homogeneous mass, free of air bubbles ready for use.

Whiting
Calcium carbonate. A material which is frequently used as a flux in glazes and as a source of calcia in clay bodies.

Wollastonite
Calcium silicate. A natural mineral used in glazes as a source of calcia.

Zinc oxide
Used as an auxiliary flux in glazes. It has a strong effect on certain colouring oxides and is generally best with copper or cobalt. Zinc oxide is often an important constituent of crystalline glazes.

Zirconium oxide
Used as an opacifier in glazes, often as a substitute for the more expensive tin oxide. Helps to promote crystal formation and mottled colours in glazes.

SUGGESTED FURTHER READING

BOOKS

Åse, Arne, *Water Colour on Porcelain* (Norwegian University Press, 1989)

Axel, Jan and Karen McCready, *Porcelain, Traditions and New Visions* (Watson Guptill, 1981)

Billington, Dora, *The Technique of Pottery,* (Batsford, London, 1966)

Blackman, Audrey, *Rolled Pottery Figures* (Pitman/A&C Black, London, 1978)

Casson, Michael, *The Craft of the Potter* (BBC Publications, London, 1977)

Clark, Kenneth, *The Potter's Manual,* (Macdonald, 1983)

Clays and Glazes (The Ceramic Review Book of Clay Bodies and Glaze Recipes, 1988)

Colbeck, John, *Pottery: Techniques of Decoration* (Batsford, London, 1983)

Cooper, Emmanuel, *Electric Kiln Pottery* (Batsford, London, 1982)

Cosentino, Peter, *The Encyclopaedia of Pottery Techniques* (Headline Book Publishing, 1990)

Flight, Graham, *Ceramics Manual* (Collins, London, 1990)

Fournier, Robert, *Illustrated Dictionary of Practical Pottery* (A&C Black, 1973, 1977, 1992)

Fraser, Harry, *Glazes for the Craft Potter* (A&C Black, London, 1973, 199)

Gibson, John, *Pottery Decoration: Contemporary Approaches* (A&C Black, London, 1987)

Godden, Geoffrey, *Encyclopaedia of British Porcelain Manufacturers* (Barrie & Jenkins, London, 1988)

Gompertz, G. St. G. M., *Chinese Celadon Wares* (Faber and Faber, London, 1968)

Grebanier, Joseph, *Chinese Stoneware Glazes* (Pitman, London, 1975)

Green, David, *Understanding Pottery Glazes* (Faber and Faber, London, 1963)

Green, David, *A Handbook of Pottery Glazes* (Faber and Faber, London, 1978)

Hamer, Frank and Janet *The Potter's Dictionary of Materials and Techniques* (A&C Black, London, 1975, 1986, 1991, 1993, 19)

Hamilton, David *Stoneware and Porcelain* (Thames and Hudson, London, 1982)

Hopper, Robin, *The Ceramic Spectrum* (Chilton Book Company, USA, 1984)

Lane, Peter, *Studio Porcelain* (Pitman/A&C Black, London and Chilton Book Company, USA, 1980)

Lane, Peter, *Studio Ceramics* (Collins, London and Chilton Book Company, USA, 1983)

Lane, Peter, *Ceramic Form: Design & Decoration* (Collins, London and Rizzoli, New York, 1988) and New edition 1998.

Leach, Bernard, *A Potter's Book* (Faber and Faber, London, 1945)

Medley, Margaret, *The Chinese Potter* (Phaidon, Oxford, 1976)

Nelson, Glenn C., *Ceramics* (Holt, Rinehart & Winston, New York, 1978)

Parmelee, Cullen W., *Ceramic Glazes* (Industrial Publications, Chicago, 1951)

Rhodes, Daniel, *Clay and Glazes for the Potter* (Chilton, USA and Pitman/A&C Black, London, 1973)

Rhodes, Daniel, *Stoneware and Porcelain* (Chilton, USA and Pitman, London, 1960)

Rhodes, Daniel, *Kilns: Design, Construction and Operation* (Chilton, USA, 1969)

Savage, George, *Porcelain through the Ages* (Penguin, London, 1954)

Scott, Paul, *Ceramics and Print* (A&C Black, London, 1994, rev. ed; 2002)

Wood, Nigel, *Oriental Glazes* (Pitman/A&C Black, London, 1978)

PERIODICALS

American Craft (Published by the American Crafts Council, New York)

Ceramics: Art and Perception (35 William Street, Paddington, Sydney NSW 2021, Australia)

Ceramics Technical Perception (35 William Street, Paddington, Sydney NSW 2021, Australia)

Ceramics Monthly (Columbus, Ohio, USA)

Ceramic Review (Published by The Craft Potters' Association, London)

Crafts Magazine (Published by the Crafts Council, London)

Pottery in Australia (Published by The Potters' Society of Australia, Sydney)

La Revue de la Ceramique et du Verre, (France)

Czech Design and Art. Ceramics & Glass (Czech Republic)

Neue Keramik (Berlin)

Kerameiki Techni (Piraeus, Greece)

Studio Pottery (Exeter, UK)

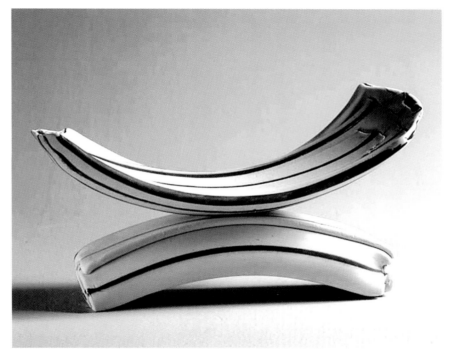

Untitled, by Aline Favre (France), 2002. Porcelain sculpture, 60 x 40 x 30 cm (23 ½ x 15 ¾ x 11 ¾ in.). *Photograph by Jean-François Claustre.*

INDEX

Page numbers in italics indicate illustrations